The Benedict Option

The Benedict Option

A STRATEGY FOR CHRISTIANS IN A POST-CHRISTIAN NATION

Rod Dreher

SENTINEL

An imprint of Penguin Random House LLC
375 Hudson Street
New York, New York 10014

Most Sentinel books are available at a discount when purchased in quantity for sales promotions or corporate use. Special editions, which include personalized covers, excerpts, and corporate imprints, can be created when purchased in large quantities. For more information, please call (212) 572-2232 or e-mail specialmarkets@penguinrandomhouse.com. Your local bookstore can also assist with discounted bulk purchases using the Penguin Random House corporate Business-to-Business program. For assistance in locating a participating retailer, e-mail B2B@penguinrandomhouse.com.

Library of Congress Cataloging-in-Publication Data
Names: Dreher, Rod, author.
Title: The Benedict option : a strategy for Christians in a post-Christian nation / Rod Dreher.
Description: New York : Sentinel, 2017.
Identifiers: LCCN 2016053888 (print) | LCCN 2017001377 (ebook) | ISBN 9780735213296 (hardcover) | ISBN 9780735213319 (e-book)
Subjects: LCSH: Christianity and culture—United States. | Benedict, Saint, Abbot of Monte Cassino. Regula. | Benedictines—Rules. | Monasticism and religious orders—Rules.
Classification: LCC BR526 .D735 2017 (print) | LCC BR526 (ebook) | DDC 261.0973—dc23
LC record available at https://lccn.loc.gov/2016053888

Scripture quotations taken from the New American Standard Bible® (NASB), Copyright © 1960, 1962, 1963, 1968, 1971, 1972, 1973, 1975, 1977, 1995 by The Lockman Foundation. Used by permission. www.Lockman.org.

Printed in the United States of America

Book design by Cassandra Garruzzo

For Ken Myers

Contents

Contents

Let us arise, then, at last,

For the Scripture stirs us up, saying,

"Now is the hour for us to rise from sleep." (Romans 13:11)

—Rule of Saint Benedict

Introduction: The Awakening

For most of my adult life, I have been a believing Christian and a committed conservative. I didn't see any conflict between the two, until my wife and I welcomed our firstborn child into the world in 1999. Nothing changes a man's outlook on life like having to think about the kind of world his children will inherit. And so it was with me.

As Matthew grew into toddlerhood, I began to realize how my politics were changing as I sought to raise our child by traditionalist Christian principles. I began to wonder what, exactly, mainstream conservatism was conserving. It dawned on me that some of the causes championed by my fellow conservatives—chiefly an uncritical enthusiasm for the market—can in some circumstances undermine the thing that I, as a traditionalist, considered the most important institution to conserve: the family.

I also came to see the churches, including my own, as largely ineffective in combating the forces of cultural decline. Traditional, historic Christianity—whether Catholic, Protestant, or Eastern Orthodox—ought to be a powerful counterforce to the radical individualism and secularism of modernity. Even though conservative Christians were said to be fighting a culture war, with the exception of the abortion and gay marriage issues, it was hard to see my people putting up much of a fight. We seemed content to be the chaplaincy to a consumerist culture that was fast losing a sense of what it meant to be Christian.

In my 2006 book *Crunchy Cons*, which explored a countercultural, traditionalist conservative sensibility, I brought up the work of philosopher Alasdair MacIntyre, who declared that Western civilization had lost its moorings. The time was coming, said MacIntyre, when men and women of virtue would understand that continued full participation in mainstream society was not possible for those who wanted to live a life of traditional virtue. These people would find new ways to live in community, he said, just as Saint Benedict, the sixth-century father of Western monasticism, responded to the collapse of Roman civilization by founding a monastic order.

I called the strategic withdrawal prophesied by MacIntyre "the Benedict Option." The idea is that serious Christian conservatives could no longer live business-as-usual lives in America, that we have to develop creative, communal solutions to help us hold on to our faith and our values in a world growing ever more hostile to them. We would have to choose to make a decisive leap into a truly countercultural way of living Christianity, or we would doom our children and our children's children to assimilation.

Over the last decade, I have been writing on and off about the Benedict Option, but it never took off outside a relatively small circle of Christian conservatives. Meanwhile the Millennial generation began to abandon the church in numbers unprecedented in U.S. history. And they almost certainly did not know what they were discarding: new social science research indicated that young adults are almost entirely ignorant of the teachings and practices of the historical Christian faith.

The steady decline of Christianity and the steady increase in hostility to traditional values came to a head in April 2015, when the state of Indiana passed a version of the federal Religious Freedom Restoration Act. The law merely provided a valid religious liberty defense for those sued for discrimination. It did not guarantee that those defendants would prevail. Gay rights activists loudly protested, calling the law bigoted—and for the first time ever, big business took sides in the culture war, coming down firmly on behalf of gay rights. Indiana backed down under corporate pressure—as did Arkansas a week later.

This was a watershed event. It showed that if big business objected, even Republican politicians in red states would not take a stand, even a mild one, for religious freedom. Professing orthodox biblical Christianity on sexual matters was now thought to be evidence of intolerable bigotry. Conservative Christians had been routed. We were living in a new country.

And then two months later the U.S. Supreme Court declared a constitutional right to same-sex marriage. The decision was popular with the American people, which had, over the previous decade, undergone a staggering shift on gay rights and same-sex marriage. No sooner was the right to gay marriage achieved than activists and their political allies, the Democratic Party, began pushing for transgender rights.

Post-*Obergefell*, Christians who hold to the biblical teaching about sex and marriage have the same status in culture, and increasingly in law, as racists. The culture war that began with the Sexual Revolution in the 1960s has now ended in defeat for Christian conservatives. The cultural left—which is to say, increasingly the American mainstream—has no intention of living in postwar peace. It is pressing forward with a harsh, relentless occupation, one that is aided by the cluelessness of Christians who don't understand what's happening. Don't be fooled: the upset presidential victory of Donald Trump has at best given us a bit more time to prepare for the inevitable.

I have written *The Benedict Option* to wake up the church and to encourage it to act to strengthen itself, while there is still time. If we want to survive, we have to return to the roots of our faith, both in thought and in practice. We are going to have to learn habits of the heart forgotten by believers in the West. We are going to have to change our lives, and our approach to life, in radical ways. In short, *we are going to have to be the church*, without compromise, no matter what it costs.

This book does not offer a political agenda. Nor is it a spiritual how-to manual, nor a standard decline-and-fall lament. True, it offers a critique of modern culture from a traditional Christian point of view, but more importantly, it tells the stories of conservative Christians who are pioneering creative ways to live out the faith joyfully and counter-culturally in these darkening days. My hope is that you will be inspired by them and collaborate with like-minded Christians in your local area to construct responses to the real-world challenges faced by the church. If the salt is not to lose its savor, we have to act. The hour is late. This is not a drill.

Alasdair MacIntyre said that we await "a new—doubtless very different—St. Benedict." The philosopher meant an inspired, creative leader who will pioneer a way to live the tradition in community, so that it can survive through a time of great testing. Pope Emeritus Benedict XVI foretells a world in which the church will live in small circles of committed believers who live the faith intensely, and who will have to be somewhat cut off from mainstream society for the sake of holding on to the truth. Read this book, learn from the people you meet in it, and be inspired by the testimony of the lives of the monks. Let them all speak to your heart and mind, then get active locally to strengthen yourself, your family, your church, your school, and your community.

In the first part of this book, I will define the challenge of post-Christian America as I see it. I will explore the philosophical and theological roots of our society's fragmentation, and I will explain how the Christian virtues embodied in the sixth-century Rule of Saint Benedict, a monastic guidebook that played a powerful role in preserving Christian culture throughout the so-called Dark Ages, can help all believers today.

In the second part, I will discuss how the way of Christian living prescribed by the Rule can be adapted to the lives of modern conservative Christians of all churches and confessions. To avoid political confusion, I use the word "orthodox"—small "o"—to refer to theologically traditional Protestants, Catholics, and Eastern Orthodox Christians. The Rule offers insights in how to approach politics, faith, family, community, education, and work. I will detail how they manifest themselves in the lives of a diverse number of Christians who have lessons to teach the entire church. Finally, I will consider the critical importance of believers thinking and acting radically in the face of the two most powerful phenomena directing contemporary life and pulverizing the church's foundations: sex and technology.

In the end, I hope you will agree with me that Christians are now in a time of decision. The choices we make today have consequences for the lives of our descendants, our nation, and our civilization. Jesus Christ promised that the gates of Hell would not prevail against His church, but He did not promise that Hell would not prevail against His church *in the West*. That depends on us, and the choices we make right here, right now.

I invite you, the reader, to keep in mind as you make your way through these pages that maybe, just maybe, the new and quite different Benedict that God is calling to revive and strengthen His church is . . . *you*.

—Rod Dreher

CHAPTER 1

The Great Flood

No one saw the Great Flood coming.

The newspaper said heavy rains were headed to south Louisiana that weekend in August 2016, but it was nothing unusual for us. Louisiana is a wet place, especially in summer. The weatherman said we could expect three to six inches over a five-day period.

By the time the rain stopped, the deluge had dropped over thirty inches of water on the greater Baton Rouge area. Places that no one ever imagined would see high water disappeared beneath the muddy torrent as rivers and creeks hemorrhaged and burst their banks. People fled their houses and made it to high ground with minutes to spare. Some had not even that much time and were lucky to clamber with their families onto their roofs, where rescuers found them.

I spent the Sunday of the flood at a makeshift shelter in Baton Rouge. My son Lucas and I helped unload the rescued from National Guard helicopters, and we joined scores of other volunteers in feeding and helping the thousands of refugees flowing in from the surrounding area. Men, women, families, the elderly, the well-off, the very poor, white, black, Asian, Latino—it was a real "here comes everybody" moment. And nearly every one of them looked shell-shocked.

Serving jambalaya to hungry and dazed evacuees, one heard the same story over and over: *We have lost everything. We never expected this. It has never flooded where we live. We were not prepared.*

These confused and homeless evacuees could be forgiven their lack of preparation. Few had thought to buy flood insurance, but why would they? The Great Flood was a thousand-year weather event, and nobody in recorded history had ever seen this land underwater. The last time something like this happened in Louisiana, Western civilization had not yet reached American shores.

We Christians in the West are facing our own thousand-year flood—or if you believe Pope Emeritus Benedict XVI, a fifteen-hundred-year flood: in 2012, the then-pontiff said that the spiritual crisis overtaking the West is the most serious since the fall of the Roman Empire near the end of the fifth century. The light of Christianity is flickering out all over the West. There are people alive today who may live to see the effective death of Christianity within our civilization. By God's mercy, the faith may continue to flourish in the Global South and China, but barring a dramatic reversal of current trends, it will all but disappear entirely from Europe and North America. This may not be the end of the world, but it is the end of *a* world, and only the willfully blind would deny it. For a long time we have downplayed or ignored the signs. Now the floodwaters are upon us—and we are not ready.

The storm clouds have been gathering for decades, but most of us believers have operated under the illusion that they would blow over. The breakdown of the natural family, the loss of traditional moral values, and the fragmenting of communities—we were troubled by these developments but believed they were reversible and didn't reflect anything fundamentally wrong with our approach to faith. Our religious leaders told us that strengthening the levees of law and politics would keep the flood of secularism at bay. The sense one had was: There's nothing here that can't be fixed by continuing to do what Christians have been doing for decades—especially voting for Republicans.

Today we can see that we've lost on every front and that the swift and relentless currents of secularism have overwhelmed our flimsy barriers. Hostile secular nihilism has won the day in our nation's government, and the culture has turned powerfully against traditional Christians. We tell ourselves that these developments have been imposed by a liberal elite, because we find the truth intolerable: The American people, either actively or passively, approve.

The advance of gay civil rights, along with a reversal of religious liberties for believers who do not accept the LGBT agenda, had been slowly but steadily happening for years. The U.S. Supreme Court's *Obergefell* decision declaring a constitutional right to same-sex marriage was the Waterloo of religious conservatism. It was the moment that the Sexual Revolution triumphed decisively, and the culture war, as we have known it since the 1960s, came to an end. In the wake of *Obergefell*, Christian beliefs about the sexual complementarity of marriage are considered to be abominable prejudice—and in a growing number of cases, punishable. The public square has been lost.

Not only have we lost the public square, but the supposed high ground of our churches is no safe place either. Well, so what if those around us don't share our morality? We can still retain our faith and teaching within the walls of our churches, we may think, but that's placing unwarranted confidence in the health of our religious institutions. The changes that have overtaken the West in modern times have revolutionized everything, even the church, which no longer forms souls but caters to selves. As conservative Anglican theologian Ephraim Radner has said, "There is no safe place in the world or in our churches within which to be a Christian. It is a new epoch."[1]

Don't be fooled by the large number of churches you see today. Unprecedented numbers of young adult Americans say they have no religious affiliation at all. According to the Pew Research Center, one in three 18-to-29-year-olds have put religion aside, if they ever picked it up in the first place.[2] If the demographic trends continue, our churches will soon be empty.

Even more troubling, many of the churches that do stay open will have been hollowed out by a sneaky kind of secularism to the point where the "Christianity" taught there is devoid of power and life. It has already happened in most of them. In 2005, sociologists Christian Smith and Melinda Lundquist Denton examined the religious and spiritual lives of American teenagers from a wide variety of backgrounds. What they found was that in most cases, teenagers adhered to a mushy pseudoreligion the researchers deemed Moralistic Therapeutic Deism (MTD).[3]

MTD has five basic tenets:

- A God exists who created and orders the world and watches over human life on earth.
- God wants people to be good, nice, and fair to each other, as taught in the Bible and by most world religions.
- The central goal of life is to be happy and to feel good about oneself.
- God does not need to be particularly involved in one's life except when he is needed to resolve a problem.
- Good people go to heaven when they die.

This creed, they found, is especially prominent among Catholic and Mainline Protestant teenagers. Evangelical teenagers fared measurably better but were still far from historic biblical orthodoxy. Smith and Denton claimed that MTD is colonizing existing Christian churches, destroying biblical Christianity from within, and replacing it with a pseudo-Christianity that is "only tenuously connected to the actual historical Christian tradition."

MTD is not entirely wrong. After all, God does exist, and He does want us to be good. The problem with MTD, in both its progressive and its conservative versions, is that it's mostly about improving one's self-esteem and subjective happiness and getting along well with others. It has little to do with the Christianity of Scripture and tradition, which teaches repentance, self-sacrificial love, and purity of heart, and commends suffering—the Way of the Cross—as the pathway to God. Though superficially Christian, MTD is the natural religion of a culture that worships the Self and material comfort.

As bleak as Christian Smith's 2005 findings were, his follow-up research, a third installment of which was published in 2011, was even grimmer. Surveying the moral beliefs of 18-to-23-year-olds, Smith and his colleagues found that only 40 percent of young Christians sampled said that their personal moral beliefs were grounded in the Bible or some other religious sensibility.[4] It's unlikely that the beliefs of even these faithful are biblically coherent. Many of these "Christians" are actually committed moral individualists who neither know nor practice a coherent Bible-based morality.

An astonishing 61 percent of the emerging adults had no moral problem at all with materialism and consumerism. An added 30 percent expressed some qualms but figured it was not worth worrying about. In this view, say Smith and his team, "all that society is, apparently, is a collection of autonomous individuals out to enjoy life."

These are not bad people. Rather, they are young adults who have been terribly failed by family, church, and the other institutions that formed—or rather, failed to form—their consciences and their imaginations.

MTD is the de facto religion not simply of American teenagers but also of American adults. To a remarkable degree, teenagers have adopted the religious attitudes of their parents. We have been an MTD nation for some time now.

"America has lived a long time off its thin Christian veneer, partly necessitated by the Cold War," Smith told me in an interview. "That is all finally being stripped away by the combination of mass consumer capitalism and liberal individualism."

The data from Smith and other researchers make clear what so many of us are desperate to deny: the flood is rising to the rafters in the American church. Every single congregation in America must ask itself if it has compromised so much with the world that it has been compromised in its faithfulness. Is the Christianity we have been living out in our families, congregations, and communities a means of deeper conversion, or does it function as a vaccination against taking faith with the seriousness the Gospel demands?

Nobody but the most deluded of the old-school Religious Right believes that this cultural revolution can be turned back. The wave cannot be stopped, only ridden. With a few exceptions, conservative Christian political activists are as ineffective as White Russian exiles, drinking tea from samovars in their Paris drawing rooms, plotting the restoration of the monarchy. One wishes them well but knows deep down that they are not the future.

Americans cannot stand to contemplate defeat or to accept limits of any kind. But American Christians are going to have to come to terms with the brute fact that we live in a culture, one in which our beliefs make increasingly little sense. We speak a language that the world more and more either cannot hear or finds offensive to its ears.

Could it be that the best way to fight the flood is to . . . stop fighting the flood? That is, to quit piling up sandbags and to build an ark in which to shelter until the water recedes and we can put our feet on dry land again? Rather than wasting energy and resources fighting unwinnable political battles, we should instead work on building communities, institutions, and networks of resistance that can outwit, outlast, and eventually overcome the occupation.

Fear not! We have been in a place like this before. In the first centuries of Christianity, the early church survived and grew under Roman persecution and later after the collapse of the empire in the West. We latter-day Christians must learn from their example—and particularly from the example of Saint Benedict.

One day near the turn of the sixth century, a young Roman named Benedict said good-bye to his hometown, Nursia, a rugged village pocketed away in central Italy's Sibylline mountain range. The son of Nursia's governor, Benedict was on his way to Rome, the place where promising young men seeking a place in the world went to complete their education.

This was no longer the Rome of imperial glory, the memory of which remained after Constantine's conversion made the empire officially Christian. Nearly seventy years before Benedict was born, the Visigoths had sacked the Eternal City. The collapse of the city of Rome was a staggering blow to the morale of citizens across the once-mighty empire.

By that time, the empire was governed in the West from Rome, which had long been in decline, and in the East from Constantinople, which thrived. Yet Christians throughout the empire mourned because Rome's suffering forced them to confront a terrible fact: that the foundations of the world they and their ancestors had known were crumbling before their eyes.

"My voice sticks in my throat; and, as I dictate, sobs choke my utterance," wrote Saint Jerome in its aftermath. "The city which had taken the whole world was itself taken." So great was the shock that Jerome's contemporary, Saint Augustine, wrote his classic *City of God*, which explained the catastrophe in terms of God's mysterious will and refocused the minds of Christians on the imperishable heavenly kingdom.

The city of Rome did not disappear, but by the time young Benedict arrived, Rome was a pathetic shadow of its former self. Once the world's largest city, with a population estimated at one million souls at the height of its power in the second century, its population plummeted in the decades after the sack. In 476, barbarians deposed the last Roman emperor of the West. By the turn of the sixth century, Rome's population had scattered, leaving only one hundred thousand souls to pick over the ruins.

The overthrow of the Western empire did not mean anarchy. To the contrary, in Italy, things went on much as they had gone for decades. Theodoric, the Visigoth king who ruled Italy in Benedict's time from his capital in Ravenna, was a heretical Christian (an Arian) but made a pilgrimage to Rome in the year 500 to pay his respects to the Pope. The king assured the Romans of his favor for them and his protection. In fact, the best he could do was to manage Rome's decline.

We know few particulars of social life in barbarian-ruled Rome, but history shows that a general loosening of morals follows the shattering of a long-standing social order. Think of the decadence of Paris and Berlin after World War I, or of Russia in the decade after the end of the Soviet empire. Pope Saint Gregory the Great never knew Benedict, but he wrote the saint's biography based on interviews he conducted with four of Benedict's disciples. Gregory writes that young Benedict was so shocked and disgusted by the vice and corruption in the city that he turned his back on the life of privilege that awaited him there, as the son of a government official. He moved to the nearby forest and later to a cave forty miles to the east. There Benedict lived a life of prayer and contemplation as a hermit for three years.

This was normal in the first centuries of the church, and it continues in some places even today. In the third century, men (and even a few women) retreated to the Egyptian desert, renouncing all bodily comfort to seek God in a solitary life of silence, prayer, and fasting. They took to an extreme the scriptural injunction to die to self to live in Christ, obeying the Lord's command to the rich young ruler to sell his possessions, give to the poor, and follow Him. Saint Anthony of Egypt (ca. 251–356) is believed to have been the first hermit. His followers founded communal Christian monasticism, but the figure of the hermit remained a part of monastic life and practice.

During Benedict's three years in the cave, a monk named Romanus, from a nearby monastery, brought him food. By the time Benedict emerged from the cave, he had a reputation for sanctity and was invited by a monastic community to be their abbot. Eventually Benedict founded twelve monasteries of his own in the region. His twin sister, Scholastica, followed in his footsteps, beginning her own community of nuns. To guide the monks and nuns in living simple, orderly lives consecrated to Christ, Benedict wrote a slim book, now known as the Rule of Saint Benedict.

For the early monastics, a "rule" was simply a guide to living in Christian community. The one Benedict wrote is a more relaxed form of a very strict earlier one from the Christian East. In his Rule, Benedict described the monastery as a "school for the Lord's service." In that sense, his Rule is simply a training manual. Modern readers who turn to it looking for mystical teaching of fathomless spiritual depth will be disappointed. Benedict's spirituality is wholly practical—and he originally wrote it not for the clergy but for laymen.

When he left fallen Rome for the wilderness, Benedict had no idea that his founding of his schools for the Lord's service would over time have such dramatic impact on Western civilization. Europe in the early Middle Ages was reeling from the calamitous end of the empire, which left in its wake countless local wars as barbarian tribes fought for dominance. Rome's fall left behind a staggering degree of material poverty, the result of both the disintegration of Rome's complex trade network and the loss of intellectual and technical sophistication.

In these miserable conditions, the church was often the strongest—and perhaps the only—government people had. Within the broad embrace of the church, monasticism provided much-needed help and hope to the peasantry, and thanks to Benedict, a renewed focus on spiritual life led many men and women to leave the world and devote themselves wholly to God within the walls of monasteries under the Rule. These monasteries kept faith and learning alive within their walls, evangelized barbarian peoples, and taught them how to pray, to read, to plant crops, and to build things. Over the next few centuries, they prepared the devastated societies of post-Roman Europe for the rebirth of civilization.

It all grew from the mustard seed of faith planted by a faithful young Italian who wanted nothing more than to seek and to serve God in a community of faith constructed to withstand the chaos and decadence all around them. Benedict's example gives us hope today, because it reveals what a small cohort of believers who respond creatively to the challenges of their own time and place can accomplish by channeling the grace that flows through them from their radical openness to God, and embodying that grace in a distinct way of life.

In his book *After Virtue*, philosopher Alasdair MacIntyre likened the present cultural moment to the fall of the Roman Empire in the West. He argued that the West has abandoned reason and the tradition of the virtues in giving itself over to the relativism that is now flooding our world today. We are governed not by faith, or by reason, or by any combination of the two. We are governed by what MacIntyre called *emotivism*: the idea that all moral choices are nothing more than expressions of what the choosing individual feels is right.

MacIntyre said that a society that governed itself according to emotivist principles would look a lot like the modern West, in which the liberation of the individual's will is thought to be the greatest good. A virtuous society, by contrast, is one that shares belief in objective moral goods and the practices necessary for human beings to embody those goods in community.

To live "after virtue," then, is to dwell in a society that not only can no longer agree on what constitutes virtuous belief and conduct but also doubts that virtue exists. In a post-virtue society, individuals hold maximal freedom of thought and action, and society itself becomes "a collection of strangers, each pursuing his or her own interests under minimal constraints."

Achieving this kind of society requires

- abandoning objective moral standards;
- refusing to accept any religiously or culturally binding narrative originating outside oneself, except as chosen;
- repudiating memory of the past as irrelevant; and

- distancing oneself from community as well as any unchosen social obligations.

This state of mind approximates the condition known as barbarism. When we think of barbarians, we imagine wild, rapacious tribesmen rampaging through cities, heedlessly destroying the structures and institutions of civilization, simply because they can. Barbarians are governed only by their will to power, and neither know nor care a thing about what they are annihilating.

By that standard, despite our wealth and technological sophistication, we in the modern West are living under barbarism, though we do not recognize it. Our scientists, our judges, our princes, our scholars, and our scribes—they are at work demolishing the faith, the family, gender, even what it means to be human. Our barbarians have exchanged the animal pelts and spears of the past for designer suits and smartphones.

MacIntyre concluded *After Virtue* by looking back to the West after barbarian tribes overthrew the Roman imperial order. He wrote,

A crucial turning point in that earlier history occurred when men and women of good will turned aside from the task of shoring up the Roman imperium and ceased to identify the continuation of civility and moral community with the maintenance of that imperium. What they set themselves to achieve instead—often not recognizing fully what they were doing—was the construction of new forms of community within which the moral life could be sustained so that both morality and civility might survive the coming ages of barbarism and darkness.[5]

In MacIntyre's reading, the post-Roman system was too far gone to be saved. Saint Benedict had taken the proper measure of Rome. He acted wisely by leaving society and starting a new community whose practices would preserve the faith through the trials ahead. Though not then a Christian, MacIntyre called on traditionalists who still believe in reason and virtue to form communities within which the life of virtue can survive the long Dark Age to come.

The world, said MacIntyre, awaits "another—doubtless very different—St. Benedict." Christians besieged by the raging floodwaters of modernity await someone like Benedict to build arks capable of carrying them and the living faith across the sea of crisis—a Dark Age that could last centuries.

In this book, you will meet men and women who are today's Benedicts. Some live in the countryside. Others live in the city. Still others make their homes in the suburbs. All of them are faithful orthodox Christians—that is, theological conservatives within the three main branches of historic Christianity—who know that if believers don't come out of Babylon and be separate, sometimes metaphorically, sometimes literally, their faith will not survive for another generation or two in this culture of death. They recognize an unpopular truth: politics will not save us. Instead of looking to prop up the current order, they have recognized that the kingdom of which they are citizens is not of this world and have decided not to compromise that citizenship.

What these orthodox Christians are doing now are the seeds of what I call the Benedict Option, a strategy that draws on the authority of Scripture and the wisdom of the ancient church to embrace "exile in place" and form a vibrant counterculture. Recognizing the toxins of modern secularism, as well as the fragmentation caused by relativism, Benedict Option Christians look to Scripture and to Benedict's Rule for ways to cultivate practices and communities. Rather than panicking or remaining complacent, they recognize that the new order is not a problem to be solved but a reality to be lived with. It will be those who learn how to endure with faith and creativity, to deepen their own prayer lives and adopting practices, focusing on families and communities instead of on partisan politics, and building churches, schools, and other institutions within which the orthodox Christian faith can survive and prosper through the flood.

This is not just about our own survival. If we are going to be for the world as Christ meant for us to be, we are going to have to spend more time away from the world, in deep prayer and substantial spiritual training—just as Jesus retreated to the desert to pray before ministering to the people. We cannot give the world what we do not have. If the ancient Hebrews had been assimilated by the culture of Babylon, it would have ceased being a light to the world. So it is with the church.

The reality of our situation is indeed alarming, but we do not have the luxury of doom-and-gloom hysteria. There is a hidden blessing in this crisis, if we will open our eyes to it. Just as God used chastisement in the Old Testament to call His people back to Himself, so He may be delivering a like judgment onto a church and a people grown cold from selfishness, hedonism, and materialism. The coming storm may be the means through which God delivers us.

Growing up in south Louisiana, whenever a hurricane was coming, somebody would take out the cast-iron kettle, make a big pot of gumbo, and after battening down the hatches, invite the neighbors over to eat, tell stories, make merry, and ride out the storm together. This spirit ruled the response to the Great Flood of 2016. Even as the waters rose, little platoons all over south Louisiana rushed out to rescue the trapped, shelter the homeless, feed the hungry (with mountains of jambalaya, mostly), and comfort the broken and broken-hearted.

This was not a response ordered from on high. It emerged spontaneously, out of the love local people had for their neighbor, and the sense of responsibility they had to care for those left poor and naked by the flood. Men and women of virtue—the Cajun Navy, church folks, and others—did not wait to be told what to do. They recognized the seriousness of the crisis, and they moved.

The grave spiritual and cultural crisis that has overtaken us did not come from nowhere. Though its pace has quickened over the past fifty years, the crisis has been gestating for many centuries. If we are going to figure out how to make it through the storm and the fog to safe harbor, we have to understand how we got here. Ideas, as we will see, have consequences.

CHAPTER 2

The Roots of the Crisis

On a warm evening in the late autumn, a recently retired woman sits on the front porch of her neighbor's house, talking about the ways of the world. It is two weeks before the Trump-Clinton election, and everything seems to be going to pieces, the neighbors agree. How did our country get to this place? they wonder. Both of the women are working class by culture, but thanks to economic and cultural changes in the mid-twentieth century, they are now entering their golden years as members of a modest middle class. America has been very good to them and their families.

Yet neither woman is confident about the future for their grand-children. One tells the other that in the past year, she has gone to six baby showers for young women in her family and social circles. None of the expectant mothers had husbands. Some had more than one child out of wedlock. The gray-haired women know what poverty and insecurity are like, and they can't believe that these young women would bring children into the world without fathers in the home, given how much more likely children in those situations are to be poor. And where are the fathers, anyway? What is wrong with young men these days?

These women are pro-life Christian conservatives who would never countenance abortion. They would rather see babies born than exterminated in the womb, no matter what the cost. Still, the normalization of having children outside of marriage is hard for them to take. In the 1940s, when they were born, the out-of-wedlock birth rate among whites was 2 percent. It is now nearly 30 percent (the overall birth rate to unwed mothers is 41 percent).[1] "It's like the whole world is coming apart," sighed one of the women.

"I'm glad I'm not going to be around to see it," said the other.

Those women aren't imagining things. Their whole world really is unraveling. Political scientist Charles Murray documented it in his aptly titled 2012 book *Coming Apart: The State of White America 1960–2010*. Murray focused his study on the white working class, but the social and cultural trends that have undone them are not confined to whites alone. Nor were the 1960s the beginning of our unraveling, though they were a turning point. We are living with the consequences of ideas accepted many generations ago, and as a result of those decisions, we are losing our religion—a far greater crisis than merely losing the habit of churchgoing.

The word *religion* comes from the Latin word *religare*, meaning "to bind." From a sociological point of view, religion is a coherent system of beliefs and practices through which the community of believers know who they are and what they are to do. These beliefs and practices are held to be rooted in and expressive of the sacred order both grounding and transcending existence. They tell and enact the story that holds the community together.

The loss of the Christian religion is why the West has been fragmenting for some time now, a process that is accelerating. How did it happen? There were five landmark events over seven centuries that rocked Western civilization and stripped it of its ancestral faith:

- In the fourteenth century, the loss of belief in the integral connection between God and Creation—or in philosophic terms, transcendent reality and material reality
- The collapse of religious unity and religious authority in the Protestant Reformation of the sixteenth century
- The eighteenth-century Enlightenment, which displaced the Christian religion with the cult of Reason, privatized religious life, and inaugurated the age of democracy
- The Industrial Revolution (ca. 1760–1840) and the growth of capitalism in the nineteenth and twentieth centuries
- The Sexual Revolution (1960–present)

This outline of Western cultural history since the High Middle Ages admittedly leaves out a great deal. And it is biased toward an intellectual understanding of historical causation. In truth, material consequences often give birth to ideas. The discovery of the New World and the invention of the printing press, both in the fifteenth century, and the invention of the birth control pill and the Internet in the twentieth, made it possible for people to imagine things they never had before and thus to think new thoughts. History gives us no clean, straight causal lines binding events and giving them clear order. History is a poem, not a syllogism.

That said, outlining the role ideas—especially ideas about God—played in historical change gives us a conceptual understanding of the nature of our present crisis. It's important to grasp this picture, however incomplete and oversimplified, to understand why the humble Benedictine way is such a potent counterforce to the dissolving currents of modernity.

The people of the Middle Ages lived in what philosopher Charles Taylor calls an "enchanted world"—one so unlike ours that we struggle to imagine it. We in the modern West are on a distant shore, and the worldview of our medieval ancestors is over the horizon, far from view.

Medievals experienced the divine as far more present in their daily lives. As it has been for most people, Christian and otherwise, throughout history, religion was everywhere, and—this is crucial—as a matter not merely of belief but of experience. In the mind of medieval Christendom, the spirit world and the material world penetrated each other. The division between them was thin and porous. Another way to put this is that the medievals experienced everything in the world *sacramentally*.

We associate that word with church and rightly so. Baptism is a sacrament, for example, as is Communion. These are special rituals in which God's grace is present in a particular way, effecting a real transformation on those participating in it. But sacramentalism had a much broader and deeper meaning in the mind of the Middle Ages. People of those days took all things that existed, even time, as in some sense sacramental. That is, they believed that God was present everywhere and revealed Himself to us *through* people, places, and things, through which His power flowed.

The power of sacred places and the relics of saints had such potency to the medievals because God wasn't present in a vague spiritual sense, like a butler watching silently over a manor house. He was there, writes Taylor, "as immediate reality, like stones, rivers, and mountains."[2] The specific sense in which He was present was a mystery—and a source of speculation and contention even back then—but *that* He was truly present was not disputed. The only reason the material world had any meaning at all was because of its relationship to God.

Medieval man held that reality—what was *really* real—was outside himself and that dwelling in the darkness of the Fall, he could not fully perceive it. But he could relate to it intellectually through faith and reason, and know it through conversion of the heart. The entire universe was woven into God's own Being, in ways that are difficult for modern people, even believing Christians, to grasp. Christians of the Middle Ages took Paul's words recorded in Acts—"in Him we live and move and have our being"—and in his letter to the Colossians—"He is before all things and in Him all things hold together"—in a much more literal sense than we do.

Medieval man did not see himself as fundamentally separate from the natural order; rather, the alienation he felt was an effect of the Fall, a catastrophe that, as he understood it, made it difficult for humans to see Creation as it really is. His task was to join himself to the love of God and harmonize his own steps with the great cosmic dance. Truth was guaranteed by the existence of God, whose Logos, the divine principle of order, was made fully manifest in Jesus Christ but is present to some degree in all Creation.

Medieval Europe was no Christian utopia. The church was spectacularly corrupt, and the violent exercise of power—at times by the church itself—seemed to rule the world. Yet despite the radical brokenness of their world, medievals carried within their imagination a powerful vision of integration. In the medieval consensus, men construed reality in a way that empowered them to harmonize everything conceptually and find meaning amid the chaos.

The medieval conception of reality is an old idea, one that predates Christianity. In his final book *The Discarded Image*, C. S. Lewis, who was a professional medievalist, explained that Plato believed that two things could relate to each other only through a third thing. In what Lewis called the medieval "Model," everything that existed was related to every other thing that existed, through their shared relationship to God. Our relationship to the world is mediated through God, and our relationship to God is mediated through the world.

Humankind dwelled not in a cold, meaningless universe but in a *cosmos*, in which everything had meaning because it participated in the life of the Creator. Says Lewis, "Every particular fact and story became more interesting and more pleasurable if, by being properly fitted in, it carried one's mind back to the Model as a whole."[3]

For the medievals, says Lewis, regarding the cosmos was like "looking at a great building"—perhaps like the Chartres cathedral—"overwhelming in its greatness but satisfying in its harmony."

The medieval model held all of Creation to be bound in a complex unity that encompassed all of time and space. It reached its apogee in the highly complex, rationalistic theology known as Scholasticism, of which the brilliant thirteenth-century Dominican friar Thomas Aquinas (1225–1274) was the greatest exponent.

The core teachings of Scholasticism include the principle that all things exist and have a God-given essential nature independent of human thought. This position is called "metaphysical realism." From this principle comes what Charles Taylor identifies as the three basic bulwarks upholding the medieval Christian "imaginary"—that is, the vision of reality accepted by all orthodox Christians from the early church through the High Middle Ages:

- The world and everything in it is part of a harmonious whole ordered by God and filled with meaning—and all things are signs pointing to God.
- Society is grounded in that higher reality.
- The world is charged with spiritual force.

These three pillars had to crumble before the modern world could arise from the rubble, Taylor says. And crumble they did. It did not happen at once, and it did not happen straightforwardly. But it happened. Theologian David Bentley Hart describes the transformation as opening an "imaginative chasm between the premodern and modern worlds. Human beings now in a sense inhabited a universe different from that inhabited by their ancestors."[4]

The theologian who did the most to topple the mighty oak of the medieval model—that is, Christian metaphysical realism—was a Franciscan from the British Isles, William of Ockham (1285–1347).

The ax he and his theological allies created to do the job was a big idea that came to be called *nominalism*.

Realism holds that the essence of a thing is built into its existence by God, and its ultimate meaning is guaranteed by this connection to the transcendent order. This implies that Creation is comprehensible because it is rationally ordered by God and a revelation of Him.

"The heavens declare the glory of God, and the sky above proclaims his handiwork," says the Psalmist. The sense that the material world discloses the workings of the transcendent order was present in ancient philosophy and in many world religions, even nontheistic ones like Taoism. Metaphysical realism tells us that the awe we feel in the presence of nature, beauty, or goodness—the feeling that there must be more than what we experience with our senses—is a reasonable intuition. It doesn't tell us who God is, but it tells us that we are not imagining things: something—or Someone—is there.

Aquinas puts it like this: "To know that someone is approaching is not the same as to know that Peter is approaching, even though it is Peter who is approaching." Through prayer and contemplation, we may build on that intuition and come to know the identity of the One we sense. For example, the yearning for meaning and truth that all humans have, says David Bentley Hart, "is simply a manifestation of the metaphysical structure of all reality."

But if the infinite God reveals Himself through finite matter, does that not imply limitation? Ockham thought so. He denied metaphysical realism out of zeal to protect God's sovereignty. He feared that realism restricted God's freedom of action. For Ockham, if something is good, it is because God desired it to be so. The meaning of all things derives from God's sovereign will—that is, not because of what He is, or because of His participation in their being, but because of what He commands. If He calls something good today and the same thing evil tomorrow, that is His right.

This idea implies that objects have no intrinsic meaning, only the meaning assigned to them, and therefore no *meaningful* existence outside the mind. A table is just wood and nails arranged in a certain way, until we give it meaning by naming it "table." (*Nomen* is the Latin word for "name," hence *nominalism*.)

In Ockham's thought, God is an all-powerful entity who is totally separate from Creation. God has to be, taught Ockham, or else His freedom to act would be bound by the laws He made. A truly omnipotent God cannot be restrained by anything, in his view. If something is good, therefore, it is good because God said so. God's will, therefore, is more important than God's intellect.

This sounds like angels-dancing-on-the-head-of-a-pin stuff, but its importance cannot be overstated. Medieval metaphysicians believed nature pointed to God. Nominalists did not. They believed there is no inner meaning existing objectively within nature and discoverable by reason. Meaning is extrinsic—that is, imposed from the outside, by God—and accessible to humans by faith in Him and His revelation alone.

If this sounds like plain good sense to you, then you begin to grasp how revolutionary nominalism was. What was once a radical theory would, in time, become the basis for the way most people understood the relationship between God and Creation. It made the modern world possible—but as we will see, it also set the stage for man enthroning himself in the place of God.

Ideas don't occur in a vacuum. As C. S. Lewis put it, "We are all, very properly, familiar with the idea that in every age the human mind is deeply influenced by the accepted Model of the universe. But there is a two-way traffic; the Model is also influenced by the prevailing temper of mind."[5] Nominalism emerged from a restless civilization whose people were questing for something different. The Middle Ages were an age of intense faith and spirituality, but as even the art and poetry of the fourteenth century showed, humanity began turning its gaze away from the heavens and toward this world.

After Ockham, the so-called natural philosophers—thinkers who studied nature, the precursors of scientists—began to shed the metaphysical baggage bequeathed to them by Aristotle and his medieval Christian successors. They discovered that one didn't need to have a philosophical theory about a natural phenomenon's being in order to examine it empirically and draw conclusions.

Meanwhile, in the world of art and literature, a new emphasis on naturalism and individualism emerged. The old world, with its metaphysical certainties, its formal hierarches, and its spiritual focus gradually ceased to hold the imagination of Western man. Art became less symbolic, less idealized, less focused on religious themes, and more occupied with the life of man.

The Model shuddered under philosophical assault, but horrifying events outside the world of art and ideas also shook it to the core. War—especially the Hundred Years War between France and England—wracked western Europe, which also suffered a catastrophic fourteenth-century famine. Worst of all was the Black Death, a plague that killed between one-third and one-half of all Europeans before burning itself out. Few civilizations could withstand those kinds of traumas without tremendous upheavals.

For all these reasons, the Model broke apart. Metaphysical realism had been defeated. What emerged was a new individualism, a this-worldliness that would inaugurate the historical period called the Renaissance. The defeat of metaphysical realism inaugurated a new and dynamic phase of Western history—one that would culminate in a religious revolution.

Renaissance and Reformation

Renaissance is a French word meaning "rebirth." It refers to the cultural efflorescence that accompanied the West's rediscovery of the Greek and Roman roots of its civilization. It is important to note that the term was not applied to the period bridging the end of the Middle Ages and the beginning of the modern era until the nineteenth century. It contains within it the secular progressive belief that the religiously focused medieval period was a time of intellectual and artistic sterility—a ludicrous judgment but an influential one.

Nevertheless, the Renaissance does mark a distinct change in European culture, which shifted its focus from the glory of God to the glory of man. "We can become what we will," said Pico della Mirandola (1463–94), the archetypal Renaissance philosopher. It was not an open form of satanic defiance—indeed, Pico uttered that famous line in an oration in which he cautioned against abusing God's gift of free will—but those words express the Renaissance's optimism about human nature and its possibilities.

What was being reborn in the Renaissance? The classical spirit of ancient Greece and Rome, which had gone into eclipse following the fifth-century collapse of the Western Roman Empire, and the subsequent advent of the Christian medieval period. While the late medieval period concentrated on the rediscovery of Greek philosophical texts, Italian scholars of the fourteenth century led the way in reviving ancient literature and history. "Man is the measure of all things," said the ancient Greek philosopher Protagoras, in a line that also described the spirit of the new age dawning upon Europe.

Renaissance humanism began to consider the world through classical insights and emphasized the study of poetry, rhetoric, and other disciplines we now call the humanities. Though humanist culture was not as narrowly focused on the faith as its medieval predecessor, it was by no means anti-Christian. The Renaissance brought into Western Christianity a greater concern for the individual, for freedom, and for the dignity of man as bearing the image of God.

Medieval Christianity focused on the fall of man, but the more humanistic Christianity of the Renaissance centered on man's potential. Christian humanism was far more individualistic than what came before it, and it sought to Christianize the classical model of the hero, the man of virtue. Scholasticism emphasized reason and intellect as the way to relate to God; Christian humanism focused on the will.

The danger was that Christian humanists would become too enamored of human potential and man's capacity for self-creation and lose sight of his chronic inclination toward sin. This was a temptation to which the Italian humanists were particularly susceptible. They were all too pleased to cast off the sackcloth and ashes of medieval asceticism and revel in the glory and vigor of the sensual life. Not so with the humanists of northern Europe, who were more modest in their piety and restrained in their optimism about human nature. They were more drawn to Scripture than to philosophy and were concerned primarily with reforming the church toward a more rigorous morality and a more democratic religious life. They viewed with skepticism, even disdain, the sensuality that had overtaken European life, especially in the church.

Renaissance Rome was a cesspit of vice, and the corruption reached far beyond the papal court and the Vatican walls. Many bishops were despised for their worldliness, while drunken and ignorant parish clergy, indifferent to the Gospel, were disrespected by their angry flocks. As the church hemorrhaged spiritual and moral authority, the clamor for change rose. But the Renaissance popes, prisoners of their own greed and tastes for opulence, refused to listen. They thought what they had would last forever.

It took an Augustinian monk named Martin Luther to shatter their illusions—and with it, the religious unity of the West. The Reformation, as we call the revolution he started, was not the first protest movement against Catholic Church corruption, but it was the first to hack at the theological and ecclesiological roots of Roman Catholicism itself.

Luther built his revolution not only on protests against church corruption but also on theological and philosophical developments that had already occurred within Latin Christianity. In 1517, Luther proclaimed his "Ninety-Five Theses" questioning the sale of indulgences, a feature of the Catholic penitential system that allowed the living to buy relief for relatives believed to be suffering punishment in Purgatory.

In fact, Luther aimed his formidable rhetorical cannon at Rome's entire structure defining sin, forgiveness, and ecclesial authority. In

1520, the Vatican excommunicated Luther for refusing to recant his belief that Scripture alone—as distinct from Scripture and the authoritative interpretation of the Roman church—was the source of Christian truth. Thus was the Protestant Reformation born.

Though there was a great deal of local diversity across Catholic Europe, fidelity to the Roman Catholic institution and its authority to proclaim objective religious truth had been a unifying principle. The Reformation destroyed that unity and stripped those under its sway of many symbols, rituals, and concepts that had structured the inner lives of Christians. Reformation-era Christians—Protestants—would no longer bow before what the Reformers believed to be superstition and idolatry. Scripture was their only authority in religious matters.

The question immediately arose: whose interpretation of Scripture? No Reformer believed in private interpretation of Scripture, but they had no clear way to discern whose interpretation was the correct one. The Reformers quickly discovered that casting off Rome's authority solved one problem but created another. As historian Brad Gregory puts it, "Because Christians disagreed about what they were to believe and do, they disagreed about what the fruits of a Christian life *were*."[6] And so it remains in our day.

Because religion was inseparable from politics and culture, the Reformation, and the Catholic Counter-Reformation, quickly led to a series of savage wars that shredded Europe. To be fair, the Wars of Religion were as political, social, and economic as they were religious. But the religious basis for the wars caused weary European intellectuals to explore ways of living peaceably with the schism between Rome and the Reformers.

The Dawn of the Enlightenment

The Scientific Revolution indirectly suggested a possible way out.

Even as the Wars of Religion raged, science made rapid advances.

The Scientific Revolution was a roughly two-hundred-year period of staggering advances in science and mathematics that began with Copernicus (1473–1543), who showed that the earth was not the fixed center of Creation, and ended with Newton (1642–1727), whose breakthrough discoveries laid the foundation for modern physics. The era overturned the Aristotelian-Christian cosmos—a hierarchical model of reality in which all things exist organically through their relationship to God—in favor of a mechanical universe ordered by laws of nature, with no necessary grounding in the transcendent.

Most leaders of the Scientific Revolution were professing Christians, but the revolution's grounding lay undeniably in nominalism. If the material world could be studied and understood on its own, without reference to God, then science can exist on its own, free of theological controversy.

This practical proposition allowed science to develop unhindered by metaphysical and religious suppositions. Science focused on facts about the material world that could be demonstrated, and it had an empirical method of testing hypotheses to prove or disprove their claims.

And science *worked,* in practical ways. Sir Francis Bacon, an important late Renaissance philosopher and founder of the scientific method, famously said that scientific discovery ought to be applied "for the relief of man's estate"—that is, to improve the lives of humans by reducing their pain, suffering, and poverty. This was a turning point in the history of ideas. The natural world was to be taken no longer as something to be contemplated as in any way an icon of the divine, but rather as something to be understood and manipulated by the will of humankind for its own sake. In this way, the Scientific Revolution further distanced God from Creation in the minds of men.

The Scientific Revolution culminated in the life and work of Sir Isaac Newton, a physicist, mathematician, and unorthodox Christian who fabricated a new model of the universe that explained its physical workings in a wholly mechanical way. Newton certainly believed that the laws of motion he discovered had been established by God. Yet Newton's God, in contrast to the God of traditional Christian metaphysics, was like a divine watchmaker who fashioned a timepiece, wound it, and let it carry on without his further involvement.

The explosion of science changed Western epistemology, the study of how we know what we know. Aristotelian science, which dominated the Middle Ages, was based on metaphysical concepts about the essential nature of things. The new science jettisoned the metaphysical baggage and reasoned from empirical observations alone. Philosopher and mathematician René Descartes (1596–1650) would change the approach to the epistemological question even further. Whereas Bacon said we should develop models by reasoning from empirical observation, Descartes took a more purely rationalistic approach.

Descartes taught that the best method was to begin by accepting as true only clear ideas that were beyond doubt. You should accept nothing as truth on the basis of authority, and you should even doubt your senses. Only those things of which you can be certain are true. And the first principle of all under this method is, "I think, therefore I am."

That is, the only thing that cannot be doubted is one's own existence. That is the foundation of all other thought, according to Descartes, who in this way made the autonomous, thinking individual into the determiner of truth. Descartes was a rationalist but not a moral relativist—indeed, he considered himself a faithful Catholic whose mission in part was to reconcile science to faith.

What Descartes did—and what makes him the father of modern philosophy—was to invert the medieval approach to knowledge. To the Scholastics, reality was an objective state, and humankind's role was first to understand the metaphysical nature of reality. Only then could humans begin to explore knowledge of the world and everything within it. Descartes, on the other hand, began all inquiry with radical subjectivity, declaring that the first principle of knowledge was that the Self is conscious of itself.

Descartes's philosophy opened the door to the world-changing project dubbed "the Enlightenment" by its cheerleaders, eager to contrast it to the supposedly dark days when revealed religion had its death grip on the Western mind. At its core, the Enlightenment was an attempt by European intellectuals to find a common basis outside religion for determining moral truth. The success of science led moral philosophers to explore how disinterested reason, which was so successful in the realm of science, could show the West a nonsectarian way to live.

The philosophers of the Enlightenment sought to use reason alone to establish a new basis for political and social life, one that was separated from the past. They tried to create a secular morality that any reasonable person could understand and affirm, and they believed that this was possible. They also advocated science and technology as a way to impose man's rational will upon nature, and they extolled the freely choosing individual.

For our purposes, the Enlightenment matters because it was the decisive break with the Christian legacy of the West. God, if He was mentioned at all, was not the God of Abraham, Isaac, and Jacob but the nondescript divinity of the Deists. Deism, a rationalistic school of thought that emerged in the Enlightenment, holds that God is a cosmic architect who created the universe but does not interact with it. Deism rejects biblical religion and the supernatural and bases its principles on what can be known about God—the "Supreme Being"—through reason alone.

Most of the American Founding Fathers were either confessed Deists like Benjamin Franklin (also a Freemason) or strongly influenced by Deism (e.g., Thomas Jefferson). Deism was a powerful intellectual force in eighteenth-century American life. John Locke, the English political philosopher whose teaching was a great influence on the American founding, was technically not a Deist—his belief in miracles contradicted the Deists' watchmaker God—but his philosophy was strongly consonant with Deist principles.

Locke believed that the autonomous individual, born as a blank slate, with no innate nature, is the fundamental unit of society. The purpose of the government, according to Locke, is not to pursue virtue but rather to establish and guard a social order under which individuals can exercise their will within reason. Government exists to secure the rights of these individuals to life, liberty, and property. The authors of the Declaration of Independence changed this formulation to "life, liberty, and the pursuit of Happiness," a phrase every American schoolchild learns in his civic catechism.

The U.S. Constitution, a Lockean document, privatizes religion, separating it from the state. Every American schoolchild learns to consider this a blessing, and perhaps it is. But segregating the sacred from the secular in this way profoundly shaped the American religious consciousness.

For all the good that religious tolerance undoubtedly brought to a young country with a diverse and contentious population of Protestant sectarians and a Catholic minority, it also laid the groundwork for excluding religion from the public square by making it a matter of private, individual choice. In the American order, the state's role is simply to act as a referee among individuals and factions. The government has no ultimate conception of the good, and it regards its own role as limited to protecting the rights of individuals.

When a society is thoroughly Christian, this is an ingenious way to keep the peace and allow for general flourishing. But from the Christian point of view, Enlightenment liberalism contained the seeds of Christianity's undoing.

In a letter to soldiers in 1798, John Adams, a Founding Father and practicing Unitarian, remarked:

> We had no government armed with power capable of contending with human passions unbridled by morality and religion. Avarice, ambition, revenge, or gallantry, would break the strongest cords of our Constitution as a whale goes through a

36

net. Our Constitution was made only for a moral and religious people. It is wholly inadequate to the government of any other.[7]

Adams understood that liberty under the Constitution could only work if the people were virtuous, restraining their passions and directing them toward the good—as defined, presumably, by Adams's rationalistic religious belief. Fortunately, having gone through the First Great Awakening of the mid-eighteenth century, America was strongly Evangelical, and citizens had a strong shared idea of the Good and a shared definition of virtue. Unfortunately, this would not last.

Democracy, Capitalism, Romanticism: The Calamitous Nineteenth Century

In the middle of the eighteenth century, new technological breakthroughs began to give man unprecedented power over nature. This led to an explosion in manufacturing and commerce, which brought revolutionary changes to society. The socially stable way of life based on farming and crafts came to an end. Peasants moved en masse to cities, where they became workers in the new factories. The social hierarchies of the traditional family and village began to dissolve.

The same was true in politics. The American Revolution in 1776 overthrew monarchy and established a constitutional republic. The far bloodier French Revolution of 1789 was much more radical, attempting near-totalitarian refashioning of French society in the name of republicanism. Its terror ended in the dictatorship of Napoleon Bonaparte, who restored order, but the violence unleashed by the revolution and its ideals rocked Europe for the rest of the century. It shook monarchies and established orders, using the ideals of liberty and democracy to batter older authoritarian structures.

Around the same time, artists and intellectuals began to rebel against Enlightenment reason and the effects of the Industrial Revolution. The Romantics, as they were called, found many aspects of the new rationalist, mechanized society distasteful but had no interest in returning to the Christian world. They prized emotion, individuality, nature, and personal freedom.

They advocated an ideal of the heroic, creative individual, one who rejects the strictures of society, one who follows his feelings and intuitions. For the Romantics, meaning and release from the ugliness of modern society was to be found in art, nature, and culture. Theirs was a primitivist reaction against the cold rationalism of the preceding age.

Though a man of the Enlightenment era, philosopher Jean-Jacques Rousseau (1712–1778) became the father of Romanticism. Rousseau advanced the idea that man is born naturally good but is corrupted by society. From Rousseau came the modern notion that the freer a society is, the more virtuous it is. The people, in expressing the "general will," are always right.

Alexis de Tocqueville, a young French aristocrat traveling through America in 1831–32, observed Rousseau's egalitarian ideals in practice. In *Democracy in America*, Tocqueville concluded that democracy was the future of Europe, but observed that with its drive for equality, which entailed making standards relative to the majority's will, democracy risked eliminating the virtues that made self-rule possible. Democracies will succeed only if "mediating institutions," including the churches, thrive.

In the nineteenth century, intellectual elites understood that the world around them was quickly fragmenting. "All that is solid melts into air," said Marx and Engels's *Communist Manifesto* (1848), which accurately observed that the Industrial Revolution had destroyed old certainties. Writing a generation after Charles Darwin published his *Origin of Species* in 1859, German philosopher Friedrich Nietzsche understood natural selection to mean that there is no divine plan guiding man's development. It is random, based on the survival of the fittest. Nietzsche drew on Darwin to formulate a philosophy extolling strength and the individual will.

"God is dead, and we have killed him," said Nietzsche, stating a blunt truth about the West's nascent atheism. Matthew Arnold captured the spirit of the age in these lines from his 1867 poem *Dover Beach*:

> The Sea of Faith
> Was once, too, at the full, and round earth's shore
> Lay like the folds of a bright girdle furled.
> But now I only hear
> Its melancholy, long, withdrawing roar,
> Retreating, to the breath
> Of the night-wind, down the vast edges drear
> And naked shingles of the world.

Despite the disillusionment of artists, philosophers, and other culture producers, the nineteenth century was a time of great religious fervor in England and America. The Victorian era in England stretched from 1837 until the turn of the twentieth century and featured a popular Christianity that was muscular, moralistic, and disciplined. It was notably civic-minded, with a strong emphasis on social reform. This reformist Evangelicalism spread to the United States, sparking the Third Great Awakening, which brought explosive growth in Protestant churches and laid the groundwork for the Social Gospel movement. Rising European immigration brought Catholics pouring into American cities by the hundreds of thousands.

The important changes, though, took place among the cultural elites, who continued to shed any semblance of traditional Christianity. In America, from 1870 through 1930, these elites worked what sociologist Christian Smith terms a "secular revolution." They harnessed the energy and tumult of industrialization to remake society along broadly "progressive" lines.

The effects of this progressive movement on American religious life were vast. It began the long liberalization of Mainline Protestantism by infusing it with a passion for social reform, over and against personal piety and evangelizing. Progressives turfed the Protestant religious establishment out of universities and other leading cultural institutions. It pushed religion to the margins of public life, advocating science as the primary source of society's values and as a guide to social change. Within Christianity, it replaced the religious model of the human person with a psychological model centered on the Self. And progressives' political ardor for greater democracy and egalitarianism found expression in church life by eroding the authority of the clergy and Scripture.

The twentieth century arrived amid a wave of optimism about the West's future. It was a time of hope and faith in progress. The dream came to a catastrophic end in 1914, with the outbreak of the deadliest war the world had ever seen.

The Triumph of Eros

The mass savagery of World War I, four years of grinding combat that consumed the lives of seventeen million soldiers and civilians, shattered European ideals and dealt a mortal blow to what remained of Christendom. The war's aftermath accelerated the abandonment of traditional sources of cultural authority. Sexual morality loosened. New styles of art and literature arose, making a conscious and definitive break with the discredited values of the prewar world.

Western civilization had been abandoning Christianity for quite some time, but it still had a sense of progress and purpose to unify it and to give its people direction and order to their lives. None of that progress—scientific, technological, economic, political, or social—prevented Europe from turning itself into a charnel house.

This was the period in which the West moved from what sociologist Zygmunt Bauman called "solid modernity"—a period of social change that was still fairly predictable and manageable—to "liquid modernity," our present condition, in which change is so rapid that no social institutions have time to solidify.[8]

Sigmund Freud, the founder of psychoanalysis, found his true genius not as a scientist but as a quasi-religious figure who discerned and proclaimed the Self as a deity to replace the Christian religion. Yet Freud's immense cultural authority depended on his role as an icon of science. Among secularized elites, who disseminated Freud's views widely through mass media, Freud's vision had the force of revelation precisely because elites believed it to be scientific.

To Freud, religion was nothing more than a man-made mechanism to cope with life and to manage instincts that, if allowed to run free, would make civilization impossible. Western man had lost God, and with that a sense that there was a higher authority to give life ultimate meaning. But man had to get on with life somehow.

Freud's answer was to replace religion with psychology. In his therapeutic vision, we should stop the fruitless searching for a nonexistent source of meaning and instead seek self-fulfillment. The pursuit of happiness was not a quest for unity with God, or sacrificial dedication to a cause greater than oneself but rather a search to satisfy the Self.

In the past, a person looked outside himself to learn what he was to do with his life. But in modernity, when we know that religion and all claims to transcendent values are an illusion, we must look into ourselves for the secret to our own well-being. Psychology did not necessarily intend to change a man's character, as in the old Christian therapies of repentance as a step toward conforming to God's will, but rather to help that man become comfortable with who he is.

Sociologist Philip Rieff, the great interpreter of Freud, described the shift in Western consciousness like this: "Religious man was born to be saved. Psychological man is born to be pleased."[9]

The 1960s were the decade in which Psychological Man came fully into his own. In that decade, the freedom of the individual to fulfill his own desires became our cultural lodestar, and the rapid falling away of American morality from its Christian ideal began as a result. Despite a conservative backlash in the 1980s, Psychological Man won decisively and now owns the culture—including most churches—as surely as the Ostrogoths, Visigoths, Vandals, and other conquering peoples owned the remains of the Western Roman Empire.

In 1966, at the beginning of this new age, Rieff published a study called *The Triumph of the Therapeutic: Uses of Faith After Freud*, a book that still stuns with its prescience. In it Rieff, an unbeliever, argued that the West, amid unprecedented liberty and prosperity, was going through a profound cultural revolution. It had not become atheist, but it had spiritualized desire and embraced a secular "gospel of self-fulfillment."

Most people understood that Western culture had been slowly moving away from Christianity since the Enlightenment, but Rieff said the process had gone much farther than most people realized.

In Rieff's theory of culture, a culture is defined by what it forbids. Each culture has its own "order of therapy"—a system that teaches its members what is permitted within its bounds and gives them sanctioned ways to let off the pressure of living by the community's rules, which are traditionally rooted in religion. Moreover, the asceticism in a culture—that is, the ideal of self-denial—cannot be an end in itself, because that would destroy a culture. Rather, it must be a "positive asceticism" that links the individual negating his own particular desires to the achievement of a higher, positive, life-affirming goal.

The main thing that helps a culture survive, Rieff wrote, is "the power of its institutions to bind and loose men in the conduct of their affairs with reasons which sink so deep into the self that they become commonly and implicitly understood." A culture begins to die, he went on, "when its normative institutions fail to communicate ideals in ways that remain inwardly compelling, first of all to the cultural elites themselves."

In other words, the Judeo-Christian culture of the West was dying because it no longer deeply believed in Christian sacred order, with its "thou shalt nots," and it had no way of agreeing on the "thou shalt nots" that every culture must have to restrain individual passions and direct them to socially beneficial ends. What made our condition so revolutionary, he said, was that for the first time in history, the West was attempting to build a culture on the *absence* of belief in a higher order that commanded our obedience. In other words, we were creating an "anti-culture," one that made the foundation for a stable culture impossible.

That is, instead of teaching us what we must deprive ourselves of to be civilized, we have a culture built on a cult of desire, one that tells us we find meaning and purpose in releasing ourselves from the old prohibitions, as we self-directed individuals choose.

"Eros must be raised to the level of a religious cult in modern society, not because we really are that obsessed with it, but because the myth of freedom demands it," says political philosopher Stephen L. Gardner. "It is in carnal desire that the modern individual believes he affirms his 'individuality.' The body must be the true 'subject' of desire because the individual must be the author of his own desire."[10]

The Romantic ideal of the self-created man finds its fulfillment in the newest vanguards of the Sexual Revolution, transgendered people. They refuse to be bound by biology and have behind them an elite movement teaching new generations that gender is whatever the choosing individual wants it to be. The advent of the birth control pill in the 1960s made it possible for mankind to extend its conquest and subjection of nature to the will to the human body itself. Transgenderism is the logical next step, after which will come the deconstruction of any obstructions, in law or in custom, to freely chosen polygamous arrangements.

Sure, there will be costs to extending the Sexual Revolution. We saw them in its first phase. The 1970s, the so-called Me Decade, was when the 1960s came to the rest of America. The divorce rate, rising in the 1960s, mushroomed in the 1970s. Abortions skyrocketed. But there was no going back. The new order found its constitutional confirmation in the Supreme Court's 1992 *Planned Parenthood vs. Casey* decision reaffirming abortion rights. Justice Anthony Kennedy, writing for the pro-choice majority, explained (no doubt unintentionally) how the Sexual Revolution depends on a radical, even nihilistic, conception of freedom:

> At the heart of liberty is the right to define one's own concept of existence, of meaning, of the universe, and of the mystery of human life.

Here is the end point of modernity: the autonomous, freely choosing individual, finding meaning in no one but himself.

Philosopher Charles Taylor describes the cultural mindset that has captured us all:

> Everyone has a right to develop their own form of life, grounded on their own sense of what is really important or of value. People are called upon to be true to themselves and to seek their own self-fulfilment. What this consists of, each must, in the last instance, determine for him- or herself. No one else can or should try to dictate its content.[11]

Of course every age has had its morally lax people, and people who have forsaken ideals and commitments to pursue their heart's desire. In fact, every one of us Christians is like that at times; it's called sin. What's distinct about the present age, says Taylor, is that "today many people feel called to do this, feel they ought to do this, feel their lives would be somehow wasted or unfulfilled if they didn't do it."

What is "it"? Following your own heart, no matter what society says, or the church, or anybody else. This kind of thinking is devastating to every kind of social stability but especially to the church. The church, a community that authoritatively teaches and disciples its members, cannot withstand a revolution in which each member becomes, in effect, his own pope. Churches—Protestant, Catholic, and Orthodox—that are nothing more than a loosely bound assembly of individuals committed to finding their own "truth," are no longer the church in any meaningful sense, because there is no shared belief.

In this sense, Christians today may think we stand in opposition to secular culture, but in truth we are as much creatures of our own time as secular people are. As Charles Taylor puts it, "The entire ethical stance of moderns supposes and follows on from the death of God (and of course, of the meaningful cosmos)." We may deny that God is dead, but to accept religious individualism and its theological support structure, Moralistic Therapeutic Deism, is to declare that God may not be quite dead, but he is in hospice care and confined to the bed.

Let's review a timeline of how the West arrived at this blasted heath of atomization, fragmentation, and unbelief.

> **Fourteenth century:** The defeat of metaphysical realism by nominalism in medieval theological debates removed the linchpin linking the transcendent and the material worlds. In nominalism, the meaning of objects and actions in the material world depends entirely on what man assigns it. War and plague brought the medieval system crashing down.
>
> **Fifteenth century:** The Renaissance dawned with a new, optimistic outlook on human potential and began shifting the West's vision and social imagination from God to man, whom it saw as "the measure of all things."
>
> **Sixteenth century:** The Reformation broke the religious unity of Europe. In Protestant lands, it birthed an unresolvable crisis in religious authority, which over the coming centuries would cause unending schisms.
>
> **Seventeenth century:** The Wars of Religion resulted in the further discrediting of religion and the founding of the modern nation-state. The Scientific Revolution struck the final blow to the organic medieval model of the cosmos, replacing it with a vision of the universe as a machine. The

mind-body split proclaimed by Descartes applied this to the body. Man became alienated from the natural world.

Eighteenth century: The Enlightenment attempted to create a philosophical framework for living in and governing society absent religious reference. Reason would be the polestar of public life, with religion—considered a burden from the Dark Ages—relegated to private life. The French and American revolutions broke with the old regimes and their hierarchies and inaugurated a democratic, egalitarian age.

Nineteenth century: The success of the Industrial Revolution pulverized the agrarian way of life, uprooted masses from rural areas, and brought them into the cities. Relations among people came to be defined by money. The Romantic movement rebelled against this alienation in the name of individualism and passion. Atheism and Marxist-influenced progressive social reform spread among cultural elites.

Twentieth century: The horrors of the two world wars severely damaged faith in the gods of reason and progress and in the God of Christianity. With the growth of technology and mass consumer society, people began to pay more attention to themselves and to fulfilling their individual desires. The Sexual Revolution exalted the desiring individual as the center of the emerging social order, deposing an enfeebled Christianity as the Ostrogoths deposed the hapless last emperor of the Western Roman Empire in the fifth century.

The long journey from a medieval world wracked with suffering but pregnant with meaning has delivered us to a place of once unimaginable comfort but emptied of significance and connection. The West has lost the golden thread that binds us to God, Creation, and each other. Unless we find it again, there is no hope of halting our dissolution. Indeed, it is unlikely that the West will see this lifeline for a very long time. It is not looking for it and may no longer have the capability of seeing it. We have been loosed, but we do not know how to bind.

"To light a candle is to cast a shadow," said the writer Ursula K. Le Guin.[12] The shadow of the Enlightenment's failure to replace God with reason has engulfed the West and plunged us into a new Dark Age. There is no way through this except to push forward to the true dawn. We who still hold the golden thread loosely in our hands must seize it more tightly and cling to it for future generations, or it will be torn from our grasp.

Christians know that there is one light that the darkness can neither comprehend nor overcome, and it is that Light to Whom we must return if we are going to make it through this time of trial. This is the Light, Jesus Christ, who illuminated the monasteries of the Middle Ages and all those who gathered around them.

The Benedictines had no secret teaching. They had what they still have: the Rule, which shows how to order one's life to be as receptive as possible to God's grace, both individually and in community. As we await a new Saint Benedict to appear in our quite different time and place and teach us how to reweave the tapestry of our Christian lives, let's make a pilgrimage to Benedict's hometown and spend time with the spiritual sons of the saints, who, in defiance of all modern expectations, are living simply but abundantly, guided by the timeless teaching of the old master.

CHAPTER 3

A Rule for Living

Y ou can't go back to the past, but you can go to Norcia. And the
glimpse of the Christian past a pilgrim gets there is also, I am
confident, a glimpse of the Christian future.

Norcia—the modern name of Benedict of Nursia's birthplace—is
a walled town that sits on a broad plateau at the end of a road that
winds for thirty-five miles through harsh mountain country. It is easy
to imagine how isolated Norcia was in Benedict's day—and why, to
our knowledge, the saint went down the mountain, never to return.

One warm February morning I traveled to the Monastery of St.
Benedict, the home of fifteen monks and their prior, Father Cassian
Folsom. Father Cassian, a sixty-one-year-old American, reopened the
monastery with a handful of brother Benedictines in December 2000,
nearly two centuries after the state shut the tenth-century prayer cita-
del's doors and dispersed its monks.

The suppression of the Norcia monastery happened in 1810 under
laws imposed by Napoleon Bonaparte, then the ruler of northern Italy.
Napoleon was a tyrant who inherited the anti-Christian legacy of the
French Revolution and used it to devastate the Catholic Church in all
territories under French imperial rule. Napoleon was the dictator of a

French state so anticlerical that many in Europe speculated that he was the Antichrist.

Legend has it that in an argument with a cardinal, Napoleon pointed out that he had the power to destroy the church.

"Your majesty," the cardinal replied, "we, the clergy, have done our best to destroy the church for the last eighteen hundred years. We have not succeeded, and neither will you."

Four years after sending the Benedictines away from their home of nearly a millennium, Napoleon's empire was in ruins, and he was in exile. Today, the sound of Gregorian chants can once again be heard in the saint's hometown, a melodious rebuke to the apostate emperor. Sometimes the past, as an American novelist famously said, is not even past.

The Monastery of St. Benedict is not the world's first Benedictine monastery. Monks did not establish themselves in this town until the tenth century (or possibly earlier; written records only go back to the 900s). Most of the men who refounded the monastery are young Americans who have chosen to give their lives wholly to God as Benedictine monks—and not just as monks but as Benedictines committed to living out the fullness of their tradition.

As I settled into the quiet of my monastery guest room after a morning in Norcia, I reflected on how unlikely it was that from this small town high in the mountains came the spark that kept the light of faith alive in Europe through very hard times. That spark shone forth in a world when, in the words of the English lay Benedictine Esther de Waal, "life was an urgent struggle to make sense of what was happening."[1] *Like today*, I thought, then drifted off to sleep.

The next morning I met Father Cassian inside the monastery for a talk. He stands tall, his short hair and beard are steel-gray, and his demeanor is serious and, well, monklike. But when he speaks, in his gentle baritone, you feel as if you are talking to your own father. Father Cassian speaks warmly and powerfully of the integrity and joy of the

Benedictine life, which is so different from that of our fragmented modern world.

Though the monks here have rejected the world, "there's not just a *no*; there's a *yes* too," Father Cassian says. "It's both that we reject what is not life-giving, and that we build something new. And we spend a lot of time in the rebuilding, and people see that too, which is why people flock to the monastery. We have so much involvement with guests and pilgrims that it's exhausting. But that is what we do. We are rebuilding. That's the *yes* that people have to hear about."

Rebuilding what? I asked.

"To use Pope Benedict's phrase, which he repeated many times, the Western world today lives as though God does not exist," he says. "I think that's true. Fragmentation, fear, disorientation, drifting—those are widely diffused characteristics of our society."

Yes, I thought, *this is exactly right.* When we lost our Christian religion in modernity, we lost the thing that bound ourselves together and to our neighbors and anchored us in both the eternal and the temporal orders. We are adrift in liquid modernity, with no direction home.

And this monk was telling me that he and his brothers in the monastery saw themselves as working on the restoration of Christian belief and Christian culture. How very Benedictine. I leaned in to hear more.

This monastery, Father Cassian explained, and the life of prayer within it, exist as a sign of contradiction to the modern world. The guardrails have disappeared, and the world risks careering off a cliff, but we are so captured by the lights and motion of modern life that we don't recognize the danger. The forces of dissolution from popular culture are too great for individuals or families to resist on their own. We need to embed ourselves in stable communities of faith.

Benedict's Rule is a detailed set of instructions for how to organize and govern a monastic community, in which monks (and separately, nuns) live together in poverty and chastity.[2] That is common to all monastic living, but Benedict's Rule adds three distinct vows: obedience, stability (fidelity to the same monastic community until death), and conversion of life, which means dedicating oneself to the lifelong work of deepening repentance. The Rule also includes directions for dividing each day into periods of prayer, work, and reading of Scripture and other sacred texts. The saint taught his followers how to live apart from the world, but also how to treat pilgrims and strangers who come to the monastery.

Far from being a way of life for the strong and disciplined, Benedict's Rule was for the ordinary and weak, to help them grow stronger in faith. When Benedict began forming his monasteries, it was common practice for monastics to adopt a written rule of life, and Benedict's Rule was a simplified and (though it seems quite rigorous to us) softened version of an earlier rule. Benedict had a noteworthy sense of compassion for human frailty, saying in the prologue to the Rule that he hoped to introduce "nothing harsh and burdensome" but only to be strict enough to strengthen the hearts of the brothers "to run the way of God's commandments with unspeakable sweetness and love." He instructed his abbots to govern as strong but compassionate fathers, and not to burden the brothers under his authority with things they are not strong enough to handle.

For example, in his chapter giving the order of manual labor, Benedict says, "Let all things be done with moderation, however, for the sake of the faint-hearted." This is characteristic of Benedict's wisdom. He did not want to break his spiritual sons; he wanted to build them up.

Despite the very specific instructions found in the Rule, it's not a checklist for legalism. "The purpose of the Rule is to free you. That's a paradox that people don't grasp readily," Father Cassian said.

If you have a field covered with water because of poor drainage, he explained, crops either won't grow there, or they will rot. If you don't drain it, you will have a swamp and disease. But if you can dig a drainage channel, the field will become healthy and useful. What's more, once the water becomes contained within the walls of the channel, it will flow with force and can accomplish things.

"A Rule works that way, to channel your spiritual energy, your work, your activity, so that you're able to accomplish something," Father Cassian said.

"Monastic life is very plain," he continued. "People from the outside perhaps have a romantic vision, perhaps what they see on television, of monks sort of floating around the cloister. There is that, and that's attractive, but basically, monks get up in the morning, they pray, they do their work, they pray some more. They eat, they pray, they do some more work, they pray some more, and then they go to bed. It's rather plain, just like most people. The genius of Saint Benedict is to find the presence of God in everyday life."

People who are anxious, confused, and looking for answers are quick to search for solutions in the pages of books or on the Internet, looking for that "killer app" that will make everything right again. The Rule tells us: No, it's not like that. You can achieve the peace and order you seek only by making a place within your heart and within your daily life for the grace of God to take root. Divine grace is freely given, but God will not force us to receive it. It takes constant effort on our part to get out of God's way and let His grace heal us and change us. To this end, what we think does not matter as much as what we do—and how faithfully we do it.

A man who wants to get in shape and has read the best bodybuilding books will get nowhere unless he applies that knowledge in eating healthy food and working out daily. That takes sustained willpower. In time, if he's faithful to the practices necessary to achieve his goal, the man will start to love eating well and exercising so much that he is not pushed toward doing so by willpower but rather drawn to it by love. He will have trained his heart to desire the good.

So too with the spiritual life. Right belief (orthodoxy) is essential, but holding the correct doctrines in your mind does you little good if your heart—the seat of the will—remains unconverted. That requires putting those right beliefs into action through right practice (orthopraxy), which over time achieves the goal Paul set for Timothy when he commanded him to "discipline yourself for the purpose of godliness" (1 Timothy 4:7).

The author of 2 Peter explains well the way the mind, the heart, and the body work in harmony for spiritual growth:

> Now for this very reason also, applying all diligence, in your faith supply moral excellence, and in your moral excellence, knowledge, and in your knowledge, self-control, and in your self-control, perseverance, and in your perseverance, godliness, and in your godliness, brotherly kindness, and in your brotherly kindness, love. For if these qualities are yours and are increasing, they render you neither useless nor unfruitful in the true knowledge of our Lord Jesus Christ. (2 Peter 1:5-8)

Though it quotes Scripture in nearly every one of its short chapters, the Rule is not the Gospel. It is a proven strategy for living the Gospel in an intensely Christian way. It is an instruction manual for how to form one's life around the service of Jesus Christ, within a strong community. It is not a collection of theological maxims but a manual of practices through which believers can structure their lives around prayer, the Word of God, and the ever-deepening awareness that, as the saint says, "the divine presence is everywhere, and that 'the eyes of the Lord are looking on the good and evil in every place'" (Proverbs 15:3).

The Rule is for monastics, obviously, but its teachings are plain enough to be adapted by lay Christians for their own use. It provides a guide to serious and sustained Christian living in a fashion that re-orders us interiorly, bringing together what is scattered within our own hearts and orienting it to prayer. If applied effectively, it disciplines the life we share with others, breaking down barriers that keep the love of God from passing among us, and makes us more resilient without hardening our hearts.

In the Benedict Option, we are not trying to repeal seven hundred years of history, as if that were possible. Nor are we trying to save the

West. We are only trying to build a Christian way of life that stands as an island of sanctity and stability amid the high tide of liquid modernity. We are not looking to create heaven on earth; we are simply looking for a way to be strong in faith through a time of great testing. The Rule, with its vision of an ordered life centered around Christ and the practices it prescribes to deepen our conversion, can help us achieve that goal.

Order

If a defining characteristic of the modern world is disorder, then the most fundamental act of resistance is to establish order. If we don't have internal order, we will be controlled by our human passions and by the powerful oustside forces who are in greater control of directing liquid modernity's deep currents.

For the traditional Christian, establishing internal order is not mere discipline, nor is it simply an act of will. Rather, it is what theologian Romano Guardini called man's efforts to "regain his right relation to the truth of things, to the demands of his own deepest self, and finally to God."[3] This means the discovery of the order, the *logos*, that God has written into the nature of Creation and seeking to live in harmony with it. It also implies the realization of natural limits within Creation's givenness, as opposed to believing that nature is something we can deny or refute, according to our own desires. Finally, it means disciplining one's life to live a life to glorify God and help others.

Order is not simply a matter of law and its enforcement. In the classical Christian view, the law itself depends on a deeper conception of order, an idea of the way ultimate reality is constructed. This order may be unseen, but it is believed and internalized by those living within a community that professes it. The point of life, for individual persons, for the church, and for the state, is to pursue harmony with that transcendent, eternal order.

To order the world rightly as Christians requires regarding all things as pointing to Christ. Chapter 19 of the Rule offers a succinct example of the connection between a disciplinary teaching and the unseen order. In it, Benedict instructs his monks to keep their minds focused on the presence of God and His Angels when they are engaged in chanting the Divine Office, called the *opus Dei* or "work of God."

"We believe that the divine presence is everywhere, and that 'the eyes of the Lord are looking on the good and the evil in every place'" (Proverbs 15:3), writes Benedict. "But we should believe this especially without any doubt when we are assisting at the Work of God." He concludes with an admonition to remember that when they pray the Psalms together, they are standing before God and must pray "in such a way that our mind may be in harmony with our voice."

Every monk's life, and all his labors, must be directed to the service of God. The Rule teaches that God must be the beginning and the end of all our actions. To bound our spiritual passion by the rhythm of daily life and its disciplines, and to do so with others in our family and in our community, is to build a strong foundation of faith, within which one can become fully human and fully Christian.

As a result of their orientation toward Christ, the monks recognize that He is the Creator, the One in Whom all things consist, and that man is not the measure of all things. Unlike the secular successors to the nominalists, the Benedictine monk does not believe that things of the world have meaning only if people choose to give them meaning. The monk holds that meaning exists objectively, within the natural world created by God, and is there to be discovered by the person who has detached themselves from their own passions and who seeks to see as God sees.

"One cannot be attached to created things, because one will end up seeing them as ordered toward oneself," said Brother Evagrius Hayden, age thirty-one. "This is wrong. We are not the ones who give things meaning. God gives things meaning."

Finally, the monks go to great lengths to make sure each detail of their lives reflects Christ as the end and as the source of all meaning. Some of these lengths seem surprisingly unspiritual. In Chapter 22, for example, Benedict gives instructions for how monks are to sleep—"clothed and girded with belts or cords."

Yet even these seemingly arbitrary rules serve a spiritual purpose. In some cases, this is because the rules free the monks for certain practical ends. For example, Benedict explains that the rules about clothing are to ensure that the monks are so dressed that they can arise in the middle of the night to pray the night offices, or scheduled prayers, without delay.

But what about rules whose rationale is less apparent? Does God really care what kind of bedding a monk uses? Or how many dishes of food are served at dinner? Why would anyone voluntarily submit to a way of life that is so regimented? Father Basil Nixen, age thirty-six, and the monastery's cook, said the Rule and even its more unusual rules don't exist for arbitrary reasons.

"The monk is deeply aware of the fact that in himself and in others, that order has been disturbed, has been disrupted by the Fall, by original sin, and by the personal sin of each person," Father Basil said. "The monk enters the monastery knowing that finding that order doesn't come easily. You have to fight for it, to work for it, and you have to be patient to achieve it. But it's worth it, because that order gives us peace."

Submitting to rules one doesn't understand is difficult, but it's a good way to counteract the carnal desire for personal independence. There may not be spiritual merit in choosing to eat two dishes instead of three at a meal, but the humility that comes with agreeing to submit to another's decision that one do so is transformative.

The order of the monastery produces not only humility but also spiritual resilience. In one sense, the Benedictine monks of Norcia are like a Marine Corps of the religious life, constantly training for spiritual warfare.

"The structure of life in the monastery, the things you do every day, is not just pointless repetition," said Brother Augustine Wilmeth, twenty-five, whose red Viking-like beard touches his chest. "It's to train your heart and your spirit so that when you need it, when you don't feel strong enough to will yourself to get through a difficult moment, you fall back on your training. You know that you wouldn't be strong enough to do it if you hadn't been kind of working at it and putting all the auxiliary things in place."

In other words, ordering one's actions is really about training one's heart to love and to desire the right things, the things that are *real*, without having to think about it. It is acquiring virtue as a habit.

You never know how God will use the little things in a life ordered by His love, to His service, to speak evangelically to others, said Brother Ignatius Prakarsa, the monastery's guest master. In the summertime, the monastery's basilica church fills up with tourists, many of whom are lapsed Christians or unbelievers, who sit quietly to watch the monks chant their regular prayers in Latin.

When Brother Ignatius meets them on the church steps later, visitors often tell him that the chanting was so peaceful, so beautiful.

"I tell them we're just praying to the Lord. We're just opening our mouths to sing the beauty that's already there in the music," he said to me. "Everything is evangelical. Everything is directed to God. Everything has to be seen from the supernatural point of view. The radiance that comes through our lives is only a reflection of God. In ourselves, we are nothing."

Prayer

That radiance is a fruit of deep and constant prayer. The Apostle Paul told the church in Thessalonica to "pray without ceasing" (1 Thessalonians 5:17). Benedictines consider their entire lives to be an attempt to fulfill this command. Strictly speaking, prayer is communication, either privately or in community, with God. More broadly, prayer is maintaining an unfailing awareness of the divine presence and doing all things with Him in mind. In the Benedictine life, regular prayer is at the center of the community's existence.

To pray is to engage in contemplation. The word has a particular meaning to monastics. It refers to what they believe is the highest state of the Christian life: to free oneself from the cares of the flesh to adore and praise God and to reflect on His truth. This is in opposition to the active life, which is to do good works in the world.

Think of the Gospel story of the sisters Martha and Mary. When Jesus came to their house, Martha busied herself with preparation, but Mary sat at Jesus's feet and listened to what He had to say. When Martha complained to Jesus that Mary wasn't helping her, the Lord responded that Mary had chosen the better path.

Why? Because as Jesus said when he rebuked Satan, "Man shall not live by bread alone, but on every word that proceeds out of the mouth of God" (Matthew 4:4). It is important to do things for the Lord, but it is more important to know him with your heart and your mind. And that is why contemplation takes priority.

"Prayer is the life of the soul, it's the life of each individual monk. It's the reason why we've come to live here," said Father Basil. "The goal of our life as monks is to deepen the life of prayer, to grow in prayer. Everything we do is structured to help favor that, to be conducive for that. Prayer puts us in communication with God."

Benedictine monks have a lot of time with God. Seven times each day they gather around the altar in the basilica to chant the appointed prayers for the Divine Office, also known as the Liturgy of the Hours. These are specific prayers that Catholic monks (and others) have recited for centuries to mark off the hours of the day. These consist of psalms, hymns, Scripture readings, and prayers.

For the monks, prayer is not simply words they speak. Each monk spends several hours daily doing *lectio divina*, a Benedictine method of

Scripture study that involves reading a Scripture passage, meditating on it, praying about it, and finally contemplating its meaning for the soul.

The idea is not to study the Bible as a scholar would but rather to encounter it as God speaking directly to the individual. In this sense, a monk immersing himself in Scripture, as directed by the Rule, is carrying out a form of prayer.

And it's not the only one.

"We sing when we pray, we stand, we sit, we bow, we kneel, we prostrate," said Father Cassian. "The body is very much involved in prayer. It's not just some kind of intellectual meditation. That's important."

When one advances in prayer, said Father Basil, one comes to understand that prayer is not so much about asking God for things as about simply being in His presence.

I told the priest how, in response to a personal crisis, my own orthodox priest back in Louisiana had assigned me a strict daily prayer rule, praying the Jesus Prayer ("Lord Jesus Christ, Son of God, have mercy on me, a sinner") for about an hour each day. It was dull and difficult at first, but I did it out of obedience. Every day, for a seemingly endless hour, silent prayer. In time, though, the hour seemed much shorter, and I discovered that the peace I had conspicuously lacked in my soul came forth.

After I was spiritually healed, my priest explained his reasoning for directing me to give myself over to that simple meditative prayer: "I had to get you out of your head."

He meant that I was captive to an intellectual tendency to try to think my way out of my troubles—a strategy that always ended in failure for me. What I really needed to do was to quiet my mind and still my heart to open it to God's grace. He was right.

"That's it," said Father Basil. "That's what pure prayer is: being with God. That can come about in many different ways, but as you discovered with the Jesus Prayer, it takes time. You have to set aside time for it."

Connecticut-born Father Benedict Nivakoff, thirty-eight, has spent nearly half his life in this monastic community. He says that "if one can accept that God's will is made manifest in everything one does all day long, then one's whole day becomes a prayer."

If we spend all our time in activity, even when that activity serves Christ, and neglect prayer and contemplation, we put our faith in danger. The 1960s media theorist Marshall McLuhan, a practicing Christian, once said that everyone he knew who lost his faith began by ceasing to pray. If we are to live rightly ordered Christian lives, then prayer must be the basis of everything we do.

Work

This does not mean the active life is to be shunned. Rather, it should be integrated into a life ordered by prayer. Good work is a fruit of a healthy prayer life. If you know anything about the Benedictines, you will probably have heard that their motto is *ora et labora*—Latin for "prayer and work." It's not strictly true. Saint Benedict never said that, and though contemporary Benedictine monks have claimed the slogan as their own, it came into use only in the nineteenth century.

Still, it's not a bad description of the general Benedictine approach to life. "Idleness is the enemy of the soul," says Saint Benedict in Chapter 48 of the Rule. The idea is that to be idle is to open the door to slothfulness. But work is not simply something you do to stay out of trouble. The saint expected each of his monasteries to be self-sustaining and, unusually for a Roman of his era, taught that manual labor could be a sanctifying act.

Though they are contemplatives, monks must not complain about manual labor, directs Benedict. "For then they are truly monastics when they live by the labor of their hands, as did our Fathers and the Apostles."

This is practical wisdom for us moderns, who tend to have a disordered relationship to our work. Some of us define ourselves by our work and devote ourselves to it immoderately, at the expense of contemplation. Others, though, see work as something we do to pay the bills, nothing more, regarding it as disconnected from the rest of life, especially our spiritual lives.

That's a mistake, says the Rule. The work must serve not ourselves but God and God alone. In a chapter instructing monastic craftsmen, Benedict says that if they come to be proud of their work, the abbot must find something else for them to do. Christian humility is that important. And monks must be scrupulously honest in their business dealings, says the saint. The reason? Because in all things God must be glorified.

This is how we must approach our jobs: as opportunities to glorify God.

More deeply, Benedictines view their work as an expression of love and stewardship of the community and as a way of reordering the natural world in harmony with God's will.

Remember that for the monk, everything is a gift from God and is meant to be treated as sacred. Every human thought and act is to be centered on and directed to God and to be united in Him and to Him. And we men and women are participants in God's unfolding Creation, by ordering the world according to His will.

Seen this way, labor takes on a new dimension. For the Christian, work has sacramental value.

"Creation gives praise to God. We give praise to God through Creation, through the material world, and into our areas of work," explained Father Martin Bernhard, thirty-two. "Any time we take something neutral, something material, and we make something out of it for the sake of giving glory to God, it becomes sacramental, it becomes a channel of grace."

The monastery cook, Father Basil, described his labors preparing meals for the brethren as a form of purification, of perfection, on both a human and a supernatural level.

"By means of the work in the kitchen, I'm establishing order. I'm exercising my God-given governance of the creative world," he said. "From a human perspective, work is so important because it helps us exercise that God-commanded dominance over the earth. And from a practical point of view, it provides for ourselves and others. It's important for us to know that through our work, we are making an important contribution to the community."

And on a supernatural level?

"Ultimately, work serves as an expression of charity, of love, and that is what all work really should be," Father Basil explained. "This is a lesson we have to work all our lives to learn. Work is not something I do in order to get something. Doing it is good for me, it's constitutive of my happiness, because in it and through it I show love for others.

"We are called to love," he added. "Work is a concerted way of showing our love for others. In that sense, it can become very transformative—and very prayerful too."

"Too often it's seen as a burden, and it doesn't have to be. If we approach work as a burden, something's wrong in here," he said, pointing to his heart. "The problem needs to be fixed primarily here, in the heart."

In the days to come, circumstances will compel Christians—particularly those in certain professions—to rethink our relationship to our work. We will be shown the door in some cases because of our beliefs. In others, the doors will never open in the first place—and if they do, men and women of conscience will not be able to walk through them. This is going to cost us money and prestige and perhaps vocational satisfaction. Reorienting the way we conceive of work in a more God-centered, Benedictine way will help us make the right decision when we are put to the test in the workplace and will strengthen us when we are forced to find another profession.

Asceticism

The closure of certain professions to faithful orthodox Christians will be difficult to accept. In fact, it's hard for contemporary believers to imagine, in part because as Americans, we are unaccustomed to accepting limits on our ambitions. Yet the day is coming when the kind of thing that has happened to Christian bakers, florists, and wedding photographers will be much more widespread. And many of us are not prepared to suffer deprivation for our faith.

This is why asceticism—taking on physical rigors for the sake of a spiritual goal—is such an important part of the ordinary Christian life. Take fasting, the most common form of Christian asceticism. Jesus showed us by his own example, when he fasted for forty days in the desert after His baptism—this, to prepare Himself for His public ministry. It was during this fast that Satan appeared to the Lord and tempted Him to turn a stone into bread to satisfy his hunger. Jesus refused, asserting the primacy of the Word of God and showing that mastering bodily desires is critically important to spiritual growth.

Asceticism comes from the Greek word *askesis*, meaning "training." The life prescribed by the Rule is thoroughly ascetic. Monks fast regularly, live simply, refuse comfort, and abide by the strict rules of the monastery. This is not a matter of earning spiritual merit. Rather, the monk knows the human heart and how its passions must be reined in through disciplined living. Asceticism is an antidote to the poison of self-centeredness common in our culture, which teaches us that satisfying our own desires is the key to the good life. The ascetic knows that true happiness can be found only by living in harmony with the will of God, and ascetical practices train body and soul to put God above self.

Asceticism, especially fasting according to the Church calendar, was for most of Christian history a normal part of every believer's life. "But you, when you fast, anoint your head and wash your face," Jesus says in the Gospel of Matthew (6:17), indicating that periodically abstaining from food for religious reasons was standard practice. In the first century, Christians fasted on Wednesdays and Fridays, in memory of Christ's betrayal and crucifixion—an ascetical practice still observed today by Eastern Orthodox Christians.

A Christian who practices asceticism trains himself to say no to his desires and yes to God. That mentality has all but disappeared from the West in modern times. We have become a people oriented around comfort. We expect our religion to be comfortable. Suffering doesn't make sense to us. And without fasting and other ascetic disciplines, we lose the ability to tell ourselves no to things our hearts desire.

To rediscover Christian asceticism is urgent for believers who want to train their hearts, and the hearts of their children, to resist the hedonism and consumerism at the core of contemporary culture. And it is necessary to teach us in our bones how God uses suffering to purify us for His purposes. Ascetical suffering is a method for avoiding becoming like those monks called "detestable" by Saint Benedict in the Rule "the worst kind of monk," namely those whose "law is the desire for self-gratification."

In the teaching of the Desert Fathers, every Christian struggles to root out all desires within their hearts that do not harmonize with God's will. Brother Augustine explained how this works.

"It's like you're strengthening your will," he said. "You may be in a time of fasting, and your stomach is growling because you can't eat until five-thirty. And then you think, 'If I can't handle not eating for a few hours, how can I expect to control my more spiritual passions, like anger, envy, and pride? How can I expect to have any spiritual and moral self-discipline if I don't start with the more tangible, material desires first?'"

Besides, as Father Benedict put it, asceticism can be a wake-up call for the spiritually slothful. "We are often further away from God than we realize," he said. "Asceticism serves as a healthy reminder of how things are. It's not a punishment for being so far away."

The overweight person diets not to punish him- or herself for being heavy but to become healthier. The athlete works out not because he feels guilty for sitting around watching TV but to train his body for competition. So it is with monks and their asceticism—and so it must be with us lay Christians. We practice self-denial to strengthen ourselves in the love and service of Christ and His people.

"Suffering is part of the pursuit of Jesus Christ, who suffered first before His glory," said Brother Ignatius. "To encounter God, you too need to suffer, and to be willing to experience suffering."

Relearning asceticism—that is, how to suffer for the faith—is critical training for Christians living in the world today and the world of the near future. "There is no greatness which is not grounded deep in self-conquest and self-denial," said Romano Guardini, who explained that all forms of order must begin with mastering the self and its desires.[4]

"The Christian call is a paradox: We are called to be in the world but not of the world," says Brother Evagrius. "That paradox was lived out in the early church, in the Roman Empire, where it was a pagan culture through and through, yet you had individuals and families feeling the call of Christ and abandoning everything to follow Him, even to be martyred.

"Until we actually return to that model," he said, "nothing we do will ever bear fruit."

Stability

Along those lines, a tree that is repeatedly uprooted and transplanted will be hard pressed to produce healthy fruit. So it is with people and their spiritual lives. Rootlessness is not a new problem. In the first chapter of the Rule, Saint Benedict denounced the kind of monk he called a "gyrovague."

"They spend their whole lives tramping from province to province," he wrote, adding that "they are always on the move, with no stability, they indulge their own wills"—and are even worse, the saint said, than the hedonistic monks whose only law is desire.

If you are going to put down spiritual roots, taught Benedict, you need to stay in one place long enough for them to go deep. The Rule requires monks to take a vow of "stability"—meaning that barring unusual circumstances, including being sent out as a missionary, the monk will remain for the rest of his life in the monastery where he took his vows.

"This is where the Benedictine life is probably the most counter-cultural," said Father Benedict. "It's the life of Mary, not Martha: to stay put at the foot of Christ no matter what they say you're not doing."

The Bible shows us that God calls some people to pick up and move to achieve His purposes, Father Benedict acknowledged. "Still, in a culture like ours, where everyone is always on the move, the Bene-dictine calling to stay put no matter what can call forth new and im-portant ways of serving God."

Zygmunt Bauman says that liquid modernity compels us to refuse stability because it's a fool's game. "The hub of postmodern life strategy is not identity building but avoidance of fixation," he writes.[5] In Bau-man's pitiless analysis, to succeed today, you need to be free of all com-mitments, unbound by the past or the future, living in an everlasting present. The world changes so quickly that the person who is loyal to anything, even to her own identity, takes an enormous risk.

Instead of believing that structure is good and that duties to home and family lead us to live rightly, people today have been tricked by liquid modernity into believing that maximizing individual happiness should be the goal of life. The gyrovague, the villain of Saint Bene-dict's Rule, is the hero of postmodernity.

For most of my life, it would have been fair to call me a gyrovague. I moved from job to job, climbing the career ladder. In only twenty years of my adult life, I changed cities five times and denominations twice. My younger sister Ruthie, by contrast, remained in the small Louisiana town in which we were raised. She married her high school sweetheart, taught in the same school we attended as children, and brought up her kids in the same country church.

When she was stricken with terminal cancer in 2010, I saw the immense value of the stability she had chosen. Ruthie had a wide and deep network of friends and family to care for her and her husband and kids during her nineteen-month ordeal. The love Ruthie's community showered on her and her family made the struggle bearable, both in her life and after her death. The witness to the power of stability in the life of my sister moved my heart so profoundly that my wife and I decided to leave Philadelphia and move to south Louisiana to be near them all.

Not everybody is called to return to their hometown, of course, but everybody should think deeply about the spiritual and emotional costs of the gyrovague's liberty that we contemporary Americans take as our birthright. In a sense, what looks like freedom can really be a form of bondage.

Father Martin said that those who think stability is meant to hold you back, and to stifle personal and spiritual growth, are missing the hidden value in the commitment to stability. It anchors you and gives you the freedom that comes from not being subject to the wind, the waves, and the currents of daily life. It creates the ordered conditions in which the soul's internal pilgrimage toward holiness becomes possible.

Or as Father Martin put it, "Stability give us the time and the structure to go deep into who we are as sons of God."

Community

The rootlessness of contemporary life has frayed community bonds. It is common now to find people who don't know their neighbors and don't really want to. To be part of a community is to share in its life. That inevitably makes demands on the individual that limits his freedom.

The church is not always a sign of contradiction to this modern lack of community. In the first decade of my life as an adult Christian, I left church as soon as services were over. Getting involved with the people there was not interesting. Just Jesus and me was all I wanted and all I needed, or so I thought. You might say that I wasn't interested in joining their pilgrimage, that I preferred to be a tourist at church—and was too spiritually immature to understand how harmful this was.

That consumerist approach to the community of believers reproduces the fragmentation that is shattering Christianity in the contemporary world. In Benedictine monasteries, however, monks are always aware that they are not merely individuals who share living quarters with other individuals but are part of an organic whole—a spiritual family.

The Rule's instructions concerning obedience are meant to foster mutual accountability. Everyone in the monastery depends on everyone else, and all decisions of importance must be made with others and consider their interests. To live in real community is to put the good of others ahead of our own desires, when doing so serves truth and righteousness.

Many of the Rule's more stringent instructions are oriented toward protecting community life. Benedict devotes a chapter to prescribing penalties for monks who show up late to prayer services. The saint explains that if others see their bad example, they may be tempted to do evil. A school for the Lord's service cannot accomplish its mission if its students are often tardy.

Benedict devotes several short chapters to punishments for other infractions. His method is to encourage monks who have done wrong to confess at once their fault to the abbot and receive a reprimand. If the fault comes to the abbot's attention through the testimony of another, the punishment is to be greater. And if a monk's transgressions are so great that he is excommunicated from the oratory or the common table, he can be restored only after lying prostrate before the community as an act of apology and humility, until the abbot accepts his repentance.

The point of exercises like this is not to embarrass errant monks but rather to discipline them for their own good and for the good of the entire community. To be a Christian, and to be a vowed member of a religious community, incurs certain obligations to others. Rules and discipline for those who break them wear down the sharp edges of individual selfishness that stand as jagged rocks across the pilgrim's path to sanctity.

Like a wise and generous father, Saint Benedict understood that imposing rules and discipline on his spiritual children was an act not of domination but of love, one that helped them grow in charity. He ended the Rule by exhorting his followers to embrace love in community. In his penultimate chapter, the saint commanded the brethren to compete zealously to serve the others.

> Just as there is an evil zeal of bitterness which separates from God and leads to hell, so there is a good zeal which separates from vices and leads to God and to life everlasting. This zeal, therefore, the brothers should practice with the most fervent love. Thus they should anticipate one another in honor (Rom. 12:10); most patiently endure one another's infirmities, whether of body or of character; vie in paying obedience one to another—no one following what he considers useful for himself, but rather what benefits another; tender the charity of brotherhood chastely; fear God in love; love their Abbot with a sincere and humble charity; prefer nothing whatever to Christ.

That extraordinary standard is hard to achieve in any family, much less in a community of strangers, many of whom come from very different backgrounds and even different nations. Yet only by setting this goal for individuals and the community as a whole will the monastery be able to form faithful servants of Christ.

Life in Christian community, whether in monastic or ordinary congregations, is about building the kind of fellowship that every one of us needs to complete our individual pilgrimage. As Dietrich Bonhoeffer said in *Life Together*, his own rule, of sorts, for living in faithful community:

> A Christian needs another Christian who speaks God's Word to him. He needs him again and again when he becomes uncertain and discouraged, for by himself he cannot help himself without belying the truth. He needs his brother man as a bearer and proclaimer of the divine word of salvation.[6]

Community life, not a dreamy ideal, said Bonhoeffer, but an often difficult initiation into the "divine reality" that is the church. That is, the church exists as a brotherhood established by Christ, even if it doesn't feel like it in a given moment. The martyred Lutheran pastor taught that struggles within the community are a gift of God's grace, because they force its members to reckon with the reality of their kinship, despite their brokenness. A community that cannot face its faults and love each other through to healing is not truly Christian.

"It's not easy," conceded Father Martin. "It's really doable only by grace, and this is the beauty of Christianity: that it can bring people of different blood relations, languages, and ethnicities together and give us a common culture."

The Norcia monastic community contains brothers from the United States, Indonesia, Brazil, Germany, and Canada. Life in common can be very difficult, the monks say, but it is essential to living out the Benedictine "conversion of life" vow.

And it teaches the individual monk more about himself. "When a man first comes to the monastery, the first thing he notices is everybody else's quirks—that is, what's wrong with everybody else," said Father Martin. "But the longer you're here, the more you begin to think: what's wrong with me? You go deeper into yourself to learn your own strengths and weaknesses. And that leads you to acceptance of others."

Father Basil says that in his years as a monk, he has come to have a much clearer understanding of what it means to live as the Body of Christ: the community as an organic whole, united in Christ, with each man committed in love to doing his own part to strengthen the whole.

"God has distributed his graces in such a way that we really need each other," said the priest. "Certainly there's the old man within me that craves individualism, but the more I live in community, the more I see that you can't have it and be faithful, or fully human."

In his travels tending to monastery affairs, Father Martin, who is its business manager, sees a vacancy in the faces of many people he encounters. They seem so anxious, so unsettled, so uncertain. The monk believes this is the result of loneliness, isolation, and the lack of deep and life-giving communal bonds. When the light in most people's faces comes from the glow of the laptop, the smartphone, or the television screen, we are living in a Dark Age, he said.

"They are missing that fundamental light meant to shine forth in a human person through social interaction," he said. "Love can only come from that. Without real contact with other human persons, there is no love. We've never seen a Dark Age like this one."

Hospitality

The Benedictine approach to prayer, work, asceticism, stability, and community requires practices that knit the monastic community together tightly. The resulting closeness and cohesion are augmented by the monks' separation from the world. But Benedict orders them in the

Rule to be aware that they live not for themselves alone but also to serve outsiders.

According to the Rule, we must never turn away someone who needs our love. A church or other Benedict Option community must be open to the world, to share the bounty of God's love with those who lack it.

The monks live mostly cloistered lives—that is, they stay behind their monastery's walls and limit their contact with the outside world. The spiritual work they are called to do requires silence and separation. Our work does not require the same structures. As lay Christians living in the world, our calling is to seek holiness in more ordinary social conditions.

Yet even cloistered Benedictines practice Christian hospitality to the stranger. The Rule commands that all those who present themselves as pilgrims and visitors to the monastery "be received like Christ, for He is going to say, because He will say, 'I was a stranger, and you took me in'" (Matt. 25:35). If you are invited to dine with the monks in the refectory, they greet you the first time with a hand-washing ceremony prescribed in the Rule.

Brother Francis Davoren, forty-four, the monastery's brewmaster, used to be the refectorian, the monk charged with overseeing the dining room. He approached that task with sacramental imagination.

"Saint Benedict says that Christ is present in the brothers, and Christ is present in our guests. Every day I would think, 'Christ is coming. I'm going to make this as pleasant for them as I can, because it showed them that we cared,'" he said. "That's a good outreach to people: to respect them, to recognize their dignity, to show them that you can see Christ in them and want to bring them into your life."

As guest master, Brother Ignatius is the point of contact between pilgrims and the monastic community. He explains why the monks take Christ's words about receiving strangers so seriously: "It is kind of a warning: if you want to be welcome in heaven, you had better welcome people as Christ himself now, even if you don't like it, even if you suffer because of those people," he said. "If your life is to seek

Christ, this is it. You will find redemption in serving these guests, because Christ is coming in them."

Saint Benedict commands his monks to be open to the outside world—to a point. Hospitality must be dispensed according to prudence, so that visitors are not allowed to do things that disrupt the monastery's way of life. For example, at table, silence is kept by visitors and monks alike. As Brother Augustine put it, "If we let visitors upset the rhythm of our life too much, then we can't really welcome anyone." The monastery receives visitors constantly who have all kinds of problems and are seeking advice, help, or just someone to listen to them, and it's important that the monks maintain the order needed to allow them to offer this kind of hospitality.

Rather than erring on the side of caution, though, Father Benedict believes Christians should be as open to the world as they can be without compromise. "I think too many Christians have decided that the world is bad and should be avoided as much as possible. Well, it's hard to convert people if that's your stance," he said. "It's a lot easier to help people to see their own goodness and then bring them in than to point out how bad they are and bring them in."

The power of popular culture is so overwhelming that faithful orthodox Christians often feel the need to retreat behind defensive lines. But Brother Ignatius, at age fifty-one, warned that Christians must not become so anxious and fearful that they cease to share the Good News, in word and deed, with a world held captive by hatred and darkness. It is prudent to draw reasonable boundaries, but we have to take care not to be like the unfaithful servant in the Parable of the Talents, who was punished by his master for his poor, fearful stewardship of the master's property.

"The best defense is offense. You defend by attacking," Brother Ignatius said. "Let's attack by expanding God's kingdom—first in our hearts, then in our own families, and then in the world. Yes, you have to have borders, but our duty is not to let the borders stay there. We have to push outward, infinitely."

Balance

The Benedictine life is rigorous, but if lived according to the Rule, it is also free from fundamentalism and extremism. "We hope to ordain nothing that is harsh or burdensome," wrote Benedict. The point of the Rule, he said—and indeed the point of their life—however, is that "our hearts expand, and we shall run the way of God's commandments with unspeakable sweetness of love."

Said Father Basil: "Saint Benedict takes the image that Scripture uses to speak about Christ himself. 'A bruised reed he will not break, a smoldering wick he will not quench.' Humanity is already fragile. We need to treat it with care, with concern, with delicacy."

This orientation toward community life stands in stark contrast to a number of other Christian intentional communities that have fallen apart or become cultlike because an authoritarian leader obsessed with purity abused power.

Brother Francis put it like this: If a community relaxes its discipline too much, it will dissolve. But if it is too rigid, it will make people crazy. "If you want to judge a community, you need to see what their fruit is," he said. "Are they growing? Are they cheerful? Are they happy? Are they doing good and helping people? Look at what a community produces to see what kind of balance they have."

Balance, then—or put another way, prudence, mercy, and good judgment—is key to governing the life of a Christian community. So too is keeping the necessities of daily monastic living—eating, sleeping, praying, working, reading—in harmonious relationship, so that none overtakes a monk's life and all are integrated into a healthy whole.

But Father Benedict insisted that no one should think the Rule is about living a balanced life in the sense of satisfying oneself with half measures and spiritual mediocrity. The balance is not one between good and bad but between different kinds of good.

Benedict did not want to create wishy-washy monks. "He wants people to be saints. Saints are not usually very balanced people," said Father Benedict, laughing. "He was creating a radical life: total detachment and emphasis on conversion. It's giving everything to God, all the time."

The laity can benefit from the Rule, he said, if they understand what is radical about Saint Benedict's life: total abandonment of the self-will for the will of God. The method may require balance in its application, but the goal given to us by the Lord is extraordinary: to be perfect, even as our Father in heaven is perfect.

Because Jesus is one with the Father, those who seek perfection must try to imitate Him. It is heresy, of course, to believe that we can achieve this perfection on our own or on this side of heaven. It is a paradox of the Christian life that the holier one becomes, the more acutely aware one is of one's lack, and therefore one's total dependence on God's mercy. That said, the ideal person is one who is Christ-like in all things, as she fulfills the Lord's calling. Whether she is called to the monastery or to the world, to family or to the single life, to manual labor or to a desk job, to stay at home or to travel the world, she must strive to her utmost to be like Jesus. By methodically and practically ordering our bodies, souls, and minds to a harmonious life centered on the Christ who is everywhere present and filling all things, the Benedictine way offers a spirituality accessible to anyone. For the Christian who follows the way of Saint Benedict, everyday life becomes an unceasing prayer, both an offering to God and a gift from Him, one that transforms us bit by bit into the likeness of His son.

The Only Great Tragedy in Life

The Benedictine example is a sign of hope but also a warning: no matter what a Christian's circumstances, he cannot live faithfully if God is only a part of his life, bracketed away from the rest. In the end, either Christ is at the center of our lives, or the Self and all its idolatries are. There is no middle ground. With His help, we can piece together the fragments of our lives and order them around Him, but it will not be easy, and we can't do it alone. To strive for anything less, though, is to live out the saying of the French Catholic writer Léon Bloy: "The only real sadness, the only real failure, the only great tragedy in life, is not to become a saint."[7]

As I was preparing to leave the Monastery of St. Benedict after my stay, I mentioned to Father Martin how unusual it is for a place like this to exist at all in the modern world. Young men taking up a tradition of prayer, liturgy, and ascetic communal life that dates back to the early church—and doing so with such evident joy? It's not supposed to happen in these times.

But here they are: a sign of contradiction to modernity.

Father Martin flashed a broad grin from beneath his black beard and said that all Christians can have this if they are willing to do what it takes to mount the recovery, "to pick up what we have lost, and to make it real again.

"There's something here that's very ancient, but it's also new," Father Martin said. "People say, 'Oh, you're just trying to turn back the clock.' That makes no sense. If you're doing something right now, it means you're doing it *right now*. It's new, and it's alive! And that's a very powerful thing."

Leaving Norcia and going back down the mountain, a pilgrim might envy the monks the simplicity of their lives in the quiet village. The serenity and solidity of Norcia and its Benedictines seem so far from the tumultuous world below, and you shouldn't be surprised if you miss it before you've even reached the train station in Spoleto. But if you have received the gift of Norcia rightly, you do not leave empty-handed and unprepared for what lies ahead.

For the brothers and fathers there will have given you a glimpse of what life together in Christ can be. They will have shown you that traditional Christianity is not dead, and that Truth, Beauty, and Goodness can be found and brought to life again, though doing so will cost you nothing less than everything. And they will have shared their ancient teaching, tendered by the hands of monks and nuns from generations of generations for a millennium and a half—wisdom that can help ordinary believers, doing battle in the modern world, not only hold firm through the new Dark Age but actually to flourish in it.

How do we take Benedictine wisdom out of the monastery and apply it to the challenges of worldly life in the twenty-first century? It is to this question that we now turn. The way of Saint Benedict is not an escape from the real world but a way to see that world and dwell in it as it truly is. Benedictine spirituality teaches us to bear with the world in love and to transform it as the Holy Spirit transforms us. The Benedict Option draws on the virtues in the Rule to change the way Christians approach politics, church, family, community, education, our jobs, sexuality, and technology.

And it does so with urgency. When I first told Father Cassian about the Benedict Option, he mulled my words and replied gravely, "Those who don't do some form of what you're talking about, they're not going to make it through what's coming."

CHAPTER 4

A New Kind of Christian Politics

L ike the people of other Western democracies, Americans are living through a political earthquake shaking the foundations of the postwar order. The old, familiar categories that framed political thought and discourse are dead or dying. Where do orthodox Christians fit into this emerging reality? Which side should we be on? Or do we have a side at all?

The answer will not satisfy conservative Christians who understand the church as the Republican Party at prayer, or who go into the voting booth with more conviction than they show at Sunday worship. Though there remain a few possibilities for progress in traditional politics, growing hostility toward Christians, as well as the moral confusion of values voters, should inspire us to imagine a better way forward.

The Benedict Option calls for a radical new way of doing politics, a hands-on localism based on pioneering work by Eastern bloc dissidents who defied Communism during the Cold War. A Westernized form of "antipolitical politics," to use the term coined by Czech political prisoner Václav Havel, is the best way forward for Orthodox Christians seeking practical and effective engagement in public life without losing our integrity, and indeed our humanity.

The Rise and Fall of Values Voters

As recently as the 1960s, with the notable exception of civil rights, moral and cultural concerns weren't make-or-break issues in U.S. politics. Americans voted largely on economics, as they had since the Great Depression. There was sufficient moral consensus in the culturally Christian nation to keep sex and sexuality apolitical.

The sexual revolution changed all that. Beginning with the *Roe v. Wade* abortion decision in 1973, Americans began sorting themselves politically according to moral beliefs. The religious right began to rise in the Republican Party as 'the secular left did the same among the Democrats. By the turn of the century, the culture war was undeniably the red-hot center of American politics.

"Whereas elections once pitted the party of the working class against the party of Wall Street," wrote journalist Thomas Byrne Edsall in the *Atlantic*, "they now pit voters who believe in a fixed and universal morality against those who see moral issues, especially sexual ones, as elastic and subject to personal choice."

That was 2003. Today the culture war as we knew it is over. The so-called values voters—social and religious conservatives—have been defeated and are being swept to the political margins. Moral issues may not be as central to our politics as they once were, but the American people remain fragmented, often bitterly, by these concerns. Though Donald Trump won the presidency in part with the strong support of Catholics and Evangelicals, the idea that someone as robustly vulgar, fiercely combative, and morally compromised as Trump will be an avatar for the restoration of Christian morality and social unity is beyond delusional. He is not a solution to the problem of America's cultural decline, but a symptom of it.

The diminishment in the drama of American politics has allowed the natural tensions within both parties over economic issues to assert themselves boldly. The nation is fracturing along class lines, with large numbers on both the young left and the populist right challenging the free market, globalist economic consensus that has united U.S. politics since the Reagan and Bill Clinton presidencies. In 2016, the Republican nominee ran as a nationalist opponent of trade deals while the Democratic candidate, a globalist to the fingertips, was Wall Street's favorite.

This is the first wave of a tectonic political realignment, based around competing visions of free trade and national identity. Race and class will be front and center, for better or worse, and we may look back fondly to the years when abortion and gay marriage were the things animating our fiercest fights. Welcome to the politics of post-Christian America.

Where do the erstwhile values voters fit in the new dispensation? We don't, not really. The 2016 presidential campaign made it clear—piercingly, agonizingly clear—that conservative Christians, once comfortably established in the Republican Party, are politically homeless.

Our big issues—abortion and religious liberty—were not part of the GOP primary campaign. Donald Trump captured the party's nomination without having to court religious conservatives. In his convention acceptance speech, he ignored us. During the general election campaign, some prominent Evangelicals and a handful of leading Catholics climbed aboard the Trump train out of naked fear of a Hillary Clinton administration. In his upset victory, Trump captured 52 percent of the Catholic vote, and a stunning 81 percent of the Evangelical vote.

Will Trump govern as a friend to Christian conservatives? Perhaps. If he appoints Supreme Court justices and lower court judges who are enthusiasts for religious liberty, then his administration will have been a blessing to us. Though Trump's conversion to the pro-life cause was very late and politically expedient, it's a reasonable bet that his administration will cease its predecessor's hostility to it. For Christians who anticipated four more years of losing ground under sustained assault by a progressive White House, these are no small things.

However, there are a number of dangers, both clear and hidden, from the new Washington regime. For one, Donald Trump's long public life has shown him to be many things, but a keeper of his promises is not one of them. The Psalmist's warning to "put not your trust in princes" remains excellent advice.

For another, the church is not merely politically conservative white people at prayer. Many Hispanics and other Christians of color, as well as all who, for whatever reason, did not vote for the divisive Trump, do not thereby cease to be Christian. Holding the church together during the Trump years will pose a strong challenge to us all.

Besides, fair or not, conservative Christianity will be associated with Trump for the next few years, and no doubt beyond. If conservative church leaders aren't extraordinarily careful in how they manage their public relationship to the Trump administration, anti-Trump blowback will do severe damage to the church's reputation. Trump's election solves some problems for the church, but given the man's character, it creates others. Political power is not a moral disinfectant.

And this brings us to the more subtle but potentially more devastating effects of this unexpected GOP election victory. There is first the temptation to worship power, and to compromise one's soul to maintain access to it. There are many ways to burn a pinch of incense to Caesar, and some prominent pro-Trump Christians arguably crossed that line during the campaign season. Again, political victory does not vitiate the vice of hypocrisy.

There is also the danger of Christians falling back into complacency. No administration in Washington, no matter how ostensibly pro-Christian, is capable of stopping cultural trends toward desacralization and fragmentation that have been building for centuries. To expect any different is to make a false idol of politics.

One reason the contemporary church is in so much trouble is that religious conservatives of the last generation mistakenly believed they could focus on politics and the culture would take care of itself. For the past thirty years or so, many of us believed that we could turn back the tide of aggressive 1960s liberalism by voting for conservative Republicans. White Evangelicals and Catholic "Reagan Democrats" came together to support GOP candidates who vowed to back socially conservative legislation and to nominate conservative justices to the U.S. Supreme Court.

The results were decidedly mixed on the legislative and judicial fronts, but the verdict on the overall political strategy is clear: we failed. Fundamental abortion rights remain solidly in place, and Gallup poll numbers from the *Roe v. Wade* era until today have not meaningfully changed. The traditional marriage and family model has not been protected in either law or custom, and because of that, courts are poised to impose dramatic rollbacks of religious liberty for the sake of antidiscrimination.

Again, the new Trump administration may be able to block or at least slow these moves with its judicial appointments, but this is small consolation. Will the law as written by a conservative legislature and interpreted by conservative judges overwrite the law of the human heart? No, it will not. Politics is no substitute for personal holiness. The best that Orthodox Christians today can hope for from politics is that it can open a space for the church to do the work of charity, culture building, and conversion.

Traditional Politics: What Can Still Be Done

To be sure, Christians cannot afford to vacate the public square entirely. The church must not shrink from its responsibility to pray for political leaders and to speak prophetically to them. Christian concern does not end with fighting abortion and with protecting religious liberty and the traditional family. For example, the new populism on the right may give traditionalist Christians the opportunity to shape a new GOP that on economic issues is about solidarity more with Main Street than Wall Street. Conservative Christians can and should continue working with liberals to combat sex trafficking, poverty, AIDS, and the like.

The real question facing us is not whether to quit politics entirely, but how to exercise political power prudently, especially in an unstable political culture. When is it cowardly not to cooperate with secular politicians out of an exaggerated fear of impurity—and when is it corrupting to be complicit? Donald Trump tore up the political rule book in every way. Faithful conservative Christians cannot rely unreflectively on habits learned over the past thirty years of political engagement. The times require much more wisdom and subtlety for those believers entering the political fray.

Above all, though, they require attention to the local church and community, which doesn't flourish or fail based primarily on what happens in Washington. And the times require an acute appreciation of the fragility of what can be accomplished through partisan politics. Republicans won't always rule Washington, after all, and the Republicans who are ruling it now may be more adversarial to the work of the church than many gullible Christians think.

Yuval Levin, editor of *National Affairs* magazine and a fellow of Washington's Ethics and Public Policy Center, contends that religious conservatives would be better off "building thriving subcultures" than seeking positions of power. Why? Because in an age of increasing and unstoppable fragmentation, the common culture doesn't matter as much as it used to. Writes Levin:

> The center has not held in American life, so we must instead find our centers for ourselves as communities of like-minded citizens, and then build out the American ethic from there. . . . Those seeking to reach Americans with an unfamiliar moral message must find them where they are, and increasingly, that means traditionalists must make their case not by planting themselves at the center of society, as large institutions, but by dispersing themselves to the peripheries as small outposts. In

this sense, focusing on your own near-at-hand community does not involve a withdrawal from contemporary America, but an increased attentiveness to it.[1]

Though orthodox Christians have to embrace localism because they can no longer expect to influence Washington politics as they once could, there is one cause that should receive all the attention they have left for national politics: religious liberty.

Religious liberty is critically important to the Benedict Option. Without a robust and successful defense of First Amendment protections, Christians will not be able to build the communal institutions that are vital to maintaining our identity and values. What's more, Christians who don't act decisively within the embattled zone of freedom we have now are wasting precious time—time that may run out faster than we think.

Lance Kinzer is living at the edge of the political transition Christian conservatives must make. A ten-year Republican veteran of the Kansas legislature, Kinzer left his seat in 2014 and now travels the nation as an advocate for religious liberty legislation in statehouses. "I was a very normal Evangelical Christian Republican, and everything that comes with that—particularly a belief that this is 'our' country, in a way that was probably not healthy," he says.

That all fell apart in 2014, when Kansas Republicans, anticipating court-imposed gay marriage, tried to expand religious liberty protections to cover wedding vendors, wedding cake makers, and others. Like many other Republican lawmakers in this deep-red state, Kinzer expected that the legislation would pass the House and Senate easily and make it to conservative Governor Sam Brownback's desk for signature.

It didn't work out that way at all. The Kansas Chamber of Commerce came out strongly against the bill. State and national media exploded with their customary indignation. Kinzer, who was a pro-life leader in the House, was used to tough press coverage, but the firestorm over religious liberty was like nothing he had ever seen.

The bill passed the Kansas House but was killed in the Republican-controlled Senate. The result left Kinzer reeling. "It became very clear to me that the social conservative–Big Business coalition politics was frayed to the breaking point and indicated such a fundamental difference in priorities, in what was important," he recalls. "It was disorienting. I had conversations with people I felt I had carried a lot of water for and considered friends at a deep political level, who, in very public, very aggressive ways, were trying to undermine some fairly benign religious liberty protections."

Kinzer had already decided to leave state politics anyway, to return to his law practice and spend more time with his family. The debacle over religious liberty legislation confirmed that he had made the right decision.

It wasn't simply exhaustion with the political process but more a recognition that given "the reality of the cultural moment," it was more important to shore up his local church community than to continue his legislative work. Though a lifelong churchgoer—he and his family worship at a Presbyterian Church in America congregation in Overland Park, a Kansas City suburb—Kinzer concluded that he ought to do more locally.

"It's easy when you've chosen politics as a vocation to convince yourself that you're doing fundamental work for the Kingdom by what you're doing in the legislature," he said. "I started to question that. It's not whether or not it was worthwhile to have worked on those issues, but rather a growing sense inside of me that there's a real work of cultural reclamation and renewal, not outside the church but *inside* the church, that really needs to happen first, before we can think about much longer-term goals."

Even though Kinzer and his family attend a conservative church within a conservative denomination, he found that many of his fellow congregants were largely unaware of their own Reformed tradition—and in turn, were oblivious to the wealth of resources that that tradition offered to ground them more deeply in the faith.

"I grew up very much with the idea church was a place you go for teaching and fellowship, but you're really there for a kind of pep talk before you go out there and live your real life the rest of the week," he says.

Given the post-Christian turn in American culture, that is no longer enough. Kinzer has plunged more deeply into the life of his congregation, teaching a class on Augustine's *City of God* and organizing a new prayer meeting for men and women. The former legislator sees this as vital work to prepare his own congregation for the new reality—one that American Christians still don't grasp.

"The big challenge, especially for Evangelicals who always believed that there was some sort of silent majority with them, is to come to terms with the fact that this is just not true," he says. "This is difficult, this is disorienting. Internalizing the fact that that is not the case is difficult, is disorienting to a lot of people.

"By the same token, I think it's vital for the health of Christianity, and even for Christian engagement in the political sphere, for them to do just that," he continues. "And it needs to be more than just an intellectual exercise. You need forms of living that reinforce your distinctiveness, that reinforce the kind of 'strangers in exile' sense that's well grounded in Scripture."

Yet Kinzer has not left politics entirely. The first goal of Benedict Option Christians in the world of conventional politics is to secure and expand the space within which we can be ourselves and build our own institutions. To that end, he travels around the country advocating for religious liberty legislation in state legislatures. Over and over he sees Republican legislators who are inclined to support religious liberty taking a terrible pounding from the business lobby. He doesn't know how much longer they will be able to hold out. Pastors and lay Christian leaders need to prepare their congregations for hard times.

"It's important to avoid being alarmist, but people really do need to recognize the seriousness of the threats that Christians face, and the real, deep difficulty of the political environment," Kinzer says. "They need to internalize what it really means to be in a minority posture, and beginning to think like that is really critical. If we don't, we're going to continue to operate out of a playbook that has very little to do with the game that's actually being played."

Kinzer contends that even as Christians refocus their attention locally and center their attention on building up their own local church communities, they cannot afford to disengage from politics completely. The religious liberty stakes are far too high. What does this mean at the grassroots level? He offers these suggestions:

- Get active at the state and local level, engaging lawmakers with personal letters (not cut-and-paste mailings from activist groups) and face-to-face meetings.
- Focus on prudent, achievable goals. Don't fight the entire culture war or waste scant political capital on meaningless or needlessly inflammatory gestures.
- Nothing matters more than guarding the freedom of Christian institutions to nurture future generations in the faith. Given our political weakness, other objectives have to take a back seat.
- Reach out to local media and invite coverage of the religious side in particular religious liberty controversies.
- Stay polite and respectful. Don't validate opponents' claims that "religious liberty" is nothing more than an excuse for bigotry.
- Because Christians need all the friends we can get, form partnerships with leaders across denominations and from non-Christian religions. And extend a hand of friendship to gays and lesbians who disagree with us but will stand up for our First Amendment right to be wrong.

Most American Christians have no sense of how urgent this issue is and how critical it is for individuals and churches to rise from their slumber and defend themselves while there is still time. We do not have the luxury of continuing to fight the last war.

"We are facing the real risk that the work of the church, and its ability to form our children according to the things we believe are most important in life, is under threat by a hostile government," warns Kinzer. "And I don't think it's alarmist to say so."

True. As important as religious liberty is, though, Christians cannot forget that *religious liberty is not an end in itself* but a means to the end of living as Christians in full. Religious liberty is an important component in permitting us to get on with the real work of the church and with the Benedict Option. If protecting religious liberty requires us to compromise the moral beliefs that define us as Christians, then any victories we achieve will be hollow. The church's mission on earth is not political success but fidelity.

Antipolitical Politics

The Benedict Option calls for a new Christian politics, one that grows out of our own relative powerlessness in contemporary America. It might sound strange to call the Rule of Saint Benedict a political document, but it is nothing less than a constitution governing the shared life of a particular community. Because it dictates how Benedictine virtues are to be lived by monastic communities, the Rule is political.

The concept is hard to grasp because when we think about politics, we imagine campaigns, elections, activism, lawmaking—all the elements of statecraft in a democracy. In the most basic philosophical sense, though, politics is the process by which we agree on how we are going to live together.

As we have seen, the politics of a Benedictine monastery are very different from the politics of a liberal democracy. This is how it should be. The *telos*, or ultimate goal, of a monastic life is not the same as the *telos* of life in a secular state.

Nevertheless both communities—like all communities—are governed by a vision of order constructed according to some shared sense of the Good. All laws reflect this.

Benedict Option politics begin with recognition that Western society is post-Christian and that absent a miracle, there is no hope of reversing this condition in the foreseeable future. This means, in part, that what Orthodox Christians can accomplish through conventional politics has narrowed considerably. Most Americans will not only reject many things traditional Christians consider good but will even call them evil. Trying to reclaim our lost influence will be a waste of energy or worse, if the financial and other resources that could have been dedicated to building alternative institutions for the long resistance went instead to making a doomed attempt to hold on to power.

Instead, Christians must turn their attention to a different kind of politics. Part of the change we have to make is accepting that in the years to come, faithful Christians may have to choose between being a good American and being a good Christian. In a nation where "God and country" are so entwined, the idea that one's citizenship might be at radical odds with one's faith is a new one.

Alexis de Tocqueville was convinced that democracy could not survive the loss of Christian faith. Self-government required shared convictions about moral truths. Christian faith drew men outside themselves and taught them that laws must be firmly rooted in a moral order revealed and guaranteed by God.

If a democratic nation loses religion, he wrote, then it falls prey to inordinate individualism, materialism, and democratic despotism and inevitably "prepares its citizens for servitude." Therefore, said Tocqueville, "one must maintain Christianity within the new democracies at all cost."

We have not done that. If Tocqueville is right, conservative Christians must now prepare ourselves for very dark times. The 2016 election was a harbinger. Americans had to choose between an establishment Democrat deeply hostile to core Christian values and to religious liberty, and an outsider Republican of no particular religious commitment who sold himself as a strongman who would impose order by force of will.

What's more, we must now face a question that will strike many of us as heretical according to our civic catechism. It has previously been unthinkable, certainly to patriotic Christians. But it must be confronted.

In his 2016 book *Conserving America?: Essays on Present Discontents,* Patrick J. Deneen, a Notre Dame political theorist, argues that Enlightenment liberalism, from which both U.S. parties are descended, is built on the premise that humans are by nature "free and independent," and that the purpose of government is to liberate the autonomous individual. Making progress toward this goal, whether promoted by free-market parties of the right or statist egalitarian parties of the left, depends on denying natural limits.

This is contrary to what both Scripture and experience teach us about human nature. The purpose of civilization, in Deneen's words, "has been to sustain and support familial, social and cultural structures and practices that perpetuate and deepen personal and intergenerational forms of obligation and gratitude, of duty and indebtedness."

In other words, civilization doesn't exist to make it possible for individuals to do whatever they want to do. To believe that is an anthropological error. A civilization in which no one felt an obligation to the past, to the future, to each other, or to anything higher than self-gratification is one that is dangerously fragile. In the waning decades of the Western Roman Empire, Augustine described society as preoccupied with pleasure-seeking, selfishness, and living for the moment.

Because it prescribes government of the people, liberal democracy can be only as strong as the people who live under it. And so, the question before us now is whether our current political situation is a betrayal of liberal democracy or, given its core principles of individualism and egalitarianism, liberal democracy's inevitable fulfillment under secularism. Writes Deneen:

We have reached a culminating moment when it is less a political movement that is needed—as important as it might be to seek certain public goods—than a revival of culture, of sustainable practices and defensible ways of life born of shared experience, memory and trust. However, such a revival can't occur by attempting to go back or recover something lost. Rather, ironically what is needed is provided by the very vehicle of destruction, and found amid the strengths of liberalism itself: the creative human capacity of reinvention and new beginnings.[2]

Hence the need, not for the second coming of Ronald Reagan or for a would-be political savior, but for a new—and quite different—Saint Benedict.

What kind of politics should we pursue in the Benedict Option? If we broaden our political vision to include culture, we find that opportunities for action and service are boundless. Christian philosopher Scott Moore says that we err when we speak of politics as mere statecraft.

"Politics is about how we order our lives together in the polis, whether that is a city, community or even a family," writes Moore. "It is about how we live together, how we recognize and preserve that which is most important, how we cultivate friendships and educate our children, how we learn to think and talk about what kind of life really is the good life."[3]

In thinking about politics in this vein, American Christians have much to learn from the experience of Czech dissidents under Communism. The essays that Czech playwright and political prisoner Václav Havel and his circle produced under oppression and persecution far surpassing any that American Christians are likely to experience in the near future offer a powerful vision for authentic Christian politics in a world in which we are a powerless, despised minority.

Havel, who died in 2011, preached what he called "antipolitical politics," the essence of which he described as "living in truth." His most famous and thorough statement of this was a long 1978 essay titled "The Power of the Powerless," which electrified the Eastern European resistance movements when it first appeared.[4] It is a remarkable document, one that bears careful study and reflection by orthodox Christians in the West today.

Consider, says Havel, the greengrocer living under Communism, who puts a sign in his shop window saying, "Workers of the World, Unite!" He does it not because he believes it, necessarily. He simply doesn't want trouble. And if he doesn't really believe it, he hides the humiliation of his coercion by telling himself, "What's wrong with the workers of the world uniting?" Fear allows the official ideology to retain power—and eventually changes the greengrocer's beliefs. Those who "live within a lie," says Havel, collaborate with the system and compromise their full humanity.

Every act that contradicts the official ideology is a denial of the system. What if the greengrocer stops putting the sign up in his window? What if he refuses to go along to get along? "His revolt is an attempt to *live within the truth*"— and it's going to cost him plenty.

He will lose his job and his position in society. His kids may not be allowed to go to the college they want to, or to any college at all. People will bully him or ostracize him. But by bearing witness to the truth, he has accomplished something potentially powerful.

He has said that the emperor is naked. And because the emperor is in fact naked, something extremely dangerous has happened: by his action, the greengrocer has addressed the world. He has enabled everyone to peer behind the curtain. He has shown everyone that it *is* possible to live within the truth.

Because they are public, the greengrocer's deeds are inescapably political. He bears witness to the truth of his convictions by being willing to suffer for them. He becomes a threat to the system—but he has preserved his humanity. And that, says Havel, is a far more important accomplishment than whether this party or that politician holds power.

"A better system will not automatically ensure a better life," Havel goes on. "In fact the opposite is true: *only by creating a better life can a better system be developed*" (emphasis mine).

The answer, then, is to create and support "parallel structures" in which the truth can be lived in community. Isn't this a form of escapism, a retreat into a ghetto? Not at all, says Havel; a countercultural community that abdicated its responsibility to reach out to help others would end up being a "more sophisticated version of 'living within a lie.'"

A good example of what this better life could look like comes from the late mathematician and dissident Václav Benda. A faithful Catholic, Benda believed that Communism maintained its iron grip on the people by isolating them, fragmenting their natural social bonds. The Czech regime severely punished the Catholic Church, driving many believers to privatize their faith, retreating behind the walls of their homes so as not to attract attention from the authorities.

Benda's distinct contribution to the dissident movement was the idea of a "parallel *polis*"—a separate but porous society existing alongside the official Communist order.[5] Says Flagg Taylor, an American political philosopher and expert on Czech dissident movements, "Benda's point was that dissidents couldn't simply protest the Communist government, but had to support positive engagement with the world."

At serious risk to himself and his family (he and his wife had six children), Benda rejected ghettoization. He saw no possibility for collaboration with the Communists, but he also rejected quietism, considering it a failure to display proper Christian concern for justice, charity, and bearing evangelical witness to Christ in the public square. For Benda, Havel's injunction to "live in truth" could only mean one thing: to live as a Christian in community.

Benda did not advocate retreat to a Christian ghetto. He insisted that the parallel *polis* must understand itself as fighting for "the preservation or the renewal of the national community in the widest sense of the word—along with the defense of all the values, institutions, and material conditions to which the existence of such a community is bound.

> I personally think that a no less effective, exceptionally painful, and in the short term practically irreparable way of eliminating the human race or individual nations would be a decline into barbarism, the abandonment of reason and learning, the loss of traditions and memory. The ruling regime—partly intentionally, partly thanks to its essentially nihilistic nature—has done everything it can to achieve that goal. The aim of independent citizens' movements that try to create a parallel *polis* must be precisely the opposite: we must not be discouraged by previous failures, and we must consider the area of schooling and education as one of our main priorities.[6]

From this perspective, the parallel *polis* is not about building a gated community for Christians but rather about establishing (or reestablishing) common practices and common institutions that can reverse the isolation and fragmentation of contemporary society. (In this we hear Brother Ignatius of Norcia's call to have "borders"—formal lines behind which we live to nurture our faith and culture—but to "push outwards, infinitely.") Benda wrote that the parallel *polis*'s ultimate political goals are "to return to truth and justice, to a meaningful order of values, [and] to value once more the inalienability of human dignity and the necessity for a sense of human community in mutual love and responsibility."

In other words, dissident Christians should see their Benedict Option projects as building a better future not only for themselves but for everyone around them. That's a grand vision, but Benda knew that most people weren't interested in standing up for abstract causes that appealed only to intellectuals. He advocated *practical* actions that ordinary Czechs could do in their daily lives.

"If you didn't like how university education was going, help students find an underground seminar taught by one of these brilliant professors kicked out of university by the government," Taylor says, explaining Benda's principles. "Print good novels by *samizdat* and get them into the hands of the people, and let them see what they're missing. Support theological education in one of the underground seminaries. When people see [that] resistance is connected to something that's really meaningful to them, and that is possible only if there are a certain number of people committed to preserving it in the face of the state's opposition, they will act."

Whether you call it "antipolitical politics" or a "parallel *polis*," what might the Czech dissidents' vision look like in our circumstances? Havel gives a number of examples. Think of teachers who make sure kids learn things they won't get at government schools. Think of writers who write what they really believe and find ways to get it to the public, no matter what the cost. Think of priests and pastors who find a way to live out religious life despite condemnation and legal obstacles, and artists who don't give a rip for official opinion. Think of young people who decide not to care about success in society's eyes and who drop out to pursue a life of integrity, no matter what it costs them. These people who refuse to assimilate and instead build their own structures are living the Benedict Option.

If we hope for our faith to change the world one day, we have to start locally. Benedict Option communities should be small, because "beyond a certain point, human ties like personal trust and personal responsibility cannot work." And they should "naturally rise from *below*," which is to say, they should be organic and not handed down by central planners. These communities start with the individual heart and spread from there to the family, the church community, the neighborhood, and onward.

In order to know what our neighbors need and want, we will have to be close to them. In Benda's time, the Czech people had little concept of themselves as a community. The totalitarian government had taken that away from them. Benda's attempt to repoliticize the people consisted of activating their desire simply to be together, to be social in whatever way they found pleasing.

"Benda teaches us an important lesson," Taylor says. "In my case, I don't really know my neighbors, other than one family next door. There's no neighborhood bar for me to go see people in my community. Maybe there's something to be said for reactivating people's social natures. We probably don't know what we're missing."

A friend of mine who led a wild, hedonistic life converted to Christianity after seeing her brother's genuinely happy family and knowing the light in their faces and the love in their hearts came from faith in Christ. She told me, "I realized later that I just needed somebody to give me permission to be wholesome." As the West declines into spiritual acedia, there will be more and more people who are seeking something real, something meaningful, and yes, something wholesome. It is our mandate as Christians to offer it to them.

No matter how furious and all-consuming partisan political battles are, Christians have to keep clearly before us the fact that conventional American politics cannot fix what is wrong with our society and culture. They are inadequate because in both their left-wing and right-wing forms, they operate from the position that facilitating and expanding human choice is the proper end of our politics. The left and the right just disagree over where to draw the lines. Neither party's program is fully consistent with Christian truth.

By contrast, the politics of the Benedict Option assume that the disorder in American public life derives from disorder within the American soul. Benedict Option politics start with the proposition that the most important political work of our time is the restoration of inner order, harmonizing with the will of God—the same *telos* as life in the monastic community. Everything else follows naturally from that.

Above all, this means being ordered toward love. We become what we love and make the world according to our loves. We should act from a place not of fear and loathing but of affection and confidence in God and His will.

When we are truly ordered toward God, we won't have to worry about immediate results—and that's a good thing. In interviewing surviving dissidents from the Czech Communist era, researcher Taylor discovered something they had in common with Saint Benedict and his monks. They never expected to live to see the end of totalitarianism, and they did not really believe their activities would have any effect in the short term. But this worked to their advantage.

"They surrendered themselves to the idea that these things were worth doing in and of themselves, not because they might have definite, measurable consequences," Taylor says. "Havel, Benda, and the other dissidents made it clear that once you start down the path of consequentialism, you will always find a reason not to do anything. You have to want to do something because it's worth doing, not because you think it will make the Communist Party fall in four years."

Building Benedict Option communities may not turn our nation around, but it's still worth doing. Those engaged in building these structures should not be discouraged by failures in the short run. These are bound to happen. Rather, they must keep their balance and stay focused on, in Havel's words, "the everyday, thankless, and never-ending struggle of human beings to live more freely, truthfully, and in quiet dignity."

Don't be deceived by the ordinariness of this charge. This is politics at its most profound level. It is politics during wartime, and we are fighting nothing less than a culture war over what C. S. Lewis called "the abolition of man."

"The best resistance to totalitarianism is simply to drive it out of our own souls, our own circumstances, our own land, to drive it out of contemporary humankind," said Václav Havel. The same is true for the corrosive anti-Christian philosophy that has taken over American public life.

At their best, Benedict Option communities can provide an unintentional political witness to secular liberal culture, offering a potent contrast to a set of increasingly cold and indifferent political and economic arrangements. The state will not be able to care for all human needs in the future, especially if the current projections of growing economic inequality prove accurate. The sheer humanity of Christian compassion, and the image of human dignity it honors, will be an extraordinarily attractive alternative—not unlike the evangelical witness of the early church amid the declining paganism of an exhausted Roman Empire.

Here's how to get started with the antipolitical politics of the Benedict Option. Secede culturally from the mainstream. Turn off the television. Put the smartphones away. Read books. Play games. Make music. Feast with your neighbors. It is not enough to avoid what is bad; you must also embrace what is good. Start a church, or a group within your church. Open a classical Christian school, or join and strengthen one that exists. Plant a garden, and participate in a local farmer's market. Teach kids how to play music, and start a band. Join the volunteer fire department.

The point is not that we should stop voting or being active in conventional politics. The point, rather, is that this is no longer enough. After the 1992 *Planned Parenthood v. Casey* decision upheld abortion rights, the pro-life movement understood that it was not going to be possible in the short run to overturn *Roe v. Wade*. So it broadened its strategy. The movement retained lobbyists and activists fighting the good fight in Washington and state capitals, but at the local level, creative pro-lifers opened crisis pregnancy centers. These quickly became central to advancing the pro-life cause—and saved countless unborn lives. This is a model we traditional Christians should follow. Times have changed dramatically, and we can no longer rely on politicians and activists to fight the culture war alone on our behalf.

Many conservative Christians felt relief over the fate of the Supreme Court upon hearing the shocking (even to his supporters) news that Donald Trump had won the presidency. This is understandable, and we should urge the new administration to appoint justices strongly committed to religious liberty and protecting unborn life. But it can't be repeated often enough: believers must avoid the usual trap of thinking that politics can solve cultural and religious problems. Trusting Republican politicians and the judges they appoint to do the work that only cultural change and religious conversion can do is a big reason Christians find ourselves so enfeebled. The deep cultural forces that have been separating the West from God for centuries will not be halted or reversed by a single election, or any election at all.

We faithful orthodox Christians didn't ask for internal exile from a country we thought was our own, but that's where we find ourselves. We are a minority now, so let's be a creative one, offering warm, living, light-filled alternatives to a world growing cold, dead, and dark. We will be increasingly without influence, but let's be guided by monastic wisdom and welcome this humbly as an opportunity sent by God for our purification and sanctification. Losing political power might just be the thing that saves the church's soul. Ceasing to believe that the fate of the American Empire is in our hands frees us to put them to work for the Kingdom of God in our own little shires.

CHAPTER 5

A Church for All Seasons

Your church may be killing itself and have no idea what it's doing. Everything may look fine on the surface, but deep down a cancer could be silently metastasizing in its bones, whose fragility will become painfully clear when put to the test.

In 2004, Robert Louis Wilken reflected in *First Things* magazine on a sobering trip he had made to Europe that year. Wilken, a leading American historian of early Christianity, said that over the course of his lifetime, he had seen the "collapse of Christian civilization." In Germany that spring, he observed that even the memory of once having been Christian was fading. It was bad enough that anti-Christian secularists were hard at work to eliminate the faith from public life, but it was still worse that Christians were aiding and abetting their own extinction.

Why? Christians in the West had badly neglected sustaining their own distinct culture. Wilken wrote:

> Nothing is more needful today than the survival of Christian culture, because in recent generations this culture has become dangerously thin. At this moment in the Church's history in this country (and in the West more generally) it is less urgent

to convince the alternative culture in which we live of the truth of Christ than it is for the Church to tell itself its own story and to nurture its own life, the culture of the city of God, the Christian republic. This is not going to happen without a rebirth of moral and spiritual discipline and a resolute effort on the part of Christians to comprehend and to defend the remnants of Christian culture.[1]

In other words: *If you do not change your ways, you are going to die, and so will what's left of the Christian faith in our civilization.*

The Benedict Option is vital to the life of the local church today. Why? Benedictine spirituality is good at creating a Christian culture because it is all about developing and sustaining the Christian *cultus*, a Latin word meaning "worship." A culture is the way of life that emerges from the common worship of a people. What we hold most sacred determines the form and content of our culture, which emerges organically from the process of making a faith tangible.

If it is going to bring about a genuine renewal of Christian culture, the Benedict Option will have to be centered on the life of the church. Everything else follows.

In some sense, Christians' new minority status may help us keep our focus where it ought to be. As Southern Baptist leader Russell Moore says in his book *Onward*, by losing its cultural respectability, the church is freer to be radically faithful.

"We will engage the culture less like the chaplains of some idyllic Mayberry and more like the apostles in the book of Acts," writes Moore. "We will be speaking not primarily to baptized pagans on someone's church roll, but to those who are hearing something new, maybe for the first time. We will hardly be 'normal,' but we should never have tried to be."[2]

The best witness Christians can offer to post-Christian America is simply to be the church, as fiercely and creatively a minority as we can manage. "By this will all men know that you are my disciples," the

Lord said in the Gospel of John, and if we stand a chance today, we do only because of His love lived out through us—to our brothers and sisters in Christ and then out to the world.

But you cannot give what you do not possess. Too many of our churches function as secular entertainment centers with religious morals slapped on top, when they should be functioning as the living, breathing Body of Christ. Too many churches have succumbed to modernity, rejecting the wisdom of past ages, treating worship as a consumer activity, and allowing parishioners to function as unaccountable, atomized members. The sad truth is, when the world sees us, it often fails to see anything different from nonbelievers. Christians often talk about "reaching the culture" without realizing that, having no distinct Christian culture of their own, they have been co-opted by the secular culture they wish to evangelize. Without a substantial Christian culture, it's no wonder that our children are forgetting what it means to be Christian, and no surprise that we are not bringing in new converts.

If today's churches are to survive the new Dark Age, they must stop "being normal." We will need to commit ourselves more deeply to our faith, and we will need to do that in ways that seem odd to contemporary eyes. By rediscovering the past, recovering liturgical worship and asceticism, centering our lives on the church community, and tightening church discipline, we will, by God's grace, again become the peculiar people we should always have been. The fruits of this focus on Christian formation will result not only in stronger Christians but in a new evangelism as the salt recovers its savor.

Rediscover the Past

If the monks of Norcia woke up in a new world every day and decided that their direction would be decided by their whims, the community would fall apart, or it would at least cease to be the kind of community that forms Christian monks. Instead, they follow a Rule that has been tested by fifteen hundred years of experience. Tradition not only guides them in how to obey God's Word and be open to the Holy Spirit's leading, but it frees them from the burden of having to make things up as they go along.

This is a hard thing for modern Christians to understand. Our imaginations have been colonized by a mentality that holds older, inherited forms of worship to be impediments to authenticity. On the contrary, we need to be instructed in how to pray and worship to train our minds to think in an authentically Christian way. As Paul exhorted the Romans, we must be transformed by the renewing of our minds, by adopting thought patterns and behaviors that are not actually natural to us. This is not bondage but liberty.

When Christians ignore the story of how our fathers and mothers in the faith prayed, lived, and worshiped, we deny the life-giving power of our own roots and cut ourselves off from the wisdom of those whose minds were renewed. As a result, at best, the work of God in our lives is slower and shallower than it might otherwise be. At worst, we lose our children.

A big part of the falling away today is that our children don't know the history of Christianity or grasp why it matters. One Eastern Orthodox friend, raised an Evangelical, said she had no idea what the early church taught, or even who the fathers of the church were, until she became Orthodox—a tradition that emphasizes their writings and teachings. For this friend, the Christian faith amounted to the Bible as interpreted by the most popular Evangelical pastors of the day.

It's not that Evangelicalism rejects the foundational theological writings of early Christianity, she explained, but that it never mentions them. Nor did the church of her youth dig deeply into the Reformation tradition from which it sprang. In her church and religious school, she was fed nothing but the thin gruel of contemporary Christianity, with its shallow theology and upbeat sloganeering. As writer Walker Percy cracked about vapid contemporary Christian novelists, they've sold their birthright for "a pot of message."

This is not an exclusively Evangelical problem. Many Mainline Protestants and Catholics over the past two or three generations have been raised in near-total ignorance of the roots of their own tradition. No small number of cradle Eastern Orthodox grew up learning more about their ancestors' ethnic folkways than about the faith of their fathers. To cut a people off from their tradition is to break the chain of historical memory and deprive them of a culture. No wonder Christian culture withers in modernity.

But there are ways for determined Christians to get around this.

Once, during my Catholic days, I was complaining with a Catholic friend about how terrible the teaching was in parish life. A priest listening to us said that everything we griped about was true, but we didn't have to resign ourselves and our children to this fate.

"You could go online to Amazon.com tonight and have sent to you within a week a theological library that Aquinas would have envied," he said. "My parents raised me in the seventies, which was the beginning of the catechesis nightmare. They knew that if they were going to raise Catholic kids, they would have to do a lot of it themselves, and they did. So do you."

If you don't start something in your local church, who will? Religious liberty activist Lance Kinzer, whom you met in the previous chapter, started a prayer group at his church, in which they use prayers written by Calvin himself. Kinzer is also leading a Sunday school study of Augustine's writings. It is understandable that Protestants would be wary of pre-Reformation theological works of the second millennium, but the writings of the early church fathers are a gold mine of spiritual and theological wisdom.

Polycarp, Justin Martyr, Athanasius, Augustine, John Chrysostom, the Cappadocians, Jerome, Ignatius of Antioch, Clement of Alexandria, Maximus the Confessor, Irenaeus, and so many more: these voices from the first eight centuries of the Christian church still speak to us today. Christians seeking to deepen their connections to historical Christianity should read these men of God. Their writings are straightforward and accessible to the hearts of even contemporary readers. They reveal to us the Christian tradition that gave us our distinctiveness, much of which we have lost in modern times.

The church's loss of its distinct culture is also a loss for the world, which God intends to bless through the church's life. Southern Baptist literary critic Ralph Wood contends that the church's task today is "not to create a counter-culture, so much as a new culture based on one so ancient and nearly forgotten that it looks freshly minted."[3]

We Christians today can create that new culture based on returning in creative ways to that very old one. We are called to be a new—and quite different—Saint Polycarp, Saint Irenaeus, Saint Augustine, and so forth. The best way to do that is to immerse ourselves in the words and the world of the old saints.

Recover Liturgical Worship

Just as many contemporary Christians are allergic to the past, many are also wary of liturgy, but they shouldn't be. Liturgy—from the Greek word *leitourgia*, meaning "work of the people"—in Christian use means the form of common worship. There is a connection between neglecting to take liturgy seriously, or giving up liturgy altogether, and abandoning Christian orthodoxy. If we are to maintain these truths over time, we must maintain our liturgy.

The media critic Marshall McLuhan could be said to have been writing about liturgies when he said, "The medium is the message." What he meant was that the concrete form in which information is delivered is itself a message, because it shapes our ability to receive the message.

Here's an example. When my parents were growing up in Louisiana in the 1940s and '50s, Europe was so distant in their imagination as to be virtually unreal. When I was growing up in the same place in the 1970s and '80s, Europe seemed so much closer thanks to television, which beamed sounds and pictures from the continent into our home almost daily. In high school, I had a couple of Dutch pen pals. Once I screwed up the courage to call one of them on our touch-tone phone. It was such a momentous event in my mind that even thirty years later, I can still remember her family's phone number, which I had memorized like a line of poetry. The sound of her voice coming to me over the phone that first time made me feel that technology enabled me to break through to another dimension. And in a way, it had.

For my children, who are being raised in the same geographical location as both my parents and me, Europe is as real as Texas. Not only do they see Europe on the TV news and on the wide variety of programming that comes to our television over the Internet, but our family likes to speak live over the Internet, with Skype or FaceTime, with our friends in the Netherlands. McLuhan coined the term *global village* in 1964 to refer to the technology-enabled worldwide sharing of culture. Fifty years later the Internet has made that a reality.

What changed is not the "message" from Europe, in terms of the informational content. The revolutionary change in consciousness came through the electronic media—first television, then the Internet. The truly transformative message is that electronic media make the whole wide world immediately accessible.

Liturgy is like a medium of communication in the McLuhanesque sense. The effect of liturgy is both in the information it conveys and in the way it conveys it. Imagine that you are at a Catholic mass in a dreary 1970s-era suburban church that looks like a converted Pizza Hut. The next Sunday you are at a high Catholic mass in New York City, at St. Patrick's Cathedral. The Scripture reading is the same in both places, and Jesus is just as present in the Eucharist at Our Lady of Pizza Hut as at St. Patrick's. Chances are, though, that you had to work harder to conjure a sense of the true holiness of the mass in the suburban church than in the cathedral—though theologically speaking, the "information" conveyed in Word and Sacrament in both places was the same. This is the difference liturgy can make.

James K. A. Smith, an Evangelical Christian philosopher, points out that all of life is liturgical, in the sense that all our actions frame our experiences and train our desires to particular ends. Every day we are living out what he calls "cultural liturgies" of one kind or another.

The secular liturgy of the shopping mall is designed to call forth and cultivate certain desires within those who enter the mall. It promises to deliver personal fulfillment through purchasing. In Smith's telling, advertising images of beautiful people convey the subliminal message that you could be just as happy and attractive as they are if you would purchase the product. If the mall liturgy does what it is supposed to do, the desire that the images and rituals of shopping evoke will lead the shopper to exchange money for products, then leave the mall fulfilled—until longing for the same experience brings her back.[4]

The lesson here is that various elements present in the ritual of shopping at a mall activate particular desires and direct them toward certain objects, the purchase of which promises to deliver satisfaction.

Christian liturgies, on the other hand, should lead us to desire communion with God. The basis for our liturgies is the one who unites the medium and the message of the Gospel: Jesus Christ. As scholar Robert Inchausti pithily puts it, McLuhan's famous slogan is "just another way of saying 'the Word become flesh.'"[5] Our liturgies of worship, diverse as they may be, are oriented toward praising and partaking of Him.

There have been a number of liturgies throughout the history of the Christian church, but most followed a basic pattern derived from Scripture. At its most basic, Sunday liturgy begins with the formal gathering of the worshiping community, the reading of Scripture, the celebration of Communion, and the dispersal of the community to live for Christ. Sunday liturgy, then, is a gathering of the faithful to commune with God in Word and Sacrament, and their sending out into the world.

Many Christians today (including some in liturgical churches) believe that Sunday worship is merely expressive—that is, it's only about what we the people have to say to God. However, in the Christian tradition, liturgy is primarily, though not exclusively, about what God has to say to us. Liturgy reveals something of the divine, transcendent order, and when we submit to it, it draws us into closer harmony with that order.

All worship is in some sense liturgical, but liturgies that are sacramental both reflect Christ's presence in the divine order and embody it in a concrete form accessible to worshipers. Liturgy is not magic, of course, but if it is intended and received sacramentally, it awakens the sense that worshipers are communing with the eternal, transcendent realm through the ritual and its elements. The liturgy feeds the sacramental imagination, reweaving the connection between body and spirit.

As we have seen, the Benedictines order their lives around belief that matter matters, and that what we do with our bodies and the material world has concrete spiritual consequences.

The contemporary Reformed theologian Hans Boersma identifies the loss of sacramentality as the key reason why the modern church is falling apart. If there is no real participation in the eternal—that is, if we do not regard matter, and even time itself, as rooted firmly in God's being—then the life of the church can scarcely withstand the torrents of liquid modernity.

"It seems to me that contemporary Western culture looks at the things we see around us—every created object—as isolated," Boersma told me. "We typically in our culture also look at every event, whatever it may be, as an isolated event, independent of any other event. Everything in our culture is in flux. Everything is unrelated to everything else. We have no anchor, no stability."

Liturgy restores the stability we've lost by cementing the story of the gospel in our bodies. As MacIntyre has said, if we want to know what to do, we must first determine the story to which we belong. Christian worship, done properly, provides us with regular reminders that we belong to Christ and to the story He is unfolding. It also teaches us, though, that we are not free to improvise the story but are bound to write our own chapters according to what has been revealed to us in the Book, and in continuity with what our fathers and mothers of the faith have written before us.

Even secular sociologists recognize the power of these physical acts to maintain cultural memory. In his book *How Societies Remember*, social anthropologist Paul Connerton studies practices that various peoples have undertaken to hold fast to their stories in the face of forgetfulness. He says that when a community wants to remember its sacred story, the one that gives it meaning, it must make the story a matter of "habit-memory." That is, it must absorb the story as something "sedimented into the body."[6]

The most powerful rituals involve the body, says Connerton. They make use of all the senses to impress the sacred story upon the individuals gathered. For example, when worshippers kneel or prostrate themselves at a certain point in a ritual, they learn in their very muscles the awe-filled meaning of that sacred moment—and it helps them remember.

Connerton's study found that the most effective rituals do not vary and stand distinctly apart from daily life in their songs and language. And if a ritual is to be effective in training the hearts and shaping the imaginations of its participants, it has to be something that they are habituated to in their bodies.

Christianity is much more than an effective liturgy, of course. A rich liturgy that is not accompanied by sound teaching and strong practices would be little more than an aesthetic experience for a congregant. But if corporeality is how God created us to function, and if our tradition provides us with biblically based liturgies that cement the cultural memory of Christ's death, burial, and resurrection in our bones, why would we not implement them?

Along with helping us remember Christ, liturgy also reminds us that Christianity isn't just a philosophy but a way of life that demands everything. When my small congregation of Orthodox Christians started a mission church in our tiny Louisiana town, the Russian Orthodox Church offered to send us a priest. When Father Matthew Harrington came to town, he told us that it was the practice of the Russian church to insist that its members come to vespers (evening prayer) on Saturday night if they want to receive communion on Sunday morning.

This was new to us. All of us (including Father Matthew) were converts, but most of us had not come into Orthodoxy through the Russian tradition. Did we really have to do this? Yes, said Father Matthew. It's not negotiable.

So we all submitted to the discipline. It was hard, and I resented it. The vespers service was inconvenient. We ended up arriving late at Saturday night barbecues and dinner parties. That was forty-five minutes out of my weekend that I did not want to give up.

After six months of this, I realized that vespers had become . . . normal. And not only normal, I actually looked forward to the service. The simple practice of starting Saturday evening with communal prayer in church taught me (and my children) that God comes first in our lives. More to the point, it helped reinforce the truth that Orthodox Christianity is a way of life, and embracing it means we do things that set us apart from the crowd.

The need for liturgy is becoming clear to more and more Protestant theologians. Perhaps surprisingly for a Pentecostal, Simon Chan, a noted theologian, scholar, and writer based in Singapore, is one of a growing number of Evangelical church leaders who argue that their churches must return to the richness of liturgical worship. Evangelical ecclesiology is inadequate to the task of meeting postmodernity's challenges, he has written.

This is in part because Evangelicalism has historically been focused not on institution building but on revivalism, making it inherently unstable. It has also taken an individualistic approach to faith that leaves it vulnerable to pop culture trends. Plus, Evangelicalism developed partly in reaction to liberalism within Mainline Protestant denominations, whose more formal worship style led Evangelical dissenters to associate (wrongly, in Chan's view) liturgy with spiritual deadness.

Chan believes that a worship approach that focuses on seeking spiritual highs—church as pep rally—is unsustainable. If you want to build faith capable of maintaining stability and continuity, you need to regularly attend a church that celebrates a fixed liturgy. That's how individuals come to be "shaped by the Christian story."

"Liturgical rhythm is a kind of music by which the truth of the gospel is inculcated over time," writes Chan in his book *Liturgical Theology*.[7] He adds that the liturgy is a "journey toward an intended end" and constitutes "the living out of our baptismal faith in the body."[8]

(Chan's words bring to mind a coffee shop conversation I had with a Millennial Evangelical in Colorado Springs, in which she explained to me why she left her church to attend a more liturgically focused one. "I just got tired of sitting there," she said. "I wanted to worship with my body.")

Scott Aniol, who teaches worship at Southwestern Baptist Theological Seminary, argues that not all liturgies are equally effective. All divine liturgies convey God's truth in a particular way, but some forms of worship convey those truths and realities better than others. Aniol says this is because liturgy trains us to imagine God in particular ways—ways that make believers better disciples.

Liturgies do more than pass on information about God. They form our imaginations and our hearts. Nothing is more effective at doing so in a way faithful to Scripture than ancient forms of Christian worship, says Aniol. What many Protestants reject as "vain repetition" in liturgical forms of worship is actually the quality of liturgy that makes it so effective at discipleship.

"The issue is not whether people will be formed by liturgy, but which liturgies will form them," says Aniol. This is where conservative Christians today have much to learn from our ancestors in the faith.

In Aniol's view, we must not reject Christian liturgical tradition for the sake of being "relevant" or anything else—not if we understand worship as primarily formative, not expressive. He teaches both his Baptist seminarians and the congregation at his local church to go deep within the Christian tradition to recover old liturgical forms.

Ryan Martin pastors a rural fundamentalist church in Minnesota, one that does not have a high smells-and-bells liturgy but nevertheless observes a more traditional worship form. They believe this is a biblical mandate.

"We detest entertainment as worship. We believe that God is to be worshipped in a way that communicates his transcendence, as well as the warmth of the Gospel," Martin says. "Contemporary worship manipulates. God is not a fad or a hipster deity. To attach him to our own little slice of popular culture fails to do justice to him as the transcendent God over all history and cultures."

Ben Haguewood used to go to mainstream Evangelical churches, where he appreciated the seriousness with which the congregation took Scripture, but he grew to dislike the lack of reverence. "In the name of relevance and welcoming people that associated church with judgment and negativity, they offered worship that looked more like a watered-down version of pop culture to me," he says.

Haguewood now worships at Redeemer Presbyterian, a conservative Presbyterian Church in America (PCA) congregation in Austin, Texas, that observes a more formal liturgy. He says the worship form is beautiful, the teaching is clear, and there is "never any equivocation" on the church's first mission: to worship God in Word and Sacrament. "It could not be more 'irrelevant' to modern culture," Haguewood says—and that's why he loves it.

It is beyond the scope of this book to tell other Christians how they should celebrate their liturgies while still being faithful to their theological tradition. That said, it would do low-church believers well to rethink their dismissal of traditional liturgies as nothing but "smells and bells." The aroma of incense, the sound of church bells, the glow from candles, and the vivid hues of icons—all these make a powerful, prerational impression on the mind and prepare us for communion with the Lord in Word and Sacrament.

When you enter into an Eastern Orthodox church, for example, you know at once that you are in a sacred space. The burning candles symbolize the Light of Christ. The icons remind us of the communion of saints and the theological truth that we are surrounded by "so great a cloud of witnesses," as Paul wrote to the Hebrews (12:1). And the incense stands for the presence of the Holy Spirit. All these simple, sensual things work together to integrate our bodies into Christian worship, to put us into a contemplative frame of mind, and to prepare the ground to receive the seed of Scripture and Holy Communion. They are not decorative accoutrements accompanying worship (icons are not mere paintings, for example) but a crucial part of the worship itself.

We are supposed to feel that gathering in a church as a community to offer worship to our God is something set apart from ordinary life. This is what gives rich liturgies their power. Nonliturgical churches are experimenting with adding historic liturgical prayers and other elements from the Christian tradition, including candles and incense, to their services. This is encouraging.

Now, low-church Evangelicals are absolutely right to say that liturgy itself won't save you. Only conversion of the heart will. Liturgy is necessary for worship to do what it must do to fulfill its potential, but liturgy alone is not sufficient, for the same reason a Bach concerto performance means nothing to a deaf man. If a believer's body is worshipping but his heart and the mind are elsewhere, what good does that do? The goal is to integrate all parts of the Christian person. It takes faith and reason to form and to disciple a Christian.

That said, there can be no doubt that the form worship takes is a powerful weapon, both against modernity (in building a bulwark against its disintegrating forces) and for modernity (by leaving churches without adequate defenses).

Relearn the Traditional Christian Habits of Asceticism

Few modern lay Christians outside Eastern Orthodox circles (and too few within them) undertake regular fasting and other tangible forms of asceticism. As we learned in an earlier chapter, *asceticism* comes from the Greek word *askesis*, which means "training." It refers to giving up material pleasures, permanently or periodically, for spiritual strengthening.

Asceticism is a vital part of a Christian life that, in the words of theologians Stanley Hauerwas and Will Willimon, is about "disciplining our wants and needs in congruence with a true story, which gives us the resources to lead truthful lives."[9]

Benedictine monks take seriously the New Testament's teaching that attachment to wealth and earthly things impedes the journey to holiness. Brother Ignatius explains that monks place high value on ascetical discipline. He describes it as spiritual housecleaning—one that can have an evangelical effect, if done with humility.

"You're so busy cleaning up your own house that you have no time to look at your neighbor's house," says the monk. "Perhaps when my neighbor sees that I'm serious in cleaning my house, they might follow me and start to clean their own houses. If I invite them over, they might say, 'Nice house. How do you take care of it?'"

In a society that values comfort and well-being over anything else, there may be no more essential Christian formative practice than regular fasting. Observant Eastern Orthodox Christians typically eat modestly, avoiding meat, dairy, oil, and wine on Wednesdays (in remembrance of Christ's betrayal) and on Fridays (in remembrance of His Crucifixion). We similarly fast during prescribed seasons preceding important holy days, like the forty days before Pascha (Easter) known as Great Lent.

Fasting like this is not easy, especially at first. Eastern Orthodox priests ordinarily prescribe light fasts to spiritual beginners. The point is not to abstain from certain foods for legalistic reasons but to break the power our bodily desires have over us. "I have been crucified with

Christ; and it is no longer I who live, but Christ lives in me," the Apostle Paul wrote to the Galatians (2:20). Fasting is a spiritual exercise whose purpose is to subject the body to the liberating yoke of Jesus. As Wendell Berry puts it, denying bodily desire for the sake of spiritual growth is "a refusal to allow the body to serve what is unworthy of it."[10]

This is true not only of the individual body but also of the church, the Body of Christ. During Great Lent in the Eastern Orthodox Church, the entire congregation engages in long, demanding penitential prayer services, often involving full bodily prostrations in church. Though no parishioner checks to see who else is fasting as observantly, if at all, there is a strong sense that we are all on this trying journey of repentance together. In this way, the ardors of fasting can build community.

Everyday asceticism may include keeping a regular prayer rule, committing to daily Scripture reading, gathering nightly with the family for dinner, and setting a time each night to turn off the television or the computer—and sticking to it. Over time, these exercises will become effortless. The goal is not only to acquire spiritual discipline but also to have it become second nature, so that one no longer thinks about acquiring it.

A runner could not hope to complete a marathon without preparing for it through hours of training. In the same way, if we don't train ourselves to give up small things now, we will not be prepared to give up big things when put to the test. Near the end of his life, Saint Paul wrote to Timothy (4:7), "I have fought the good fight, I have finished the course, I have kept the faith." If we hope to say the same thing, we have to practice every day of our lives.

Tighten Church Discipline

What is true for individual Christian bodies is also true for the Body of Christ, the church. We are not just a group of individuals who come together once a week to share the same worship space. Scripture makes it plain that we are part of one organic system, each with our own role to play. As we discipline our physical bodies to submit them to spiritual truths, so must we discipline our collective church body—and not only by fasting together and engaging in penitential prayers as an assembly.

As Benedict Option Christians build healthier church communities, they'll also have to tighten church discipline. Gays, lesbians, and their allies are not wrong to question why conservative Christians are quick to condemn their sin but overlook rampant divorce and sexual sin among straights in our own congregations. The early church maintained fairly strict discipline among its congregations. They believed that the Way led somewhere and that those who refused to walk the Way needed to be brought back to it or, if they persisted in sin, be sent away from their own congregations.

The rationale was neither meanness nor self-righteousness but accountability. Besides, the church, as a community of practice and formation, could not do what it was supposed to do if it could not maintain good order. Benedictine monks who refuse to live by the Rule are compelled to leave, for the sake of the community's integrity.

Denny Burk, a seminary professor and Southern Baptist pastor in Kentucky, says the lack of church discipline in churches across his denomination have left congregations completely unprepared for the aftermath of the Sexual Revolution. When churches are undisciplined, the members will be undisciplined too. It creates a climate conducive to immorality and crumbling marriages. It welcomes congregants who are Christians in name only. The problem became so acute that the Southern Baptist governing body passed a resolution in 2008 calling on the churches to renew "the practice of lovingly correcting wayward church members" and "to recover and implement our Savior's teachings on church discipline."

The congregation Burk helps lead today requires members to sign a covenant defining the obligations of their fellowship. "Everyone who

joins the church knows what they're getting into, not just to be a follower of Christ, but to be a follower of Christ within our church," he
told me. "Failure to uphold these things means that the church will
call you to repent. Any member who refuses to turn away from sin and
to follow Christ will eventually be excommunicated."

This happened to a couple in Burk's church who were divorcing after
over four decades of marriage. They refused counseling from the pastors
to help them put their marriage back together again. They even refused
assistance from other friends and church members. After months of
intervention aimed at healing their marriage, the pastors reached an
impasse with the couple. The couple simply would not cooperate. Eventually, the congregation met and voted to excommunicate them.

"It's one thing to form a moral majority and lobby politically for
public morality, but nobody really cares if the churches themselves
have no integrity," says Burk. "If that doesn't happen, there will be no
difference between the church and the world."

Evangelize with Goodness and Beauty

Fortunately, when churches are properly ordered toward Christ
through liturgy, with life maintained through asceticism and discipline, the result is a beauty in sharp contrast to the world. As times get
uglier, the church will become brighter and brighter, drawing people
to its light. As this happens, we Christians should not be afraid to
consider beauty and goodness our best evangelistic tools.

"Art and the saints are the greatest apologetic for our faith," said
Cardinal Joseph Ratzinger, the future Pope Benedict XVI. Why? Because seeing examples of great beauty and extraordinary goodness
bypasses our rational faculties and strikes the heart. We immediately
respond to beauty and goodness and desire what they reveal. As philosopher Matthew Crawford puts it, "Only beautiful things lead us out
to join the world beyond our heads."[11]

Crawford is half right. Observing acts of goodness can change your life too. Watching the way the people of my hometown, a south Louisiana village, loved and cared for my late sister during her cancer fight prompted me to do something I swore I never would: return after nearly three decades away.

Art and the saints—material instantiations of beauty and goodness—prepare the way for propositional truth because they appeal to our inner desire. Not every act that pierces our heart and awakens our desire is truly beautiful or good. Reason helps us to rightly order those desires.

Put more plainly, unbelievers today who cannot make sense of the Gospel's propositions may yet have a life-changing wordless encounter with the Gospel through Christian art or works of Christian love that pull them outside themselves and confront them with the reality of Christ.

The first Christians gained converts not because their arguments were better than those of the pagans but because people saw in them and their communities something good and beautiful—and they wanted it. This led them to the Truth.

"Apologetics then and now has a limited role," Robert Louis Wilken, the early church historian, has said. "We must speak what is true, but finally the appeal must be made to the heart, not the mind. We're really leading people to change their love. To love something different. Love is what draws and holds people."[12]

I have been surprised by how few people I have met over the years who were brought to conversion by apologetics alone, whether spoken or through books. It happens, obviously, but it rarely happens on its own. In my own case, my adult conversion to Catholicism was primarily intellectual, but the long road began at seventeen, when I had a road-to-Damascus moment in the medieval cathedral of Chartres. Nothing in my experience had prepared me for the beauty of that French cathedral. I walked into it a sniffy teenage agnostic and walked out craving to be part of the church tradition that built such a magnificent temple for God.

Seven fraught and winding years later, my mind was ready, thanks to all the reading I had done, but I was afraid to take the first real steps. What prompted me to act on all the things I was reading was my unlikely friendship with an elderly Catholic priest who was spending the last days of his life in assisted living. Monsignor Carlos Sanchez never tried to evangelize me. He just treated me like a friend and told me stories of his life, including his own dramatic midlife conversion. The peace that that gentle, luminous priest had was a thing of beauty, and I desired to possess it—and soon did.

So I was initially drawn out of my head and toward Christianity by the form of love called eros. My desire to know Christ more intimately was sparked and deepened by my sudden passionate desire to stand in relationship to the God who revealed Himself through the beauty of the cathedral and to the Christ who revealed Himself through the friendship of a ninety-nine-year-old Guatemalan immigrant priest.

The lesson here is that in an era in which logical reason is doubted and even dismissed, and the heart's desire is glorified by popular culture, the most effective way to evangelize is by helping people experience beauty and goodness. From that starting point, we help them to grasp the truth that all goodness and beauty emanate from the eternal God, who loves us and wants to be in relationship with us. For Christians, this might mean witnessing to others through music, theater, or some other form of art. Mostly, though, it will mean showing love to others through building and sustaining genuine friendships and through the example of service to the poor, the weak, and the hungry. As Brother Ignatius of Norcia reminds us, everything is evangelical.

Embrace Exile and the Possibility of Martyrdom

Just as beauty and charity stand as witnesses to the Gospel, so martyrdom has traditionally been the seed of the church. In the early church, the willingness to suffer, even to the point of laying down one's life, for Christ was seen as the most powerful testimony to the truth of Christ. Today's churches will not be equipped if we do not keep this in mind and live lives prepared to suffer severe hardship, even death, for our faith.

Rarely do American Christians think of the martyrs of church history, those who gave their lives in witness to the faith. Stories of brave men and women who suffered physical torment and death rather than betray Christ don't fit easily into the upbeat vibe in many American churches. But these are our people, too, and they have important lessons for us—lessons that we desperately need to hear.

They embody heroic faith, and a love of Christ so profound they were willing to give their own lives. Their number includes the forty-eight believers tortured publicly and massacred in the Gallic city of Lyon in the year 177, and Polycarp, ordained a bishop by the Apostle John, and burned at the stake at age eighty-six for refusing to burn a pinch of incense to Caesar.

Closer to our own time, Christians like Lutheran pastor Dietrich Bonhoeffer returned to Germany to resist Hitler and was hanged by the Nazis. In 1996, seven Trappist monks were kidnapped in Algeria by Islamic rebels and murdered. They had refused to leave the country and the service of Muslim villagers among whom they lived.

In the Christian tradition, a confessor is a believer who suffered greatly for the faith but was not put to death. The Orthodox priest Gheorghe Calciu and the Lutheran pastor Richard Wurmbrand both survived unspeakable torture in Communist Romania. Their testimonies after release from prison and exile testify not only to their courage to speak the truth despite fear of arrest, and to the strength of their endurance in prison, but also and even more powerfully to their ability to love those who tortured them.

Once he was free, Wurmbrand wrote that there are two kinds of Christians: "those who sincerely believe in God and those who, just as sincerely, believe that they believe. You can tell them apart by their actions in decisive moments."[13]

We should stop trying to meet the world on its own terms and focus on building up fidelity in distinct community. Instead of being seeker-friendly, we should be finder-friendly, offering those who come to us a new and different way of life. It must be a way of life shaped by the biblical story and practices that keep us firmly focused on the truths of that story in a world that wants to obscure them and make us forget. It must be a way of life marked by stability and order and achieved through the steady work, both communal and individual, of prayer, asceticism, and service to others—exactly what liquid modernity cannot provide.

A church that looks and talks and sounds just like the world has no reason to exist. A church that does not emphasize asceticism and discipleship is as pointless as a football coaching staff that doesn't care if its players show up for practice. And though liturgy by itself is not enough, a church that neglects to involve the body in worship is going to find it increasingly difficult to get bodies into services on Sunday morning as America moves further into post-Christianity.

Benedict Option churches will find ways within their own traditions to take on practices, liturgical and otherwise, for the sake of deepening their commitment to Christ by building a thick Christian culture. And Benedict Option believers will break down the conceptual walls that keep God safely confined in a church-shaped compartment. That's because a church that is a church only on Sunday and at other formal gatherings of the congregation is not only failing to be the church Christ calls us all to be; it is also not going to be a church with the strength and the focus to endure the trials ahead.

CHAPTER 6

The Idea of a Christian Village

During Bill Clinton's presidency, First Lady Hillary Clinton kicked over a hornet's nest among conservatives by promoting an apocryphal African proverb: "It takes a village to raise a child." Social conservatives like me took it as Mrs. Clinton's nanny-state attempt to justify the government poking its nose into the business of the family.

A few years later, married and expecting my firstborn child, I was corresponding with the conservative radio talker Michael Medved and received an e-mail from him that I have never forgotten. I had mentioned to him that my wife and I were planning to homeschool our children. Well and good, Medved replied, but you should both understand that homeschooling is only a partial measure.

"You need to make sure you live in a community that shares your faith and your values," he advised. "When your child leaves home to go play with the neighborhood kids, you have to be able to trust that the values in your home are not undermined by the company he keeps."

That made me see Hillary Clinton's African proverb in a new light. Today that firstborn child of mine, Matthew, is seventeen, and he has a younger brother and sister. Everything that practical parenting experience has taught me confirms Medved's counsel. It really does take a village—that is to say, a community—to raise a child.

Does that surprise you? It shouldn't. God created us to be social beings. Jesus said that the sum of the Law and the Prophets is that we should love the Lord our God with all our heart, soul, and mind and love our neighbors as ourselves. To love requires loving others and letting others love you. Unless you have the rare calling to be a hermit, obeying God and being true to our divinely given nature mean engaging in community life.

The fate of religion in America is inextricably tied to the fate of the family, and the fate of the family is tied to the fate of the community. In her 2015 book *How The West Really Lost God*, cultural critic Mary Eberstadt argues that religion is like a language: you can learn it only in community, starting with the community of the family. When both the family and the community become fragmented and fail, the transmission of religion to the next generation becomes far more difficult. All it takes is the failure of a single generation to hand down a tradition for that tradition to disappear from the life of a family and, in turn, of a community. Eberstadt is one of a long line of religious thinkers to recognize that when concrete embodiments of the relationship to God crumble, it becomes very hard to hold on to Him in the abstract.[1]

For decades conservative Christians have behaved as if the primary threats to the integrity of families and communities could be effectively addressed through politics. That illusion is now destroyed. If there is going to be authentic renewal, it will have to happen in families and local church communities. In fact, as the threat to orthodox Christianity grows at the hands of hostile government, Christians should take seriously a Tocquevillian contention made by the sociologist Robert Nisbet, who said that religious liberty itself depends on strong religious communities. Despots, he said, "have never worried about religion that is confined mutely to individual minds. It is religion as community, or rather as a plurality of communities, that has always bestirred the reprisals of rulers engaged in the work of political tyranny."[2]

Strengthening families and communities, and thickening our ties to each other and to our churches, requires us to shake off our passivity. It's unrealistic to hope or expect to live as intensely in community as monks under the Rule do, but in the Benedict Option, we cannot be laissez-faire about the ties that bind us to each other. With so many forces in contemporary culture pulling families and communities apart, we can't assume that everything will work out if we just go with the flow.

Benedict Option Christians have a lot to learn from our Orthodox Jewish elder brothers in the faith, who have faced horrifying attempts over millennia to destroy their families and communities.

Orthodox Rabbi Mark Gottlieb says that Christians living apart from mainstream culture need "raw, roll-up-your-sleeves dedication to create deep structures of community." If we are to survive, we need to develop a "laser-like focus and dedication to seeing themselves as the next link in the chain of the Christian story."

"That sense of urgency, making family come first in your life, strikes me as one starting point and foundational requirement for faithful Christians," Gottlieb says. "There has to be a very deliberate commitment to the growth of one's family and the development of healthy and faithful service to one's family."

The power of secular culture to break the chains anchoring us firmly in the biblical story is immense. But we are not powerless in the face of the threat.

Turn Your Home into a Domestic Monastery

Just as the monastery's life is ordered toward God, so must the family home be. Every Christian family likes to think they put God first, but this is not always how we live. (I plead guilty.) If we are the abbot and abbess of our domestic monastery, we will see to it that our family's life is structured in such a way as to make the mission of knowing and serving God clear to all its members.

That means maintaining regular times of family prayer. That means regular readings of Scripture and stories from the lives of the saints—Christian heroes and heroines from ages past. "Christian kids need Christian heroes," says Marco Sermarini, a lay Catholic community leader in Italy. "They need to know that following Jesus radically is not an impossible dream."

Living in a domestic monastery also means putting the life of the church first, even if you have to keep your kid out of a sports program that schedules games during your church's worship services. Even more importantly, your kids need to see you and your spouse sacrificing attendance at events if they conflict with church. And they need to see that you are serious about the spiritual life.

Catholic writer Rachel Balducci lives with her husband Paul and five children (a sixth is in college) in the same intentional Christian community in which she and Paul were raised. She remembers what an impression her father's faith made on her. "I grew up here watching my dad do the right thing, even when nobody was looking. I know now that seeing him up in the morning spending time in prayer made a big difference in my life," she said.

A monastery is a place of hierarchical order, but all members are valued and united in a bond of love. Saint Benedict instructs the abbot to consult even the youngest member of the brotherhood, for he might have wisdom that eludes the older ones. In my own family, we practice the habit of asking forgiveness when we sin against each other. It is hard for me, as a father, to humble myself before my children when I have wronged them, but it's necessary for my own humility, and it's important that the kids see that their parents order their lives to Christ as well. A culture of obedience is the mark of a healthy monastery and a healthy family, but members of both communities must see that those given authority over them also subject themselves to a higher authority.

Hospitality is a central principle of the Benedictine life, but I didn't learn it from the monks. I got it from my folks. My mother and father had a well-deserved reputation for welcoming others to their hearth and table. Southerners, of course, have a reputation for hospitality, but my parents' open door was particularly pronounced. It is one of the childhood lessons for which I am most grateful, and my wife Julie and I have tried to put it into practice in our own family's life. We hope our children will remember the laughter and conversation around our hearth and table with travelers and other guests and associate that with what it means to be a Christian family, sharing our blessings with others and receiving in turn the blessing of their company.

A monastery keeps outside its walls people and things that are inimical to its purpose, which is to form its members in Christ. For families, this means strictly limiting media, especially television and online media, both to keep unsuitable content out and to prevent dependence on electronic media. It is also important for parents to do the same for themselves. True, adults should not be expected to keep their movie and TV watching to the level of children, but neither should they feel free to watch whatever they like. Too much exposure to morally compromising material will, over time, dull one's moral instincts. Remember, life in monastic community is for the abbot's formation too.

Don't Be Afraid to Be Nonconformist

Raise your kids to know that your family is different—and don't apologize for it. It's not a matter of snobbery. It's about imbuing kids with the conviction that there are some things that people in our family just do not do—and that's okay.

"My son has a peanut allergy, and from his very earliest days, we've had to teach him to stay away from certain foods," says Denny Burk, a Southern Baptist pastor and seminary professor in Kentucky. "He's only five, but he gets it and doesn't complain about it. He has a great attitude.

"But from the earliest days, we have been talking to him about it. At the church potluck every week, he doesn't touch the table without checking with us first," Burk continues. "We Christians have to cultivate our children about morals in the same way. They have to know that it's fine to be a nonconformist. If you start early with them, it will be easier when they become teenagers."

The teen years are when kids become intensely aware of their parents' anxiety about making their children seem like outcasts, or themselves look weird in the eyes of their own parental peers. If Mom and Dad don't stand firm and are not willing to be thought of as peculiar by their own friends for their strictness, then the kids don't stand a chance.

Don't Take Your Kids' Friends for Granted

It's important your kids have a good peer group. By "good," I mean one in which its members, or at least most of them, share the same strong moral beliefs. Though parental influence is critical, research shows that nothing forms a young person's character like their peers. The culture of the group of which your child is a part growing up will be the culture he or she adopts as their own.

Engaged parents can't outsource the moral and spiritual formation of their kids to their church or parachurch organization. Interviewing a wide variety of Christians for this book, I often heard complaints that church-affiliated youth groups were about keeping kids entertained more than disciplined. One older Evangelical teenager told me she dropped out of her local chapter of a national parachurch group because she grew weary of her peers smoking, drinking, and having sex. "Honestly, I would rather hang out with the kids who don't believe," she told me. "They accept me even though they know I'm a believer. At least around them, I know what being a Christian really is."

Peer pressure really begins to happen in middle childhood. Psychology researcher Judith Rich Harris, in her classic book *The Nurture Assumption*, says that kids at that age model their own behavior around their peer group's. Writes Harris, "The new behaviors become habitual—internalized, if you will—and eventually become part of the public personality. The public personality is the one that a child adopts when he or she is not at home. It is the one that will develop into the adult personality."[3]

Harris points to the example of immigrants and their children. Study after study shows that no matter how strong the home culture, first-generation offspring almost always conform to the values of the broader culture. "The old culture is lost in a single generation," she writes. "Cultures are not passed on from parents to children; the children of immigrant parents adopt the culture of their peers."[4]

On the other hand, says Harris, is that in most cases, it's not too late for kids who have been exposed to bad influences. Researchers find that damage to a child's moral core can often be repaired if he is taken away from a bad peer group. What's more, determined parents who run a disciplined home, and who immerse their children in a good peer group, can lay a good foundation, no matter how lax they have been until now.

The bad news about the fragility of culture is also good news, according to Harris: "Cultures can be changed, or formed from scratch, in a single generation."[5]

Don't Idolize the Family

I was raised in a good family headed by a strong, loving patriarch, a traditional southern gentleman who valued family and place above all things. From him I learned how to love the good things that are family and place. What I did not realize until much later in my life was that he lived as if family and place were more important than God and the liberty of his children. This caused me grief and suffering later in life, but ultimately it brought me to a much deeper faith and a profound reconciliation with my father before his death.

One of the things I learned in that healing process was that one should never expect more from family than it can possibly give. Even at its best, the family will have its flaws. A healthy family will be a humble and forgiving one—something that is surprisingly hard for many to achieve. Ideally, the family should be an icon of faith, through which the love of God shines to illuminate its members. When members of the family consider its existence to be an end in itself, as opposed to a means to the end of unity with God, the family risks becoming tyrannical.

It sometimes happens that mothers and fathers think they're serving God by their austere discipline but in fact are driving their children away from Him. I spoke to a high school senior I will call Ellen, an agonized young atheist who had been brought up in a strict home by fanatically religious parents.

"My parents are very paranoid people. They're conspiracy theorists. They're afraid that if they exposed their children to the outside world, we were going to be corrupted, because they see the world as this filthy, filthy place," she told me. "That total sheltering is very damaging, and cutting yourself off from the world like that is exactly the kind of environment you need to develop a cult."

Ellen says her two older siblings are also atheists, and she expects her younger siblings to follow in the same path, because their mother and father raised them with such fear and anxiety. "I wish you good luck with the Benedict Option," she told me. "But please tell parents that if they want their kids to stay Christian, not to do what mine did. They smothered us and made us into rebels."

Live Close to Other Members of Your Community

Geography is one secret to the strength and resilience of Orthodox Jewish communities. Because their faith requires them to walk to synagogue on the Sabbath, they must live within walking distance. This is also convenient for their communal prayer life.

"My day is built around the prayers," Rabbi Mark Gottlieb told me. "Morning prayers: wake up, go to synagogue. Afternoon prayers: go down the street from where I work in midtown Manhattan. Evening prayers: back home in my New Jersey neighborhood. The ritual of prayer structures every day and every month.

"It's not enough to say that you go to synagogue on Sabbath," said the rabbi. "You often see that Jews who are able to go to synagogue two or three times a day, in addition to the Sabbath, are also those most able to maintain a healthy distance from the most nefarious elements of modern culture. It's a matter not just of theological commitment but of practices and of seeing yourself as part of a larger Jewish community in relationship with God. This is not just for rabbis and scholars but also for the average observant Jew."

Christians don't have the geographical requirement that Orthodox Jews do, but many of those who choose to live in proximity have found it a blessing. As newcomers to Eastern Orthodox Christianity, Alaskans Shelley and Jerry Finkler found that living twenty minutes from the cathedral in Eagle River inhibited their ability to partake of the fullness of church life. A number of cathedral families live within walking distance of the cathedral, on land purchased by church members decades ago, when it was affordable.

The Finklers initially thought living in a neighborhood with their church family was weird. Circumstances caused them to live temporarily in the church neighborhood, and they discovered what a difference it made in their family's life. Later, when they returned to their house in the exurbs, the Finklers missed what they had back in Eagle

River. Everybody in the exurban settlement knew each other and were of the same class, but it wasn't the same.

"There wasn't the sense of the common good that you have when you're living around people who share your faith," Shelley Finkler once told me. "That made a big difference when it came to reaching out to help each other."

The Finklers soon sold their house and moved again, this time much closer to their church.

When our Eastern Orthodox mission church had to close, my wife and I took stock of how much we and our children had grown in faith and discipleship from four years of praying communally and liturgically with our congregation. We decided that we could not be without an Orthodox parish nearby, so we could be there at every opportunity. That's one reason we packed up our things and moved to Baton Rouge, forty-five minutes away. We knew that there would be no way to practice our faith properly in community while living so far from the church.

Why be close? Because as I said earlier, the church can't just be the place you go on Sundays—it must become the center of your life. That is, you may visit your house of worship only once a week, but what happens there in worship, and the community and the culture it creates, must be the things around which you order the rest of the week. The Benedictines structure all their life—their work, their rest, their reading, their meals—around prayer. Christians in the world are not expected to live at the same level of focus and intensity as cloistered monks, but we should strive to be like them in erasing as much as possible the false distinction between church and life.

Recall that Brother Martin of Norcia believes that after experiencing life in Christian community, it's hard to be fully Christian, or fully human, without it. The Latter-day Saints (LDS, or Mormons) may not be Orthodox Christians, but they are exceptionally good at doing the kind of community building that the monk suggests is a vital part of being a Christian.

Terryl L. Givens, a professor of literature and religion at the University of Richmond and an expert on the LDS faith, says this is because Mormon theology and ecclesiology forge unusually strong social bonds within local churches (or "wards"). Mormons don't believe in ward hopping. They are assigned their ward based on where they live and have no right of appeal. This compels them to work together to build a unified community of believers, not to wander in search of one. Givens calls this "Zion-building, not Zion-hunting"—a reference to the Mormon belief that adherents must lay the foundations for Zion, the community that Jesus Christ will establish at His return.

American Christians have a bad habit of treating church like a consumer experience. If a congregation doesn't meet our felt needs, we are quick to find another one that we believe will. I'm as guilty of this as anybody else. But Rachel Balducci can testify to the benefits, spiritual and otherwise, of grounding oneself in a committed community.

She lives with her husband Paul and their kids in the Alleluia Community, a covenanted lay community of charismatic Catholics and Protestants founded in 1973. Paul and Rachel's parents were among the early settlers of a distressed neighborhood in Augusta, Georgia, where the new community's members could afford housing. They helped each other fix up their places and began life in common.

Today the Alleluia Community has around eight hundred members, many of whom remain in Faith Village, which is what they call the original settlement. When they married and decided to start a family, the Balduccis realized that what they had been given as children was something worth passing on to the family they hoped to start one day.

Community itself won't make you holy if you aren't committed to prayer and cultivating a personal relationship with Jesus, Rachel cautions. Echoing Father Martin's observation, she says the gift of community is that it builds a social structure in which it is easier for Christians to hear and respond to God's voice and in which others hold them accountable if they lose the straight path. Living so closely with others can strain one's patience, concedes Rachel, but it has been good for her and her family.

"If I were a hermit, just God and me, it would be easier to be a saint," she says. "Living this way is good for my humility. It's like being in a rock tumbler. It polishes you and wears away your rough edges."

Chris Currie amplifies Father Martin's teaching that God disciples us through living in community. Currie, a Catholic in Hyattsville, Maryland, believes that the atomizing structures of American suburban life make it harder to be truly Christian. "A lot of the choices we make about how we live have tremendous consequences spiritually," says Currie. "The way postwar America decided it wanted to live accelerated the process of cultural disintegration and alienation we've all experienced. Secular writers have written about this, but Christians need to understand that as well.

"We were not called to be isolated materialists disengaged with neighbors and accumulating things in our castles," he continues.

In 1997, Currie and his wife, newlyweds, relocated to the inner-ring Washington suburb. Housing was affordable in the heart of the town, which had been founded in the late nineteenth century, but in the late 1990s it was in decline. The Curries bought a Victorian fixer-upper, and Chris got involved in local civic efforts to revitalize the community along New Urbanist lines.

Soon Hyattsville began its renaissance, and Christians were a big part of it. The pioneering Curries invited other young orthodox Catholic families to join them in the historic district, which was developed before the automobile and was therefore highly walkable. Though Hyattsville is now less affordable than it once was, more than one hundred Catholic families have relocated there, in large part because they wanted to be part of a thick community with a good parish—and now a good school.

The Hyattsville Catholics are not part of a formal organization. Many are rooted in nearby St. Jerome Parish, but some go to other area parishes. Bible studies, prayer groups, and book clubs happen in people's homes. But the community is also a practical aid to its members, as they assist each other with child care and repair projects, help each other through illness, and meet all kinds of challenges together in ways that living in geographical community makes possible.

Living so close to "the imperial city," as Currie calls Washington, means that most of his community members work in the nation's capital. Their close-knit Catholic neighborhood gives them the nurturing they need to be strong witnesses to the faith in the secular city. "We're not battening down the hatches, hunkering down, and keeping quiet about our faith," says Currie. "We don't do it in a belligerent way, but we are not ashamed of who we are."

He believes the St. Jerome's Parish community has been called to be a presence in the greater Washington area. The only way they can resist the pressures of worldliness and secularization is by living near each other and reinforcing their religious identity through life lived in common. Their thick community is a strong model of being in the world but not of it. Striking the balance between being an evangelical presence to the wider community while protecting what makes them distinctly and authentically Christian is difficult—but Currie believes that this is the Gospel's calling.

"Ultimately I think Christians have to understand that yes, we have to be countercultural, but no, we don't have to run away from the rest of society," he says. "We have to be a sign of contradiction to the surrounding society, but at the same time we have to be engaged with that society, while still nurturing our own community so we can fully form our children."

Make the Church's Social Network Real

In his first letter to the church in Corinth, Paul urged the believers there to "have the same care for one another.

"If one member suffers, all suffer together," the apostle wrote. "If one member is honored, all rejoice together. Now you are the Body of Christ, and individually members of it."

The LDS Church lives out that principle in a unique way. The Mormon practice of "home teaching" directs two designated Mormon holders of the church's priestly office to visit every individual or family in a ward at least once a month, to hear their concerns and offer counsel. A parallel program called Relief Society involves women ministering to women as "visiting teachers." These have become a major source of establishing and strengthening local community bonds.

"In theory, if not always in practice, every adult man and woman is responsible for spiritually and emotionally sustaining three, four, or more other families, or women, in the visiting teaching program," says the LDS's Terryl Givens. He adds that Mormons frequently have social gatherings to celebrate and renew ties to community. "Mormonism takes the symbolism of the former and the randomness of the latter and transforms them into a deliberate ordering of relations that builds a warp and woof of sociality throughout the ward," he says.

Non-Mormons can learn from the deliberate dedication that wards—at both leadership and lay levels—have to caring for each other spiritually. The church community is not merely the people one worships with on Sunday but the people one lives with, serves, and nurtures as if they were family members. What's more, the church is the center of a Mormon's social life.

"The consequence is that wherever Mormons travel, they find immediate kinship and remarkable intimacy with other practicing Mormons," Givens says. "That is why Mormons seldom feel alone, even in a hostile—increasingly hostile—world."

Reach Across Church Boundaries
to Build Relationships

A generation ago two conservative Christian leaders—Evangelical Chuck Colson and Roman Catholic Richard John Neuhaus—launched an initiative called Evangelicals and Catholics Together. The idea was to foster better relations between Christians in two church traditions that had been mutually suspicious. Colson and Neuhaus realized earlier than many that the post-1960s cultural changes meant that conservative Evangelicals and orthodox Catholics now had more in common with each other than with liberals in their own church traditions. They called their kind of partnership, born in part out of pro-life activism, an "ecumenism of the trenches."

Times have changed, and so have some of the issues conservative Evangelicals and Catholics face. But the need for an ecumenism of the trenches is stronger than ever. Metropolitan Hilarion Alfeyev, a senior bishop in the Russian Orthodox Church, has on several occasions appealed to traditionalists in the West to form a "common front" against atheism and secularism. To be sure, the different churches should not compromise their distinct doctrines, but they should nevertheless seize every opportunity to form friendships and strategic alliances in defense of the faith and the faithful.

Erin Doom, a longtime employee of the legendary Eighth Day Books, a Christian bookstore in Wichita, Kansas, founded the Eighth Day Institute (EDI) as the store's nonprofit educational arm. Committed to small-o orthodox ecumenism and to building up the local Christian community, EDI hosts various symposia and events throughout the year. Its signature event, though, may be the Hall of Men, a twice-monthly gathering in EDI's clubhouse, a kind of Christian speakeasy next door to the bookstore. Catholic, Orthodox, and Protestant men have been coming together there since 2008 to pray, to discuss and debate the works of a great figure of Christian history, then to sit around the table drinking pints of beer and enjoying each other's company.

The Hall of Men, and its recently launched parallel women's organization, the Sisters of Sophia, are a way for "mere Christians" to engage the Great Tradition, to root themselves in it, and to go out into the world to renew culture. Doom says the men come together in a spirit of brotherhood, willing to talk about their theological differences in an atmosphere of Christian love. He credits the ecumenical generosity and sense of hospitality of Eighth Day Books owner Warren Farha for setting the tone.

"If we Christians are going to survive, if we're going to make a difference, we have to be able to come together. Small-o orthodoxy is vital," says Doom. "I'd like EDI to be a model for other communities. It all begins with Hall of Men, getting the guys involved. Ultimately I want to provide tools and resources for all Christian families to make their homes into little monasteries."

It's as simple as starting a book group—but one with the purpose of catechesis, discipleship, and intentional community building. It's a social event, true, but it has to have a strong focus on something more serious than socializing. The Hall of Men prays when it meets, then discusses a text from the church's Great Tradition. Participants are expected to argue from their own theological convictions, but nobody is trying to convert anybody else, and it's all in friendship.

One key to making these ecumenical groups successful is to avoid watering down doctrinal distinctives for the sake of comity. Honoring diversity means exactly that: giving others in the fellowship the grace to bring their full Christian selves to the table without fear of reproach. This mutual respect for difference creates the space where serious theological discussion and community building can occur.

"These guys aren't all part of my church tradition, but they have become my best friends," an Evangelical man told me. "Once you start reading this stuff and talking about the early church, you start to see that you have more in common with some believers outside your own tradition. It's good to be with other guys who take the Christian life as seriously as you do. You realize that we're all in this battle with the world together."

Love the Community But Don't Idolize It

Ellen, the young woman whose controlling family drove her to atheism, comes from a part of the country where religious extremism is not unusual. In fact, after their own religious awakening in adulthood, her parents moved the family to their town to join other families who share their near-apocalyptic views. She describes the besieged community her parents joined as an informal "cult."

"We were in a small, close-knit community of homeschoolers. Most people in the group were like my family or even more out there than my family. The only kids I interacted with growing up were other kids in this group," she said. "We didn't talk to the locals that much and didn't participate in town events and family events. We didn't interact with my extended family at all. I guess it was hard for them to see how my parents were bringing us up and how far they went off the deep end."

Far from being nurturing, said Ellen, her community was extremely controlling. When she began to have doubts about the way they all lived, other kids reacted angrily and shunned her. They also began to treat Ellen's parents and siblings with disdain. "We knew no one outside this cult, so you felt really pressured to conform," she said.

The greatest temptation for tight-knit communities is a compulsion to control its members unduly and to police each other too strictly for deviation from a purity standard. It is hard to know when and where to draw the line in every situation, but a community so rigid that it cannot bend will break itself or its members.

In Eagle River, Alaska, the Eastern Orthodox community around

St. John's Cathedral lost a significant number of its members after deep divisions emerged over how strictly to live the Orthodox life.

Father Marc Dunaway, the cathedral's pastor, lived through the painful departure of friends and family who left in search of a more rigorously observant Orthodoxy. In 2013, he told me, "I think the cure for any community to avoid these sad troubles is to be open and generous and to resist the urges to build walls and isolate itself.

"If you isolate yourself, you will become weird," Father Marc continued. "It is a tricky balance between allowing freedom and openness on the one hand, and maintaining a community identity on the other. The idea of community itself should not be allowed to become an idol. A community is a living organism that must change and grow and adapt."

Communities that are wrapped too tight for fear of impurity will suffocate their members and strangle the joy out of life together. Ideology is the enemy of joyful community life, and the most destructive ideology is the belief that creating utopia is possible. Solzhenitsyn said that the line between good and evil runs down the center of every human heart. That axiom must be at the center of every Christian community, keeping it humble and sane.

"It was good for us to develop friendships outside our community," said one man, still an enthusiastic member of an intentional Christian community. "When the only people you have contact with are the ones you go to church with, it's hard to know when they're asking something unreasonable. It's easy to fall into the trap of thinking that everybody outside the community is corrupt, but it's not true."

Don't Let the Perfect Be the Enemy of the Good Enough

If you spend too much time planning and trying to build the perfect Benedict Option community, you will never start. And if you wait around for the church, or someone else, to get something going, it may never happen. What are you waiting for?

It's important to have some sort of vision and a plan but also to be open to possibility.

"Only God can understand all the different factors going into the equations of your community. You will never be able to fully manipulate them, and it's harmful to try," advises Chris Currie. "Just be open to the movement of the Holy Spirit within the community so people who have a contribution to make will feel open to making it."

Then you put things to the test. What flourishes builds up the community, and what doesn't flourish, you abandon and move on. Says Currie, "We have to understand that our minds aren't primarily directing this. Ultimately, God's the architect, and we have to primarily be cooperative with grace. Ultimately we're being led on this journey by God, so we have to be humble about our own ability to shape things."

The need to control is a sign of the middle-class Christian mentality, chides Marco Sermarini. He and his community friends were raised in what Marco disdainfully calls "this bourgeois church, this church of comfort, this church where people didn't want to take any risks to live radically for the Lord Jesus."

The story of how Sermarini and his lay Catholic community began in San Benedetto del Tronto, a small city on Italy's Adriatic coast, inspires because of its improvisational quality.

Sermarini, who is also head of Italy's G. K. Chesterton Society, and his community began as an informal group of young Catholic men inspired by the example of Pier Giorgio Frassati, a twentieth-century Catholic layman and social reformer who died at the age of twenty-four. The Blessed Pier Giorgio (he has passed the first stage of canonization, earning the title) was known for helping the poor—and that's what Sermarini and his friends did in college, reaching out to at-risk youth.

After college, the men found they enjoyed each other's company, and helping the needy, so they stayed together. As they married, they brought their wives into the group. In 1993, encouraged by their local bishop, they incorporated as an official association within the Catholic Church, an association of families they jokingly called the Tipi Loschi—Italian for "the usual suspects."

Today the Tipi Loschi have around two hundred members in their community. They administer the community school, the Scuola libera G. K. Chesterton, as well as three separate cooperatives, all designed to serve some charitable end. They continue to build and to grow, driven by a sense of spiritual and social entrepreneurship and inspired by a close connection to the Benedictine monastery in Norcia, just on the other side of the Sybilline Mountains. As the Tipi Loschi's various initiatives succeeded (and despite some that didn't), the association of families came to regard each other as something more organic.

They began helping each other in everyday tasks, trying to reverse the seemingly unstoppable atomization of daily life. Now they feel closer than ever and are determined to keep reaching out to their city, offering faith and friendship to all, from within the confident certainties of their Catholic community. This is how they continue to grow.

"The possibility to live like this is for everyone," says Sermarini. "We have only to follow an old way to do things that we always had but lost some years ago. The main thing is not to go with the mainstream. Then seek God, and after that, look for others who are also serious about seeking God, and join them. We started with this desire and started trying to teach others to do the same, to receive the same gift we were given: the Catholic faith."

It's becoming clear, Sermarini says, that Christian families have to start linking themselves decisively with other families. "If we don't move in this direction, we will face more and more crises."

Though an ocean separates them, Leah Libresco (now Leah Sargeant) understands what Sermarini is talking about. She is a Catholic and an effervescent Benedict Option social entrepreneur who lives in New York City with her husband Alexi. Before they married in

2016, Libresco organized Benedict Option events among her young single Christian friends in Washington, D.C. She started doing this after becoming convinced that her circle needed more Christian cultural liturgies in their daily lives.

"I used to do things with my Christian friends, and we knew we were all Christian, but the fact that we were Christians never came up," she says. "There's something weird when none of the communal parts of your life are overtly Christian. The Benedict Option is about creating the opportunity for those things to happen. It doesn't feel urgent, but it's really important."

Libresco took a similar approach to incentivizing single Christian life as the Tipi Loschi took for Christian family life. Don't overthink it. Do activities that are pleasurable, not merely dutiful. Let things happen naturally. Be willing to take risks and to fail without falling apart.

Echoing Sermarini, Libresco says that this strategy is not a new thing at all; it only seems so because we have forgotten how to act like a community instead of a random collection of individuals.

"People are like, 'This Benedict Option thing, it's just being Christian, right?' And I'm like, 'Yes! You've figured out the koan!'" Libresco told me. "But people won't do it unless you call it something different. It's just the church being what the church is supposed to be, but if you give it a name, that makes people care."

Relearning the lost art of community is something Christians should do in obedience to the Apostle Paul, who counseled the faithful to do their parts to grow the Body of Christ "for the building up of itself in love" (Ephesians 4:15). But there are also practical reasons for doing so.

Building communities of believers will be necessary as the number of Christians becomes thinner on the ground. Communities with a strong, shared mission will be necessary to start and to sustain authentically Christian, authentically countercultural schools.

In the years to come, Christians will face mounting pressure to withdraw their children from public schools. Secular private schools may offer a better education, but their moral and spiritual ethos will likely be scarcely better. And established Christian schools may not be sufficiently orthodox, academically challenging, or morally sound. A tight communal network generates the social capital needed to launch a school, or to reform and revive an existing one.

It's hard to overstate the importance of the Christian educational mission. Aside from building up the assembly of believers in the church, there is no more important institutional work to be done in the Benedict Option.

CHAPTER 7

Education as Christian Formation

In the mid-1980s, Soviet leader Mikhail Gorbachev's liberalization within his own country inspired the same loosening of restrictions in the Warsaw Pact nations, including Czechoslovakia. With the dawn breaking from the long Communist night, Václav Benda reflected on what he and his allies in the dissident movement had accomplished to that point. Benda was disappointed by their failure to establish much of a parallel *polis*, but one failure he described as catastrophic: their inability to establish a schooling system that would provide an alternative education to the state's.

As a Christian, Benda wanted to create a counterculture that would defend and restore authentic moral and religious values to Czech society and to reknit the bonds between Czechs and their past severed by the Communists. As a university professor, he believed that education was the most important means of doing that.

Why had they failed? Their efforts had been too exclusive, and the forms too flawed. Even as it loosened the bonds in other areas of civic life, the Communist state kept its iron grip on education. And, said Benda, the destruction of the Czech family under Communism made it difficult for any educational reform to succeed.

Poland, with its thick Catholic culture, came much closer than the Czechs to realizing a parallel *polis*. From Catholic Poland came the sparks—in the form of the Solidarity labor movement and Karol Wojtyla, Pope John Paul II—that ignited the fire that burned Communism to the ground. And yet today Poles like the Catholic philosopher and former dissident Ryszard Legutko lament that the faith and culture his people preserved through the dark night of totalitarianism are dissolving thanks to the solvent of Western-style secular liberalism (which includes hedonism and consumerism).

We traditional Christians in America can learn from both Eastern European examples. We face nothing so terrible as the Czechs did under Soviet domination, of course, but the more insidious forces of secular liberalism are steadily achieving the same aim: robbing us and future generations of our religious beliefs, moral values, and cultural memory, and making us pawns of forces beyond our control.

This is why we have to focus tightly and without hesitation on education. We have far more freedom than Benda and his colleagues did, and our people, though under strain, are far less demoralized than the Czechs were.

"Education has to be at the core of Christian survival—as it always was," says Michael Hanby, a professor of religion and philosophy of science at Washington's Pontifical John Paul II Institute. "The point of monasticism was not simply to retreat from a corrupt world to survive, though in various iterations that might have been a dimension of it," he continues. "But at the heart of it was a quest for God. It was that quest that mandated the preservation of classical learning and the pagan tradition by the monks, because they loved what was true and what was beautiful wherever they found it."

As crucial as cultural survival is, Hanby warns that Christians cannot content themselves with merely keeping their heads above water within liquid modernity. We have to search passionately for the truth, reflect rigorously on reality, and in so doing, come to terms with what it means to live as authentic Christians in the disenchanted world created by modernity. Education is the most important means for accomplishing this.

"Retaining the imagination necessary to see or to search for God is going to be an indispensable element in the preservation of true freedom and Christian freedom when our freedom under law becomes more and more limited," Hanby says.

Today, across the Christian community, there is a growing movement called classical Christian education. It is countercultural in both form and content and presents to students the Western tradition— both Greco-Roman and Christian—in all its depth. Doing it right requires a level of effort and commitment that contemporary Americans are not accustomed to—but what alternative do we have?

If you want to know how critical education is to cultural and religious survival, ask the Jews. Rabbi Mark Gottlieb says, "Jews committed to traditional life put schooling above almost anything. There are families that will do just about anything short of bankrupting themselves to give their children an Orthodox Jewish education." Christians have not been nearly as alert to the importance of education, and it's time to change that.

To that end, one of the most important pieces of the Benedict Option movement is the spread of classical Christian schools. Rather than letting their children spend forty hours a week learning "facts" with a few hours of worldview education slapped on top, parents need to pull them from public schools and provide them with an education that is rightly ordered—that is, one based on the premise that there is a God-given, unified structure to reality and that it is discoverable. They need to teach them Scripture and history. And they should not stop after twelfth grade—a Christian plan for higher education is also needed.

Building schools that can educate properly will require churches, parents, peer groups, and fellow traveler Christians to work together. It will be costly, but what choice is there?

Give Your Family a Rightly Ordered Education

For serious Christian parents, education cannot be simply a matter of building their child's transcript to boost her chance of making it into the Ivy League. If this is the model your family follows (perhaps with a sprinkle of God on top for seasoning), you will be hard-pressed to form countercultural Christian adults capable of resisting the disorders of our time.

The kind of schooling that will build a more resilient, mature faith in young Christians is one that imbues them with a sense of order, meaning, and continuity. It's one that integrates knowledge into a harmonious vision of the whole, one that unites all things that are, were, and ever will be in God.

Every educational model presupposes an anthropology: an idea of what a human being is. In general, the mainstream model is geared toward equipping students to succeed in the workforce, to provide a pleasant, secure life for themselves and their future families, and ideally, to fulfill their personal goals—whatever those goals might be. The standard Christian educational model today takes this model and adds religion classes and prayer services.

But from a traditional Christian perspective, the model is based on a flawed anthropology. In traditional Christianity, the ultimate goal of the soul is to love and serve God with all one's heart, soul, and mind, to achieve unity with Him in eternity. To prepare for eternal life, we must join ourselves to Christ and strive to live in harmony with the divine will.

To be fully human is to be fully conformed to that reality—as C. S. Lewis would say, to the things that are—through cooperating with God's freely given grace. Drawn forward by the love of God, we stagger along the pilgrim's path rejoicing, filling our minds with knowledge of Him and His Creation, and allowing our hearts to be converted by radical surrender to His love. To be humanized is to grow—by contemplation and action, and through faith and reason—in the love of the Good, the True, and the Beautiful. These are all reflections of the Triune God, in Whom we live and move and have our being.

To compartmentalize education, separating it from the life of the church, is to create a false distinction. Saint Benedict, in his Rule, called the monastery "a school for the service of the Lord." This was no mere figure of speech. Benedict believed that discipleship was a matter of pedagogy, of training both the heart and the mind, so that we could grow beyond spiritual infancy. In Chapter 7 of the Rule, in an instruction on humility, Benedict told the brothers to remember that nothing is hidden from God, citing the Psalmist's description of God as a "searcher of hearts and minds."

In the Benedictine tradition, learning is wholly integrated into the life of prayer and work. Being a faithful monk required being able to read, obviously, but the ability to write was critical to the monastic life. Monasteries became places in which countless monks undertook the painstaking work of copying by hand Holy Scripture, prayer books, patristic writings, and literature of the classical world. These men of God laid the foundation for a new civilization, and they did it because they loved God.

Today our education system fills students' heads with facts, with no higher aspiration than success in worldly endeavor. Since the High Middle Ages, the pursuit of knowledge for its own sake has been slowly separated from the pursuit of virtue. Today the break is clean.

Educator Martin Cothran, a national leader in the classical Christian school movement, says that many Christians today don't realize how the nature of education has changed over the past hundred years. The progressivism of the 1920s involved using schools to change the culture. The vocationalism of the 1940s and 1950s tried to use schools to conform children to the culture. But the traditional way of education, which reigned from the Greco-Roman period until the modern era, was about passing on a culture and one culture in particular: the culture of the West, and for most of that time, the Christian West.

"The classical education of the pagans that was transformed by the church attempted to inculcate in each new generation an idea of what a human being should be, through constantly having examples of ideal humanity set in front of it, and by studying the great deeds of great men," Cothran told me. "This was a culture with a definite and distinctive goal: to pass on the wisdom of the past and to produce another generation with the same ideals and values—ideals and values based on its vision of what a human being was.

"That's what education was for over two millennia," he continued. "It is now something that retains the old label, but is not the same thing. It is not even the same *kind* of thing. It has been abandoned in the modern school—including many Christian ones. Even many Christian parents who do not accept the political correctness of today's schools have completely bought into the utilitarian concept of education."

To be sure, there is nothing wrong in principle with learning something useful or achieving excellence in science, the arts, literature, or any other field of the intellect. But mastery of facts and their application is not the same thing as education, any more than an advanced degree in systematic theology makes one a saint.

The separation of learning from virtue creates a society that esteems people for their success in manipulating science, law, money, images, words, and so forth. Whether or not their accomplishments are morally worthy is a secondary question, one that will seem naïve to many if it occurs to them at all.

If a Christian way of living isn't integrated with students' intellectual and spiritual lives, they'll be at risk of falling away through no fault of their own. As John Mark Reynolds, who recently founded Houston's Saint Constantine School, puts it, Christian young people who have had a personal, life-changing encounter with Christ, and who know Christian apologetics but have not integrated them into their lives, are more vulnerable than they think. They have to learn how to translate the conversion experience and intellectual knowledge of the faith into a Christian way of living—or their faith will remain fragile.

If it's true that a simplistic, anti-intellectual Christian faith is a thin reed in the gale of academic life, it is also true that faith that's primarily intellectual—that is, a matter of mastering information—is deceptively fragile. Equipping Christian students to thrive in a highly secularized, even hostile environment is not a matter of giving them a protective shell. The shell may crack under pressure or be discarded. Rather, it must be about building internal strength of mind and heart.

Teach the Children Scripture

Because Scripture is the living word of God, creating educational models for our children that integrate Bible knowledge and meditation into their lives is key. Unfortunately, at this point we're letting our children down.

At dinner a few years ago with three professors from a conservative Evangelical college, I mentioned how much I, a non-Evangelical, admired Evangelicals for educating their youth so well in Scripture.

The professor on my left said that I had a romanticized or at least outdated view of Evangelicals. "You would be surprised by how many of our students come here knowing next to nothing about the Bible," he said sadly.

This stunned me. I told the professors that I was used to hearing this complaint from Catholic college professors, but could it really be true of Evangelicals too? At a conservative college?

I looked around the table. Every head nodded in the affirmative. The professors explained that even though most of these kids came out of church and youth group culture, their theological background was shockingly thin. "We do the best we can, but we only have them for four years," said one professor. "You can't make up in that short time for what they never had."

Since that night, I have made a point of asking professors at every Christian college that invites me to lecture to assess the Christian knowledge of their undergraduates. In almost every case, whether the college is Catholic or Evangelical, the answer is the same: they are theologically illiterate.

"A lot of our students come here from some of the most highly regarded Catholic schools in this region," said one professor. "They don't know anything about their faith and don't see the problem. They've had it drummed into their heads that Catholicism is anything they want it to be."

None of this is a surprise to anyone familiar with the social science literature documenting the widespread ignorance among Americans of Christian basics. After all, Moralistic Therapeutic Deism comes from somewhere.

Parents looking to counteract MTD and teach their children Scripture can find a good example in Benedict. The Rule prescribes set daily times for monks to engage in *lectio divina*, the Benedictine method of reading Scripture. The saint also commanded his monks to engage in other forms of reading and study to enrich their studying of the Bible. During Lent, for example, the Rule directs each monk to receive a book from the monastery's library and read it. The Rule instructs monks to read not only Scripture but the works of the Church Fathers and the lives of the saints, for these are "tools of virtue" for the one who wishes to build a house of faith with a firm foundation.

Not only will study of Scripture lead them to God, but it will bind young Christians together in a way that helps them stand against the onslaught of secularism. Again, we can learn from Jewish education here. Charles Chaput, the Catholic archbishop of Philadelphia, witnessed the power of Orthodox Jewish education on a 2012 visit to Yeshiva University. After observing students studying Torah as part of the university's basic coursework, Chaput wrote how impressed he was by "the power of Scripture to create new life."[1]

"God's Word is a living dialogue between God and humanity. That divine dialogue mirrored itself in the learning dialogue among the students," the archbishop wrote in *First Things* magazine. "The students began as strangers, but their work in reflecting on Scripture and in sharing what they discovered with each other created something more than themselves: a friendship between themselves, and beyond themselves, with God."

The Orthodox Jewish students study Scripture not with an academic's distance but as the bread of life and the sinews that bind them together as a community. Achieving this level of devotion in education sounds like an unrealistic goal for Christian schools and colleges, but shouldn't we try? If Rabbi Gottlieb is correct, the survival of authentically Christian culture requires this or something close to it.

Immerse the Young in the History of Western Civilization

Education not only has to reset our relationship to ultimate reality, it also must reestablish our connection to our history. That is, education is key to the recovery of cultural memory. The deeper our roots in the past, the more secure our anchor against the swift currents of liquid modernity. The greater our understanding of where we came from, the more securely we can stand in the post-Christian present, and the more confidently we can chart a course for the post-Christian future.

Christianity emerged from the confluence of Hebrew religion, Greek philosophy, and Roman law. The forms and content of Western civilization come from the same roots, as well as from the encounter of the Christian faith with various European peoples. To be clear, Jesus Christ—not Aristotle, Aquinas, or Augustus Caesar—is the savior of mankind. Still, Dante's *Divine Comedy*, the medieval masterpiece and one of the pinnacles of Western civilization, shows imaginatively how God used people from the West's pagan past to prepare souls for the coming of Christ.

Classical Christian education proceeds from the conviction that God is still doing that through the art, literature, and philosophy of the past, both Greco-Roman and Christian. We cannot understand the West apart from the Christian faith, and we cannot understand the Christian faith as we live it today without understanding the history and culture of the West. If future generations fail to learn to love our Western cultural heritage, we will lose it.

Consider the recent lament of Notre Dame political theorist Patrick Deneen. In an essay published in an online education blog, Deneen said his students are nice, pleasant, decent young men and women, but they are also "know-nothings" whose "brains are largely empty" of any meaningful knowledge. "They are the culmination of Western civilization, a civilization that has forgotten nearly everything about itself, and as a result, has achieved near-perfect indifference to its own culture," he wrote.[2]

These kids aren't stupid. Deneen, who taught at Princeton and Georgetown before arriving at Notre Dame, pointed out that none of these universities are easy to get into. These students test well and know what they must do to make good grades and "build superb résumés" that propel them upward through the meritocracy. "They are the cream of their generation," he wrote, "the masters of the universe, a generation-in-waiting to run America and the world."

However intelligent and accomplished they may be, these young people could be one of the last generations of this thing called Western civilization. They don't even know what they don't know—and they don't care. Why should they? As with their scant knowledge of the Christian faith, they are only doing what their parents, their schools, and their culture have taught them.

To be sure, this is not a new crisis. In 1943, a *New York Times* story lamented the woeful ignorance of U.S. students on historical facts. The angry secular prophet Philip Rieff, surveying the wreckage of universities in the wake of the counterculture's protests, unleashed a thundering jeremiad against the higher educational establishment back in the 1970s. In his 1973 book *Fellow Teachers*, Rieff, also a college professor, excoriated educators for acquiescing to trendy student demands for "relevance." In Rieff's jaundiced view, they surrendered their magisterial authority and abdicated their responsibility to pass to the next generation their civilizational inheritance. "At the end of this tremendous cultural development, we moderns shall arrive at barbarism," Rieff wrote. "Barbarians are people without historical memory. Barbarism is the real meaning of radical contemporaneity. Released from all authoritative pasts, we progress towards barbarism, not away from it."[3]

I am a college-educated American. In all my years of formal schooling, I never read Plato or Aristotle, Homer or Virgil. I knew nothing of Greek and Roman history and barely grasped the meaning of the Middle Ages. Dante was a stranger to me, and so was Shakespeare.

The fifteen hundred years of Christianity from the end of the New Testament to the Reformation were a blank page, and I knew only the barest facts about Luther's revolution. I was ignorant of Descartes and Newton. My understanding of Western history began with the Enlightenment. Everything that came before it was lost behind a misty curtain of forgetting.

Nobody did this on purpose. Nobody tried to deprive me of my civilizational patrimony. But nobody felt any obligation to present it to me and my generation in an orderly, coherent fashion. Ideas have consequences—and so does their lack. The best way to create a generation of aimless know-nothings who feel no sense of obligation beyond themselves is to deprive them of a past.

In the twentieth century, every totalitarian government knew that controlling the people's access to cultural memory was necessary to gain dominion over them. Today in the contemporary West, our cultural memory has not been taken from us by dictators. Rather, like the comfortable, pleasure-seeking drones in *Brave New World*, we have ceased caring about the past because it inhibits our ability to seek pleasure in the present.

It is not enough to present students with facts about Western civilization—the civilization that is the father and mother of every citizen of the West, whether their ancestors immigrated from Africa or Asia, and even if, like me, their Christian confession is Byzantine. Reynolds, a veteran Christian educator and founder of Biola University's Torrey Honors Institute, says that teachers have to move beyond mere data, integrating history and culture into the students' moral imagination. "You can't just say, 'Here is the glory of Christian civilization! Stare at it, and enjoy it,'" Reynolds says.

That is, it is not likely to be love at first sight for today's students. The material may seem distant to them, especially because they have been formed by a culture that stresses contemporaneity (that is, "relevance") and that incentivizes them to be passive test-taking conformists.

In the face of those obstacles, classical Christian educators have to practice the ancient art of intellectual seduction, one perfected nearly 2,500 years ago in Greece. "You have to be more Socratic," says Reynolds, "to draw students into it, and make it part of their identity. This is the kind of education that produced C. S. Lewis and J.R.R. Tolkien. Why would we want less for our kids today?"

Pull Your Children Out of Public Schools

Because public education in America is neither rightly ordered, nor religiously informed, nor able to form an imagination devoted to Western civilization, it is time for all Christians to pull their children out of the public school system.

If those reasons weren't already enough, the corrosive effect of the toxic peer culture found among students in many public schools (as well as private ones) would confirm the case. It's true that nationwide trends on teenage sexual activity and drug and alcohol use have been moving in a positive direction. The teen pregnancy and abortion rates have declined markedly, and the number of kids having sex before the age of fifteen has gone down slightly. But the numbers are still troubling to many Christian parents. After all, is it really all that comforting to learn from the Centers for Disease Control that just over 20 percent of twelfth graders smoke pot at least once per month? That nearly six in ten high school seniors report having had sexual intercourse?[4]

Plus, public schools by nature are on the front lines of the latest and worst trends in popular culture. For example, under pressure from the federal government and LGBT activists, many school systems are now welcoming and normalizing transgenderism—with the support of many parents.

Theologian Carl Trueman discovered this when he tried to rally moms and dads in his suburban Philadelphia school district to oppose a proposed transgender policy that he contended would erode parental rights and harm women's sports.

"I was amazed that parents either saw no problem with the policy or thought it a positive good. Nobody seemed to grasp that the issue was bigger than helping a child genuinely struggling with identity issues," says Trueman. "They simply could not see that the proposals involved setting a significant precedent for the expansion of the power of schools at the expense of the rights of parents. Needless to say, the policy passed without significant opposition."

Anecdotally confirming what seems to be a trend, a woman in suburban Baltimore said to me, "All those people who say you are alarmist about the Benedict Option must not be raising children." She went on to say that at her daughter's high school, a shocking number of teenagers were going to their parents telling them that they think they are transgender and asking to be put on hormones.

What do the parents do?

"You'd be surprised how many of them do it," the woman said. "They are so afraid of losing their kids. And this is how our culture tells them to react. Parents like this become the fiercest advocates for transgenderism."

Three months after our conversation, that woman's daughter came home from high school with the news that she is really a boy, and demanding that her family treat her as such.

A reader of my blog said she sees the same sort of thing watching her daughter navigate from junior high to high school. "There's nothing like having your twelve-year-old come home from school and start ticking off which of her classmates are bi," the reader said. "I told my daughter it was statistically impossible for there to be that many bisexual students in her class, and that for most girls—and they were all girls—seventh grade was entirely too early to make pronouncements on their sexuality. In return, I got a lot of babble about gender being fluid and nonbinary."

The reader called a friend with a daughter in the same class and asked her what was going on. "Where have you been?" she laughed. "At least a third of these girls are calling themselves bi."

Few parents have the presence of mind and strength of character to do what's necessary to protect their children from forms of disordered sexuality accepted by mainstream American youth culture. For one thing, the power of media to set the terms of what's considered normal is immense, and it affects adults as well as children. For another, parents are just as susceptible to peer pressure as their children are.

"People rear their children the way their friends and neighbors are doing it, not the way their parents did it," says psychology researcher Judith Rich Harris, "and this is true not only in media-ridden societies like our own."[5]

This kind of thing is why more and more Christian parents are concluding that they cannot afford to keep their children in public schools. Some tell themselves that their children need to remain there to be "salt and light" to the other kids. As popular culture continues its downward slide, however, this rationale begins to sound like a rationalization. It brings to mind a father who tosses his child into a whitewater river in hopes that she'll save another drowning child.

Parents may try to counteract the effects of secular education with church, Sunday school, and youth group, but two or three hours of religious education weekly is unlikely to counteract the forty or more hours spent in school or school-related programming. Nor is it a good bet that such limited measures can compensate for the anti-Christian hostility, both active and passive, faced by young believers growing up in a post-Christian world. If we want our children to survive, we must act.

Don't Kid Yourself About Christian Schools

There is no such thing as a completely safe space.

When one single dad, an Evangelical and former public school teacher, became fed up with his ninth-grade daughter being teased for declining to celebrate a lesbian classmate's coming out, he transferred her to a private Christian school. The father, who asked to remain anonymous, says it has only been a partial solution.

"My daughter went from a public school where she had no believing Christian friends to a Christian one where only fifteen or twenty percent of the students seem to have any real faith life," he said. "It's better than what she had before, and at least she's getting a Bible class."

Even in many Christian schools, Christianity is a veneer over a secular way of looking at the world. It's not strong enough to withstand the onslaught of secularism. Too many parents use Christian schools as a way to shield kids from the more harmful defects of public schooling but have only a nominal interest in their receiving a Christian education.

Years ago a Christian friend in Dallas refused to consider sending her children to a couple of the most elite Christian schools in the city. As a newcomer to the city, I assumed that the high tuition cost was the reason. Not at all, she said; she did not want her kids absorbing the materialistic, status-conscious culture within the schools.

The principal of one Christian high school told me that he and his faculty are constantly battling parents who find the serious moral and theological content of the curriculum too burdensome for their children. "All they think about is getting their kids into a top university and launching them into a good career," he said. Another principal, this one at a pricey Christian academy in the Deep South, said, "Our parents think if they've paid their seventeen-thousand-dollar tuition bill, they've done all that's expected of them about their child's religious education."

In the South, some Christian schools carry a racist legacy that unfairly (but understandably) makes African Americans and others suspicious of Benedict Option education initiatives. In the late 1960s and early 1970s, as racial integration came to public schools, some white parents created all-white private schools that became derisively known as "segregation academies." Shamefully, more than a few of these schools claimed a Christian identity.

Though times have changed and many churches have as well, the stigma remains. Benedict Option schools would be wise to make special efforts toward racial reconciliation by recruiting black families, especially given that public schools are effectively resegregating. Additionally, the future of Christianity in America, both Catholic and Evangelical, is going to be a lot more Hispanic. So should the future of Christian schooling.

In any case, if a Christian school is so immersed in the world that it perpetuates the poison of secular culture and cuts students off from historic faith, it will fail the children. In those cases, even when students at Christian schools do learn the basic truths of their faith, the shallow understanding they gain doesn't do them much good in the long run. They remain what Saint Paul called "infants in Christ" (1 Corinthians 3:1). In fact, the trite theological education many received at Christian school will serve more as a vaccination against taking the faith seriously than as an incentive for it. Pull your kids out.

Start Classical Christian Schools

Fortunately, there's a good alternative to both public schools and mediocre Christian schools: classical Christian education. It's built by marrying the Greco-Roman ideal that the purpose of education is to cultivate virtue and wisdom, to the traditional Christian worldview. The CiRCE Institute, a North Carolina–based Christian organization that trains teachers in the classical model, proclaims: "The classical Christian does not ask, 'What can I do with this learning?' but 'What will this learning do to me?'"

Like the Benedictine monastery, the classical Christian school orders everything around the Logos, Jesus Christ, and the quest to know Him with one's heart, soul, and mind. Classical education accepts the Great Tradition's fundamental understanding that all of reality is grounded in transcendental ideals—in fact, in the One in Whom we move and live and have our being.

All Christian schools should take as part of their mission the cultivation of personal devotion to Christ within the hearts of their students. Classical Christian education takes a more comprehensive and universal approach. In this model, a searching love of Christ undergirds and harmonizes all classroom learning. The end is to nurture graduates whose hearts desire truth, goodness, and beauty and who use their minds to discover these things.

Classical Christian education takes a Great Books approach to the curriculum. It presents the canonical Western texts and works of art to students, using a medieval structure called the Trivium, which, as Dorothy Sayers argued in her 1947 essay "The Lost Tools of Learning" (the founding document of the current classical education movement), corresponds to the mental capacities of young people at certain ages of development.

Typically, a student's classical school career begins with the Grammar school, in which she learns and commits to memory basic facts about the world. The second part of a child's experience is the Logic school, which corresponds to the middle school years. This is when students learn how to use reason to analyze facts and discern meaning from them. The third and final stage is the Rhetoric school, which focuses on abstract thinking, on poetry, and on clear self-expression.

The classical approach presents the Western canon in a systematic fashion that's deeply integrated into a Christian anthropology and a comprehensive vision of reality. There is no more powerfully counter-cultural way to cultivate resilient Christians from their youth.

Not everybody has the opportunity to send their children to a full-time classical Christian school. Fortunately, the world of classical Christian homeschooling is burgeoning, with more teaching resources becoming available with each passing semester. There are also hybrid schools, such as the one my children attend, Baton Rouge's Sequitur Classical Academy.

Sequitur's model gathers students for half a day and counts on parents to complete the educational equation. My wife and I find that this hybrid approach retains the best of homeschooling while giving our three children an even more comprehensive education, as well as the advantages of building a community of students and families committed to the same educational mission.

A good classical Christian school not only teaches students the Bible and Western civilization but also integrates students into the life of the church. At the newly opened Saint Constantine School in Houston, a classical Christian school in the Eastern Orthodox tradition, president John Mark Reynolds's model integrates the school as much as possible with families and churches. He calls it a kind of "new monasticism" that seeks to harmonize church, school, and family life for its students.

"In the past, schools have functioned fairly independent of the family and the church. That was defensible when our culture was more Christian, but it's not really true anymore," he says. Believing that the school must reinforce the life of the church if parishioners and students are to grow in their faith, the school works around the church schedule, making sure that students have time and space on the calendar for their spiritual lives.

The spiritual results of this kind of integration are tangible. A classical Christian school headmaster in the Southwest told me that these schools are often surprised to discover themselves leading Christian families and churches back to tradition. "Though we are the only one of those three not ordained by the Bible to form our children, this is how it's turning out in lots of places," he said.

School-church integration in a post-Christian age also has a practical benefit. Existing under the umbrella of a church offers legal protection not available to other Christian schools. Legal experts say that Christian schools facing antidiscrimination challenges in court have greater protection if they can demonstrate that they are clearly and meaningfully guided by established doctrines of a particular church and can demonstrate that they enforce these doctrines.

At the same time, it's important to recognize the ways that classical Christian schools can boost a healthy ecumenism in the face of a common enemy. While there are benefits to establishing a school under a particular tradition, there is also wisdom in taking a broad-tent approach, as long as the school remains under one of the ancient creeds. "The good news is that these kinds of schools have the real opportunity to heal the old divisions, because the old divisions are dead," says the Saint Constantine School's Reynolds.

Sequitur Classical Academy is small "o" orthodox but interdenominational. Most teachers and students are Evangelicals, but my Eastern Orthodox wife teaches there, and our Eastern Orthodox children attend there. There are also traditionalist Catholics in the school community. Co-founder Brian Daigle, born Catholic and later moving through Reformed churches, says his own journey within the Christian tradition has taught him a love and respect for what each of the faith's branches brings to the school.

"Being a part of that kind of Christian academic community has given me stronger convictions in some areas and more humility in others," he says. "And it has made me a better scholar, able to read more widely across denominational lines, understanding the importance of an author's theological nuances to their literary decisions, for example."

Daigle says that intellectually honest fellowship and collaboration among orthodox Christians in schools should strengthen the witness of the local churches in these more militantly secularizing times. He is confident that studying together within the Great Tradition will forge bonds of friendship and spiritual solidarity that will stand students in good stead in the days to come. "The benefit, I hope, for our students is that we are preparing them not for jobs which don't yet exist, but for a church which doesn't yet exist," says Daigle.

The advantages of allying a classical school to a particular church can be seen in the story of St. Jerome Academy in Hyattsville, Maryland—arguably the most famous classical Christian school in the nation.

In 2010, the Catholic Archdiocese of Washington, D.C., was moving forward with plans to shutter the school attached to St. Jerome Parish in the Maryland suburb. Enrollment at the school, which goes from pre-K to eighth grade, was way down, and the school was debt-ridden. Local Catholic businessman Chris Currie, Catholic University philosophy professor Michael Hanby, and other parents approached the school's leaders and proposed a Hail Mary pass to save it: turn it into a classical school.

Principal Mary Pat Donoghue came on board with the plan. The parish pastor, despite his reservations, decided they had nothing to lose. The archdiocese gave the go-ahead for the experiment. In response, Currie, Hanby, and others hammered out a curriculum, parents and the parish raised enough money to pay off the fading school's $117,000 debt, and they hired eight new teachers committed to the classical approach.

Today the little Catholic school that was at death's door is bursting at the seams and has become a national model for using the classical model to revive declining parish schools. Currie says that the reform and rebirth of St. Jerome's would never have happened in a rich exurban Catholic school. They happened in the inner-ring suburban parish because of necessity: it was change or die.

And it started with ordinary lay members of the parish taking the initiative. As orthodox Catholics, the St. Jerome team made a point of submitting to the authority of the parish pastor and the local bishop—and were fortunate that church officials let the visionaries have free rein to try something radically different.

"You have to change the way you teach, and that means throwing out a lot of the textbooks and resources your school is used to," Currie says. "And classical education can't be a gimmick to boost enrollment. You have to have a strong connection to mission in everything you do. That's the only way to make it effective and desirable to outsiders."

The new St. Jerome Academy made a priority of reaching out to parents and involving them in the life of the school and its classical vision. And the team followed a small-c catholic educational vision, rejecting the idea that classical education was only for highly intentional Catholics.

"This doesn't mean you accept anybody into the school," says Currie. "There are some kids who may not be able to profit from a classical education and will disrupt others in their classes. But that number is very small. We're very diverse and have students from every racial and socioeconomic group. Once parents see the difference it makes in the kids, they're sold. The way we see it, this education is for people from all walks of life."

Is starting a classical Christian school in your community possible? Through its Web site, the Association of Classical and Christian Schools (accsedu.org), an orthodox Protestant organization with members in forty-five states and four foreign countries, offers a how-to package, including a series of questions local communities should ask themselves before starting this journey.

The Institute for Catholic Liberal Education (www.catholicliber

aleducation.org) is a resource-rich organization for Catholics and includes on its Web site the educational plan of St. Jerome Academy. (In fact, Mary Pat Donoghue, the principal who oversaw the Hyattsville school's transition, now works as a full-time consultant for the institute.)

No Classical Christian School? Then Homeschool

There has been an explosion of resources to help classical Christian homeschoolers. The CiRCE Institute is a major hub, through its Web site and conferences, as is the Society for Classical Learning. The Classical Conversations method is one of the most popular programs.

Schools like Baton Rouge's Sequitur Classical Academy and North Texas's Coram Deo Academy, which both provide classroom instruction supplemented by homeschooling, are also growing in popularity.

Many Christian parents find that reliably orthodox Christian schools are either unavailable locally or unaffordable. So they turn to homeschooling—a strategy that can extract meaningful costs in an economy where most families depend on two incomes.

A Silicon Valley Catholic mom I'll call Maggie told me that she and her schoolteacher husband decided to homeschool in part because they believed they could do better than the local public school. Private school was out of the question, and her experience as a student in local Catholic schools demolished her trust in them.

Though accounting for only 3.4 percent of the nation's schoolchildren, homeschooling is growing in popularity, having increased its numbers by 62 percent from 2003 to 2012, according to the U.S. Department of Education.[6] But as any homeschooling parent will tell you, it is not for everybody. It requires particular skills—organizational savvy, for example—as well as intelligence and an extraordinary capacity for patience. Plus, you need to have a two-parent family and the ability to get by on a single income—factors that put homeschooling out of reach for many families.

But it is possible for some, provided they are willing to live asceti-cally. Maggie added that she and her fellow homeschooling moms are surrendering careers, success, and given the local cost of living, signif-icant material wealth for the sake of their children.

Even though her family has to make ends meet on one salary—and that of a schoolteacher—Maggie believes it's worth it. So do the other moms in her homeschooling circle, she says.

"We just can't be sucked into the vortex that whirls madly around us, and we don't want our children sucked in either," she said. "We don't want our children to think that their only purpose in life is to get ac-cepted to Stanford and make their first million before the age of thirty. We need to serve something—I believe, God—greater than ourselves, and schools of any stripe, at least here, do not teach you to do that."

The Benedict Option and the University

The need for committed orthodox Christian peers does not end at graduation. College is also a time of moral and spiritual challenge, and not all young believers make it through with their faith intact. Christians must not only find ways to help students navigate the exist-ing university system but also look for ways to reinvent the university.

In 2016, at a closed-door discussion among conservative Evangel-ical academics, I listened as college administrators and professors spoke frankly about how their students, including seminary students, are having their convictions waylaid by progressive sexual ideology—and this is affecting their sexual behavior.

More broadly, the dramatic decline in faith among young adults (35 percent of whom identify with no religion or religious tradition at all) means that student believers face more social pressure than any previous generation to abandon Christian orthodoxy. Where can they look for hope?

Most immediately, students can join or begin Christian associations on campus—essentially finding ways to live in Benedict Option communities there.

Catholic students at non-Catholic universities often turn to their campus Newman Center, typically the nexus of college ministry. Not all Newman Centers are reliably orthodox, but St. John's, the one at the University of Illinois at Champaign-Urbana, has a reputation for being a place of solid Catholic teaching, Bible study, retreats, and fellowship for the estimated ten thousand Catholics on campus.

St. John's Newman Center also pioneered Catholic communal living on public university campuses. Its Newman Hall is a modern student residence offering housing to six hundred Catholic students, in an environment led by full-time priests and pastoral staff, with a chapel open around the clock. In 2013, Catholic leaders in Texas and Florida opened two residence halls—one at Texas A&M, the other at the Florida Institute of Technology—based on the St. John's model.

Ryan Mattingly credits his experience at St. John's for renewing his Catholic faith and helping him discover his priestly vocation. Now a seminarian scheduled for 2018 ordination, Mattingly told the *National Catholic Register* that living in that student community drew him closer to prayer and the sacraments and away from the party lifestyle. Said Mattingly, "It gave substance to my faith—just living out the faith in an everyday manner at a large, secular university, where the faith isn't that encouraged."[7]

Father Bryce Sibley, who directs Catholic campus ministry at the University of Louisiana at Lafayette (ULL), told me that the Fellowship of Catholic University Students (FOCUS), a growing national campus ministry that has a chapter in over one hundred universities, including ULL, has been key to building strong intentional Catholic student communities among Millennials.

"These young Catholics are orthodox. They want confession, they want the sacraments, they want formation," Father Sibley said. "We're not just about pizza and having fun. As a result, in the past six years, we've had almost fifty people enter seminary or religious life."

Unlike Catholic campus ministry when he was in college a generation ago, said Father Sibley, FOCUS concentrates intensely on discipleship through prayer, study, and worship—often in small groups—and preparing students for evangelization. "You talk to most Catholic campus ministers today, we're really hopeful," said Father Sibley. "These kids want the real faith, not a watered-down version. If you want to evangelize, things will change."

On the Evangelical side, the Christian Study Center movement offers a countercultural community for young believers. It began in 1968, when a group of Evangelical leaders and students at the University of Virginia started an informal association to promote Christian intellectual and cultural engagement on campus. Inspired by the L'Abri Fellowship, the international network of Evangelical study centers founded by Francis and Edith Schaeffer, the Charlottesville group eventually bought a house on Chancellor Street near campus and set up headquarters.

Though the organization went through a few name changes over the years, it's now called the Center for Christian Study. The house on Chancellor Street is a busy hive of student activity, with Christian students studying in its impressive new library, meeting in small groups, and attending lectures and Bible studies. The center also serves as headquarters for various parachurch ministries on campus.

To think of the big house on Chancellor Street as a clubhouse for Christian college students would be to vastly undersell the center. It is a vital and deeply impressive hub for serious artistic and intellectual life and fellowship among UVA's Evangelical community and anyone who wishes to drop by. The center takes applying Christian discipleship to the life of the mind seriously, and it shows.

There are now over twenty affiliated Christian Study Centers at campuses around the United States, all modeled on the original one at UVA. A phenomenon that holds great promise for building deep Christian community on campuses nationwide has emerged out of the UVA center: a network of private single-sex group housing for Christian students there.

Within easy walking distance of the center are over twenty residences where college men and women live in various forms of community during their undergraduate years. There is no Rule covering all the houses, and some houses have no Rule at all; they're just Christians living together. What they all do is build mutual support and obligation among the students who live there.

Sitting around a table in the center one autumn afternoon, I spoke with current and former residents of the Christian houses. All of them spoke with genuine warmth and affection of how life in the houses had stabilized them and deepened their faith commitment at UVA. Said one young man, "I found people who told me stories that helped me know who I am, and to make sense of the world."

Some of those present were so marked by their years living there that they stayed on in Charlottesville after graduation, finding jobs and deepening their relationship with friends they made in residence.

Sam Speers and Jed Metge are two such UVA graduates. In 2011, they were founding members of Chancellot, a male undergraduate intentional community in a house next door to the center. The men told me their community came together with around twenty guys active in the campus's InterVarsity Christian Fellowship.

The house Rule is simple. It's a community of Christian men, active in InterVarsity, committed to rooming together in a spirit of discipleship and mutual support in living out high moral standards. It is intentionally structured to include men from each year's class. The house brotherhood is "tight but welcoming," meaning that their purpose is to serve and to evangelize the broader UVA community.

The two men recalled an undergraduate who lived next door that first year. The undergraduate started spending more time in the Chancellot living room than in his own group house. They finally asked him why he hung around so much.

"He said, 'There's a different feeling about how you guys are with each other,'" Metge remembered.

The undergraduate talked about how he and his housemates were always fighting over dirty dishes and other domestic dramas. He wanted to know what made such a difference in the Chancellot men's common life.

"We told him it was Christ," said Metge. "We told him he could have that same peace too. Another housemate and I prayed with him, and we led him to Christ."

The house Rule developed over time. They tried different things out. Morning prayer together was hard to stay committed to, but evening prayer was easier. They engaged in mutual confession of their sins to the community, so they could help each other with personal struggles. ("We didn't call it confession at the time," says Speers. "We called it accountability, which was more kosher to Evangelicals.") And they required sustained group engagement in theological conversations and study.

There were small but strict rules too. No girls in private rooms with closed doors. No alcohol except in the rooms of those of legal drinking age. Some men who struggled with pornography would leave their laptops out in the common room so they would not be tempted.

It worked wonders. Metge said that life in Chancellot gave him a level of emotional and spiritual health and stability that he had never experienced. "When I reflect on my college years, my joy was so high, and it was hugely due to this house," he says. "It expanded and deepened my vision of what depth of commitment is possible for others as a Christian. Going out of that community and into the local church, and into adulthood, it helped me to see that deeper community is possible no matter what circumstance I found myself in."

While groups like Metge's will help students retain their faith in college as it is now, they may be even more vital in the future. If the much-feared attempts to strip academic accreditation from Christian colleges and universities on antidiscrimination grounds materialize and succeed, there will be many fewer places for believing students to go and for faithful professors to teach.

Christian graduate students in the humanities tell me that they can read the handwriting on the wall in academia and see no future for themselves as college professors. In the fall of 2016, some younger members of the Society of Christian Philosophers publicly assailed Richard Swinburne, one of the most eminent living philosophers, as a bigot for briefly defending the orthodox Christian teaching on homosexuality. Prominent non-Christian philosophy professors from Yale, Columbia, and Georgetown piled on, insulting Swinburne and his defenders in lewd, profane terms. This kind of thing is why one Christian Ph.D. candidate in English literature at a prestigious American university confided to me that the total left-wing ideologization of literary scholarship caused him to give up plans for an academic career.

The ground is moving swiftly and decisively under our feet. It's time for Christians to recognize the danger and begin creating a Christian academic counterculture. John Mark Reynolds is preparing for that shift. When he left the provost's job at Houston Baptist University a few years back, he was offered the presidency of a college. He turned it down, even though it was a prestigious job that paid much more money than he's making as head of the Saint Constantine School, the classical Christian academy he founded.

He wears a number of hats at the fledgling Houston school—even part-time janitor. It's a bit of a blow to his pride, but he says it has been good for him to realize how coddled he was in conventional Christian academia—and how much it made him dependent on a higher education model that he believes is financially unsustainable, and will collapse.

Reynolds explains that even Christian colleges are living on the edge of a financing bubble that is bound to burst. When he was a Christian college provost, less than one-third of the school's budget went to academics.

"College as we know it must die," he says. "I'm not willing to have an inner-city kid come to school and borrow a hundred thousand dollars to get a baccalaureate degree that may or may not lead to a job, where they don't see a full-time professor for two years. That's the real world."

The Saint Constantine School model will eventually include a four-year liberal arts college. The school is tied tightly into local churches, and its college component, when launched, will be closely affiliated with the King's College, a Christian institution in New York City. The reason, according to Reynolds: "Those Christian institutions that were accredited before the troubles that are coming will be the last to be challenged."

The Saint Constantine president reports a surfeit of excellent résumés on file, including a number from master's degree and Ph.D. holders. "There are lots of smart, conservative, orthodox Christian teachers out there who need work," he said.

Anthony Esolen agrees. A well-known literature professor, Dante translator, and orthodox Catholic, Esolen came under intense fire in the fall of 2016 within his own school, Catholic-run Providence College, for speaking out against what he believed was the administration's attempt to gut its Catholic identity for the sake of multiculturalism.

"It's long past time for administrators at Christian colleges to abandon the hiring policies that got us in this fix to begin with," Esolen told me. "We *know* that there are plenty of excellent young Christian scholars who have to struggle to find a job. Well, let's get them, and get them right away. *We* should be establishing a network for that purpose."

Esolen is right, though he is also, alas, justified in his skepticism that most Christian colleges and universities will have the good sense to do this. Even so, classical Christian schools should take advantage of this opportunity, pooling their resources and starting a job bank so talented Christian academics willing to teach in elementary and secondary schools will know where the jobs are. Christians cannot expect quality teachers to do it for pennies. Aside from parents being willing to pay tuition rates that enable schools to pay qualified teachers competitive wages, wealthy Christians should redirect some of their political contributions to classical Christian schools. They are essential to the future of Christianity in America.

Go Back to the Classics and Forward to the Future

Christians today are experiencing birth pangs of that future church—and it can be frightening. Even as old certainties are collapsing, new opportunities are emerging. Those who try holding on to pedagogical forms—public, private, and parochial—that can no longer shape the hearts and minds of the next generations in an authentically Christian way risk damaging their kids by leaving them morally and spiritually vulnerable.

Classical Christian education is the new counterculture. In just over a century, Christians have gone from the center of American culture to its margins. Let's own our status and be proud of it. "A dead thing goes with the stream, but only a living thing goes against it," said G. K. Chesterton.

That quote from *The Everlasting Man* is the motto of the Scuola libera G. K. Chesterton, the community school of the Tipi Loschi, the Catholic lay community in San Benedetto del Tronto, Italy. The school started because Marco Sermarini and his wife Federica had the courage of their countercultural Christian convictions.

Almost a decade ago Marco and Federica began to worry that the state schools and the local Catholic high school would undermine the work of Christian formation that their children received at home and within the Tipi Loschi community.

In June 2008, Marco heard a lecture by Father Ian Boyd, an American priest and Chesterton expert visiting Italy. Father Boyd said that the problem we face today is standardization by low standards. What's more, people have no time to do creative things—but they must make time, because going with the mainstream means spiritual death.

When he returned home, Marco told his wife they had to start a school. They had three months to do it. "Many people thought I was crazy, and maybe I am, but we started on the fifteenth of September," Marco said. They had four students, two of them Sermarini children. Today there are seventy students in both a middle school and a high school.

The success of the Chesterton school inspired the Tipi Loschi to dream big. "When we discovered that we could do one strange thing, we started to think about how many things we could do in an unconventional way," says Sermarini. "We knew that we couldn't live a regular life with a Christian coating, but had to change the roots."

Going against Italy's educational stream, the Tipi Loschi found not only success with their school but inspiration to be countercultural Christians in many other ways.

"Many times in this life you will think it's impossible to have any other kind of order," he continues. "But if you start changing things, and moving things where they are meant to be, and if you put God over all of it, then you will be amazed by how many things fall into place."

Building a new Christian education system will be costly and risky. It is a scary thing to challenge the status quo, I told Sermarini, especially if you aren't sure if anybody will stand with you.

"Grande Rod!" he blurted, slapping the air. "Nobody should be afraid. Have faith! We are Christians! We know that with God, all things are possible."

That's true. Christian educators, both in the home and in the classroom, need that kind of faith to keep us going when we hit the wall. It's important to remember, though, that hope has to be grounded in reality.

Years ago my friend Mitch Muncy mentored male undergraduates at the University of Dallas, a Catholic liberal arts school with a strong focus on the Great Books tradition. Back then Mitch told me that it made him happy to see how excited these young men would get about art, books, ideas, and the faith. But he had to remind them constantly of an unromantic reality: that they could not fulfill their calling to raise a family and serve God and the church in the ways they dreamed of doing if they had no ambitions beyond reading and talking about Great Books, or skills with which to realize them.

This truth ought to keep Benedict Option educational visionaries clear-sighted. Peering into the near future, the world of work looks uncertain for everyone, especially for Christians. The practical challenges facing us are unlike any that most believers in this country have ever dealt with. Schools and colleges—morally, spiritually, and vocationally—will have to prepare young believers for some increasingly harsh realities.

Because of florists, bakers, and photographers having been dragged through the courts by gay plaintiffs, we now know that some Orthodox Christians will lose their businesses and their livelihoods if they refuse to recognize the new secular orthodoxies. We can expect that many more Christians will either be denied employment opportunities by licensing or other professional requirements, because they have been driven out of certain workplaces by outright bigotry or by dint of the fact that they cannot in good conscience work in certain fields. What will they do?

As you are about to learn, it is not too early for Christians to start asking that question and making plans.

CHAPTER 8

Preparing for Hard Labor

G rowing up in Texas, Brother Francis Davoren assumed he was going to be a man who labored primarily with his mind. He was a good student, intellectually inclined, and gifted in math and science. In college, he studied physics but switched to theology when he began to wonder if God was calling him to live as a priest or a monk. He didn't realize it until later in life, but for much of his life, Brother Francis thought those who did intellectual work were better than those who worked with their hands.

Today, at forty-three, Brother Francis has a new respect for physical labor, thanks to the hard work he has to do at the monastery, such as lugging heavy sacks of grain and maintaining plumbing. "It has been great for me, because it helps me remember that the human person is body and spirit, not just a spirit," he says. "There needs to be an integration of body and soul. You can use that body to be sanctified through work. It's great to learn that you don't have to just think about things, but actually do them."

Brother Francis also takes satisfaction knowing that his labor is vital to the overall success of the monastery and its mission. Says the monk, "That's my little part in the Church. Each person has a role to hold the whole thing up."

In the age now falling upon us, Brother Francis and the Benedictine model of sanctifying ordinary labor will be a model to traditional Christians in our professional lives, in important ways. First of all, the Benedictine model reminds us that work and worship are integrated and that our careers are not separate from our faith. Second, it reminds us that manual labor is a gift—a gift that Christians may have to rediscover if post-Christianity squeezes us out of the professions. Finally, we see work as a gift given back to God and to the community. If Benedict Option communities are to survive, they're going to have to recover this kind of solidarity, not only on a "merely spiritual" level but on a practical one as well.

What Work Is For

Most Christians still use the word *calling* to refer to a conviction that God is inviting a man or a woman to full-time ministry. Roman Catholics tend to use the word *vocation*—from the Latin word *vocare*, "to call"—to refer to a calling to the priesthood or to monastic life. In the secular world, the word *vocation* has fallen out of common use, except as a synonym for job.

It wasn't always like this. In 1603, the early English Puritan theologian William Perkins delivered a sermon in which he defined *vocation* as "a certain kind of life ordained and imposed on man by God for the common good."[1] Perkins explained that every man—king, pastor, soldier, husband, father, and so on—has a God-given vocation. He likened the symphony of vocations in society to the working of a clock, each gear turning in harmony for the common purpose of keeping time.

In this older understanding, says political theorist Patrick Deneen, we see one's work not as chosen as much as received from God, for the benefit of all. A person's labor is, in ways sometimes mysterious, part of a greater undertaking, in the economy both secular and divine.

"In spite of the contemporary usage of the word 'vocational' to mean narrow training in a job choice," writes Deneen, "the origin of the term points to the way that one's work connected not only to other activities in one's life paths—one's 'career'—but, more comprehensively, how one's work related to a larger whole outside and beyond one's own life."[2]

This is a profoundly Benedictine insight. A monk learns to do the task given to him for the greater glory of God and for the support of the community of believers. In the Benedictine tradition, our labor is one way we participate in God's creative work of ordering Creation and bringing forth good fruit from it. When undertaken in the right spirit, our labor is also a means God uses to order us inwardly.

Balance is key. There's a reason why the Rule prescribes labor for only certain hours of the day. Work is a good thing, even a holy thing, but it must not be allowed to dominate one's life. If it does, our vocation could become an idol. Recall that if an abbot sees that a monk craftsman is taking undue pride in his work, the Rule requires the abbot to reassign him. It's a harsh penalty, but one that reminds all Christians that our labor derives its ultimate value only from the role it plays in God's economy.

Work is good, but it is only good relative to its participation in the unfolding of God's will and for the benefit of others. In workaholic modern America, we have lost this sense of vocational meaning. Ironically, it is still practiced, if only by custom, in secularized Europe.

Deneen's father-in-law is a small-town butcher in southern Germany and a believing Catholic. He told his American son-in-law that he thanks God for Germany's strict laws mandating shop closing times. These laws make life less convenient for consumers, the butcher conceded, but without them he would never have been able to run his mom-and-pop business while raising a family. Without the protection of that regulation, only big stores with a large number of employees could thrive. In this sense, Germany's consumer culture manages to cultivate more balanced, integrated lives for the German people.

The most important labor lesson of the Rule, though, is that a Christian must carry out work, and all other things he does, as a gift to God—as participation in His ordering of Creation. This is as true of the carpenter and the accountant as it is of the minister and the schoolteacher. If we think of work as its own end, disconnected from God's purposes, or as merely something we do to pay the bills, we put ourselves at risk of rationalizing anything to keep our jobs.

Burning Incense to Caesar

The temptation to sell out the faith for the sake of self-protection is by no means an abstract threat. We may not (yet) be at the point where Christians are forbidden to buy and sell in general without state approval, but we are on the brink of entire areas of commercial and professional life being off-limits to believers whose consciences will not allow them to burn incense to the gods of our age.

The workplace is getting tougher for orthodox believers as America's commitment to religious liberty weakens. Progressives sneer at claims of anti-Christian discrimination or persecution. Don't you believe them. Most of the experts I talked to on this topic spoke openly only after I promised to withhold their identities. They're frightened that their words today might cost them their careers tomorrow.

They're not paranoid. While Christians may not be persecuted for their faith per se, they are already being targeted when they stand for what their faith entails, especially in matters of sexuality. As the LGBT agenda advances, broad interpretations of antidiscrimination laws are going to push traditional Christians increasingly out of the marketplace, and the corporate world will become hostile toward Christian bigots, considering them a danger to the working environment.

The Human Rights Campaign Foundation, a powerful LGBT pressure group, publishes an annual Corporate Equality Index. In its

2016 report, over half of the top twenty U.S. companies have a perfect score. To fail to score high is considered a serious problem within leading corporations.

Among the criteria the foundation used in its 2016 evaluations was that "senior management/executive performance measures include LGBT diversity metrics." A company that wants to win the foundation's seal of approval will have to show concrete proof that it is advancing the LGBT agenda in the workplace. The "ally" phenomenon—straight people publicly declaring themselves to be supporters of the LGBT agenda—is one way companies can both demonstrate progress to gay rights campaigners, as well as identify dissenters who may stand in the way of progress.

I have talked to a number of Christians, in fields as diverse as law, banking, and education, who face increasing pressure within their corporations and institutions to publicly declare themselves "allies" of LGBT colleagues. In some instances, employees are given the opportunity to wear special badges advertising their allyship. Naturally if one doesn't wear the badge, she is likely to face questions from co-workers and even shunning.

These workers fear that this is soon going to serve as a de facto loyalty oath for Christian employees—and if they don't sign it, so to speak, it will mean the end of their jobs and possibly even their careers. To sign the oath, they believe, would be the modern equivalent of burning a pinch of incense before a statue of Caesar.

It will be impossible in most places to get licenses to work without affirming sexual diversity dogma. For example, in 2016 the American Bar Association voted to add an "anti-harassment" rule to its Model Code of Conduct, one that if adopted by state bars would make simply discussing issues having to do with homosexuality (among other things) impossible without risking professional sanction—unless one takes the progressive side of the argument.

Along those lines, it will be very difficult to have open dialogue in many workplaces without putting oneself in danger. One Christian professor on a secular university's science faculty declined to answer a question I had about the biology of homosexuality, out of fear that anything he said, no matter how innocuous and fact-based, could get him brought up on charges within his university, as well as attacked by social media mobs. Everyone working for a major corporation will be frog-marched through "diversity and inclusion" training and will face pressure not simply to tolerate LGBT co-workers but to affirm their sexuality and gender identity.

Plus, companies that don't abide by state and federal antidiscrimination statutes covering LGBTs will not be able to receive government contracts. In fact, according to one religious liberty litigator who has had to defend clients against an exasperating array of antidiscrimination lawsuits, the only thing standing between an employer or employee and a court action is the imagination of LGBT plaintiffs and their lawyers.

"We are all vulnerable to such targeting," he said.

Says a religious liberty lawyer, "There is no looming resolution to these conflicts; no plateau that we're about to reach. Only intensification. It's a train that won't stop so long as there is momentum and track."

David Gushee, a well-known Evangelical ethicist who holds an aggressively progressive stance on gay issues, published a column in 2016 noting that the middle ground is fast disappearing on the question of whether discrimination against gays and lesbians for religious reasons should be tolerated.

"Neutrality is not an option," he wrote. "Neither is polite half-acceptance. Nor is avoiding the subject. Hide as you might, the issue will come and find you."[3]

Public school teachers, college professors, doctors, and lawyers will all face tremendous pressure to capitulate to this ideology as a condition of employment. So will psychologists, social workers, and all in the helping professions; and of course, florists, photographers, bakers, and all businesses that are subject to public accommodation laws.

Christian students and their parents must take this into careful consideration when deciding on a field of study in college and professional school. A nationally prominent physician who is also a devout Christian tells me he discourages his children from following in his footsteps. Doctors now and in the near future will be dealing with issues related to sex, sexuality, and gender identity but also to abortion and euthanasia. "Patient autonomy" and nondiscrimination are the principles that trump all conscience considerations, and physicians are expected to fall in line.

"If they make compliance a matter of licensure, there will be nowhere to hide," said this physician. "And then what do you do if you're three hundred thousand dollars in debt from medical school, and have a family with three kids and a sick parent? Tough call, because there aren't too many parishes or church communities who would jump in and help."

In past eras, religious minorities found themselves locked out of certain professions. In medieval times, for example, anti-Semitic bigotry in Europe prevented Jews from participating in many trades and professions, shunting them off to do marginal work that Christians did not want to do. Jews entered banking, for example, because usury was considered sinful by medieval Christianity and was kept off-limits to Christians.

Similarly, orthodox Christians in the emerging era will need to adapt to an era of hostility. Blacklisting will be real. In Canada, the legal profession is trying to forbid law graduates of Trinity Western University, a private Christian liberal arts college, from practicing law—this, to punish the school for being insufficiently progressive on LGBT issues. Similarly, an LGBT activist group called Campus Pride has put more than one hundred Christian colleges on a "shame list" and called on business and industry not to hire their graduates. It is unwise to discount the influence of groups like this on corporate culture—and that, in turn, will have a devastating effect on Christian colleges.

"The challenges to Christian education—especially higher education—are about to be aggressive," one legal scholar said. "Degrees from unaccredited universities, or universities that can't place graduates or receive federal research dollars, are of very low value."

Does this mean that no Christian should go to medical school or law school or enroll in professional training to enter other fields? Not necessarily. It does mean, however, that Christians must not take for granted that within a given field, there will be no challenges to their faith so great that they will have to choose between their Christianity and their careers. Many Christians will be compelled to make their living in ways that do not compromise their religious consciences. This calls for prudence, boldness, vocational creativity, and social solidarity among believers.

Be Prudent

Not every challenge in the workplace is a hill worth dying on. Not every office is the Roman Colosseum.

David Hall, a federal employee in Illinois, put his job in danger by repeatedly refusing his employer's request to watch an LGBT diversity training video. Hall, a Christian, told his agency that signing a statement acknowledging that he had viewed the clip would be "an abomination."

Though Hall must ultimately obey his own conscience, it's hard to sympathize with someone willing to sacrifice his job over something so trivial. Signing a statement affirming one has seen a training video is not the same thing as signing a statement affirming homosexuality.

Christians must exercise wisdom in these cases. Life is full of compromises, and not every one turns a believer into Judas. Claiming religious persecution unnecessarily will not help the cause. Instead, it will provide the secular left with grounds for claiming that all concern for religious liberty is a sham.

"If possible, so far as it depends on you, be at peace with all men," instructed Saint Paul (Romans 12:18). Christians should not seek conflict and instead should submit to their workplace and legal authorities as much as possible. The lesson for believers today? Silence does not always mean acquiescence, and in some cases it may be a wiser and more loving approach. In the end, we may be required to lose our jobs and even, alas, more. But aggressive workplace challenges to our faith can sometimes be deflected or stalled by a saintly exercise in prudence. Silence can be a shield.

Christians should never deny their faith, but that doesn't mean they are obliged to be in-your-face about it either. "I do think one can be a Christian and avoid falling into traps, as long as we have the right to remain silent and exercise it prudently," says a law professor. A Catholic doctor advises Christian physicians not to go out of their way to provoke confrontation.

"If someone voices an opinion contrary to your beliefs, including a patient, but you're not actually being asked to violate your conscience, let it go," he says. "Build for the future. Develop alliances, garner goodwill, quietly educate, seek out offices, practices, and systems that you can work in without controversy."

Maintaining a Christian witness with your colleagues while avoiding religious conflict wherever possible can also be an act of love. "The more scared and paranoid we are, the harder it is to make connections and relationships with people who need Jesus," says one Christian who works in human resources at a Fortune 500 company. "If we're always on war footing, they're going to sense that."

This HR facilitator, who asked to remain anonymous, counsels Christians to lead with compassion and empathy, erring on the side of nonjudgment. He has developed friendships with LGBT colleagues, who know he's an orthodox Christian but who also understand that he doesn't wish to demonize them. This kind of friendship can give a believer valuable insights into the real-life struggles these colleagues face and let them know that they are loved by their Christian co-workers.

"What excites me about the Benedict Option is that we're maintaining a culture, so that when this social experiment in sexuality we have going on fails—and it will—these people are going to have to have someplace to go," he says. "We can't have people thinking that they shouldn't go talk to the Christians. There can't be any positive ending in that."

Be Bold

Of course, there's a time where prudence must end and boldness begin. In some situations, if Christians are courageous enough to speak up they may be able to gain time for religious liberty. "I am a sinner who is far from perfect, but I refused to be a closeted sinner," says Stephen Bainbridge, a UCLA law professor and Catholic. "I am going to go on having a picture of Saint Thomas More in my office. And I'm going to go on pushing back when people infringe on freedom of speech and religion, especially on campuses.

"And if my colleagues don't like that, all I can say is, 'Come and have a go if you think you're hard enough,'" Bainbridge continues. "After all, if I may be forgiven for quoting the great reformer, 'Here I stand; I can do no other.'"

What are some workplace issues on which a believer cannot compromise? On which "personally opposed, but" is no excuse? A Christian doctor must always and everywhere refuse to take innocent life; abortion and euthanasia are forbidden. Christian teachers in public and private schools must not acquiesce to teaching as normative the new gender ideology, as some school systems are beginning to mandate. Participating in the direct making and distribution of pornography is yet another. And any job, no matter how benign, that compels one to affirm (as distinct from withholding approval of) something un-Christian and untrue is not worth keeping, no matter what the cost.

Recognizing these challenges, Christians need to ask themselves some tough questions: *Am I called to work in this industry? If so, how do I live faithfully within it? If not, can I find a safer line of work?*

A young friend of mine, a brilliant medical student in her mid-twenties, was well on her way to becoming a research scientist. She was working on her medical degree and interning at one of the nation's top laboratories. She is also a believing Christian, but the kind of behavior she observed in the lab, as well as the research projects she expected to have to work on in the future, made her doubt her career prospects.

My friend had long wanted to be a medical scientist, but having been raised in a devoutly orthodox Christian home, and certain of her own faith convictions, she discerned that she could not in good conscience continue down this path. She changed tracks to study hospital administration instead.

"It just wasn't worth it to me," she told me at the time. "I didn't want to get far down that road, then be faced with a choice that could blow up my career or violate my conscience. And seeing how cutthroat scientists were in the lab, only to get ahead in their careers, made me afraid that if I stayed in that culture, I might become the kind of person who does the same thing and doesn't even notice a problem."

Be Entrepreneurial

Now is the time for Christians whose livelihoods may be endangered to start thinking and acting creatively in professional fields still open to us without risk of compromise. The goal is to create business and career opportunities for Christians who have been driven out of other industries and professions.

"Our churches need more entrepreneurs, and we need to teach our children how to think entrepreneurially about their futures," says Calee Lee, an Eastern Orthodox Christian in Irvine, California.

"The key to work life under the Benedict Option is no different than today: identify a need in your community, develop an excellent product or service that fills that need, and then 'work at it with your whole heart, as working for the Lord, not for men,'" Lee says, quoting Colossians. "We need to develop good business sense, not be afraid of profit, and understand that by building something valuable, whether it is a gasket or a gardening service, we are bringing a good thing to the world."

Lee started her digital children's book company, Xist Publishing, because she saw a need. Xist pairs authors with illustrators to produce the kinds of books Lee wanted her children to read. Today Xist has more than two hundred books in its online catalog and provides income to writers and visual artists—all working outside traditional publishing.

Though she did not start her company because of anti-Christian persecution or harassment in the workplace, Lee cites it as an example of how believers driven out of certain professions can take advantage of the Internet economy to support themselves in ways that are not morally compromising.

She points to the success of companies like LuLaRoe, a clothing manufacturer started in 2012 by DeAnne Stidham, a Mormon stay-at-home mom who saw a need for modest yet attractive fashions for women like her. By selling through a nationwide network of over twelve thousand consultants—usually stay-at-home moms—LuLaRoe turned itself into a niche powerhouse.

"I could decry big publishers for not putting out books I write or things I want for my children to read, or I could do it myself," Lee says. "You can be frustrated with the fashion industry, or you can *be* the fashion industry. That's the approach Christians are going to need to take when things get tough in the workplace. For example, teachers who don't want to teach in the public school system can start their own tutoring companies."

The times are going to be more difficult for orthodox Christians in the workplace, Lee acknowledges, but it's not the end of the world.

It means they have to become more commercially innovative and independent-minded.

Buy Christian, Even If It Costs More

They are also going to have to start building the Christian community's businesses through disciplined shopping—that is, by choosing to direct their patronage to Christian-owned enterprises.

Richard Starr has been a member of Grace Bible Chapel, a large Evangelical church in the northern corner of Maryland, for the past decade. The church publishes a directory of its members and their businesses, in case others in the congregation care to patronize them.

"When my water pump went out one year, and I didn't have the two thousand dollars handy to fix it, McDowell's Plumbing let me pay over two months. When I needed two new tires, I went to Steve Foster, who put on four, called me, and said 'Your girls drive this car, and I think you need them for safety. Pay me when you can,'" Starr says.

"And yeah, Foster's Auto costs a little more money than other shops, but in the long run it's worth it, not just economically, but to support a business that treats folks that way."

Nevertheless, says Starr, as a general rule, "We should commit ourselves to finding out about what good businesses are owned by our brothers and sisters in Christ, and then patronizing them." Everyday commerce conducted within the community builds social capital.

Build Christian Employment Networks

Christians also have to become far more intentional about hiring workers from within their own church community. Many churches already have informal internal networks that help members find jobs with employers that are within the community or are known to other members. For the Benedict Option to work, this approach is going to have to become more formal and sustained.

Andrew Pudewa, the homeschooling instructional guru who runs the successful Institute for Excellence in Writing (IEW), employs members of his traditionalist Catholic agrarian community in Oklahoma. Not only does IEW publish highly regarded educational material for homeschoolers nationwide, but the rapid, Internet-driven growth of IEW's publishing business provides a livelihood for a number of families in Pudewa's church circles.

Similarly, Reba Place Fellowship in suburban Chicago, a Mennonite intentional community active since the 1950s, has spun off several businesses that began as church ministries, including a bicycle shop and an Amish furniture store.

"I've patronized or known of these businesses and the real impact they provide for the community," says Chad Comello, who lives in a Reba-owned apartment. "They employ a lot of Reba's covenant members and other Reba-adjacent young people like me, for small jobs but also steady employment. Those jobs kept me afloat when unemployed and gave me some purpose during some aimless times."

Were Starr to lose his job, he is certain that he could count on the Grace Bible congregation for support until he could find another one, and that they would all help on the job search. That's the kind of Christians they are: believers who live in such close community that when one falls on hard times, the others take up the slack as much as they can.

In Italy, the Tipi Loschi created three business cooperatives to provide employment both for its members and for rehabilitated drug addicts and former prisoners. As enthusiastic supporters of Distributism, an economic model based on Catholic social teaching and favoring small cooperatives and family businesses, the Tipi Loschi hope to create more local co-ops as they grow.

Reba Place, the Tipi Loschi, and similar initiatives offer examples of how churches and other Christian associations can build economic enterprises to sustain their own communities—just as Benedictine monks have been doing for centuries. Today the changing cultural and legal climate means all Christian communities of any size must start thinking of these initiatives as central to their mission.

Beyond the local level, Communion and Liberation (CL), a global Catholic movement based in Italy, manages the Company of Works, a nationwide Italian network of small and medium-size business, charities, and nonprofit organizations. They are all run by CL members and dedicated to cooperation for the sake of living out Catholic principles in economic life. Leaders in orthodox Christian life in the United States should consider forming a similar association of businesses, for the sake of mutual support and collaboration.

Rediscover the Trades

For some Christians, the transition will be as radical as the one Brother Francis made: shifting from working with one's mind to working with one's hands. And it might be more spiritually profitable too.

Sam MacDonald is a Catholic who oversees the parochial school system in rural Elk County, Pennsylvania, two hours northeast of Pittsburgh. Though the county is not the industrial powerhouse it once was, there are still significant manufacturers there.

Elk County (population 31,479) is heavily Catholic and culturally conservative. MacDonald, a son of Elk County, was one of the good students encouraged by the culture to leave and make his way in the outside world. After earning a Yale degree in the mid-1990s and working as a journalist in Washington, D.C., he eventually returned with his wife and kids. Today he is an education innovator, working to introduce some of the county's Catholic schools to the classical model.

"I'm going to have a classical academy that builds die-setters. That's where we're headed," he says. "If you go back fifty years, the Catholic kids around here were all taught by the nuns. They were all die-setters who learned Latin and who could do trigonometry like nobody's business."

If you have a strong work ethic, can pass a drug test, and can be trusted to show up on time, Elk County has a job for you. Its local manufacturers know that within ten years, they will need ten thousand workers to replace the skilled laborers who are retiring. Too many of the current county residents who would normally fill those jobs are too dysfunctional to do them or have moved away. Rather than look at relocating the factories a decade from now, the Elk County industrialists are considering a campaign to draw good workers to the area.

"They want to hire and build up a workforce of citizen-workers," says MacDonald, "people who are not only going to be reliable employees, but who are also going to be good citizens, who go to church, and who get involved with the community."

MacDonald says there's already a good basis for a Catholic Benedict Option community there. There are plenty of churches, a great Catholic school system that's improving, and a culturally conservative ethos that's family-friendly. Plus, it's affordable: you can get a good house for around sixty thousand dollars, which is not much more than many skilled laborers make in a year.

The catch is that you have to work in a factory, though that's a much more appealing alternative these days than in decades past, when factory floors were grimy. And you have to live in a place MacDonald describes as "in the middle of nowhere."

It's a matter of priorities.

"If you're in a place in your life where you decide that you can't work for your company because you can't be an ally, Elk County might make sense," he says. "Nobody's going to ask a die-setter to be an ally. They don't care."

Tradition-minded Christians who have immersed themselves in the writings of Wendell Berry should understand that agrarianism is no panacea. "You can't make a living as a farmer, but you can make a living as a die-setter," says MacDonald. "Industrialism is the new agrarianism. It's not back to the land, but back to the trades."

The challenge for some Benedict Option Christians will be to find and relocate to the Elk Counties all over America—faraway places on the margins of the Empire. Funny thing is, the "margins of the Empire" could be as near as the boundaries of what is acceptable employment in one's social class. Faithful Christians who foresaw a professional career for themselves or their children will need to give the trades a second look. Better to be a plumber with a clean conscience than a corporate lawyer with a compromised one.

Prepare to Be Poorer and More Marginalized

In the end, it comes down to what believers are willing to suffer for the faith. Are we ready to have our social capital devalued and lose professional status, including the possibility of accumulating wealth? Are we prepared to relocate to places far from the wealth and power of the cities of the Empire, in search of a more religiously free way of life? It's going to come to that for more and more of us. The time of testing is at hand.

"A lot of Christians see no difference between being faithfully Christian and being professionally and socially ambitious," says a religious liberty activist. "That is ending."

True story: a couple in suburban Washington, D.C., approached their pastor asking him to help their college student daughter, who felt a calling to be an overseas missionary.

"That's wonderful!" said the pastor.

"Oh no, you misunderstand," said the parents. "We want you to help us talk her out of ruining her life."

Christians like that couple won't make it through what's to come. Christians with sacrificial hearts like their daughter's will. But it's going to cost them plenty.

A young Christian who dreams of being a lawyer or doctor might have to abandon that hope and enter a career in which she makes far less money than a lawyer or doctor would. An aspiring Christian academic might have to be happy with the smaller salary and lower prestige of teaching at a classical Christian high school.

A Christian family might be forced to sell or close a business rather than submit to state dictates. The Stormans family of Washington state faced this decision after the U.S. Supreme Court upheld a state law requiring its pharmacy to sell pills the family considers abortifacient. Depending on the ultimate outcome of her legal fight, florist Barronelle Stutzman, who declined for conscience reasons to arrange flowers for a gay wedding, faces the same choice.

When that price needs to be paid, Benedict Option Christians should be ready to support one another economically—through offering jobs, patronizing businesses, professional networking, and so forth. This will not be a cure-all; the conversion of the public square into a politicized zone will be too far-reaching for orthodox Christian networks to employ or otherwise financially support all their economic refugees. But we will be able to help some.

Given how much Americans have come to rely on middle-class comfort, freedom, and stability, Christians will be sorely tempted to say or do anything asked of us to hold on to what we have. That is the way of spiritual death. When the Roman proconsul told Polycarp he would burn him at the stake if he didn't worship the emperor, the elderly second-century bishop retorted that the proconsul threatened temporary fire, which was nothing compared with the fire of judgment that awaited the ungodly.

If Polycarp was willing to lose his life rather than deny his faith, how can we Christians today be unwilling to lose our jobs if put to the test? If Barronelle Stutzman is prepared to lose her business as the cost of Christian discipleship, how can we do anything less?

We will be able to choose courageously and correctly in the moment of trial only if we have prepared ourselves in every possible way.

We can start by thinking of our work as a calling, as a vocation in the older sense: a way of life given to us by God for His own glory and for the common good. There is no reason why we can't serve the community and our own desire for professional excellence as doctors, lawyers, teachers, or almost anything else—as long as we know in our hearts that we are the Lord's good servants first.

We have talked so far in this book about what it means to create the structures and take on the practices that train our hearts to be the Lord's good servants first, even to the point of sacrifice. This is what the Benedict Option is supposed to do: help us to order all parts of our lives around Him. None of these strategies will work, however, unless Christians think radically different about the two most powerful forces shaping and driving modern life: sex and technology.

CHAPTER 9

Eros and the New Christian Counterculture

The opportunity to work is a gift from God that, when rightly employed, serves life and draws us back to Him. However, if work—or family, community, school, politics, or any other good thing—becomes an end in itself, it turns into an idol. It will eventually become a prison, a desert, even a graveyard of the spirit. These things serve the truth and human flourishing only if they are icons through which the light of Christ shines forth, making them a means by which the kingdom of God flourishes.

So it is with sex, a divine gift that, if cherished properly, becomes a source of joy, abundance, and flourishing—of the couple and their community. When bound to God's purposes, sex unites a man and a woman physically and spiritually, and from that fertile union new life may come, creating a family.

But if we use sex in a disordered way, it can be one of the most destructive forces on earth. Look around you at the suffering of children brought up without fathers, the scourge of pornography destroying the imaginations of millions, the families broken by infidelity and abuse, and on and on.

For a Christian, there is only one right way to use the gift of sex: within marriage between one man and one woman. This is heresy to the modern world, and a hard saying upon which hearts, friendships, families, and even churches have been broken. There is no core teaching of the Christian faith that is less popular today, and perhaps none more important to obey.

It's easy to get why secular people don't understand the reasons for Christian sexual practices: many Christians today don't understand them either. For generations, the church has allowed the culture to catechize its youth without putting up much of a fight. The Benedictine life offers a better way.

Why should Christians pay attention to teachings on sexuality of monastics, who live in chastity? Don't they hate sex?

Of course they don't, any more than they hate good food because they often fast, hate words because they live in great silence, hate families because they don't marry, or hate material things because they live simply. We should listen to the monks on sexuality for the same reason we should listen to them on wealth and poverty: because their asceticism is a testimony to the goodness of those divine gifts.

Remember that all Christians are called to live with some degree of sexual abstinence. Benedictines commit themselves to a life of sexual purity as part of their radical discipleship. Their celibacy testifies to the sanctity of sex in the Christian cosmos as the property of the married state alone. And their example of bodily purity transforming the erotic instinct into spiritual passion demonstrates to laypersons that living within God-ordained bounds of sexuality, even in the most extreme circumstance, is not only possible but necessary to enjoy the fullest fruits of life in Christ. As Wendell Berry puts it, "The point about temperance, including sexual discipline, is not that it reduces pleasure, but that it safeguards abundance."[1]

The radical witness of Christian monks is a special grace to lay Christians in these times. There is no other area in which orthodox Christians will have to be as countercultural as in our sexual lives, and we are going to have to support each other in our unpopular stances. We have to understand the rich Christian view of sexuality, grasp how the Sexual Revolution undermines it, recognize our own culpability, and be prepared to fight to keep our children orthodox.

Sexual practices are so central to the Christian life that when believers cease to affirm orthodoxy on the matter, they often cease to be meaningfully Christian. It was the countercultural force of Christian sexuality that overturned the pagan world's dehumanizing practices. Christianity taught that the body is sacred and that the dignity possessed by all humans as made in the image of God required treating it as such.

This is why the modern repaganization called the Sexual Revolution can never be reconciled with orthodox Christianity. Alas, that revolution has toppled the church's authority in the broader culture and is now shaking the church itself to its foundations. Christians living the Benedict Option must commit themselves resolutely to resistance and to helping each other do the same.

Sex and the Incarnation

I once heard an Evangelical woman, in a group conversation about sexuality, blurt out, "Why do we have to get stuck on sex? Why can't we just get back to talking about the Gospel?"

Christianity is not a disembodied faith but an incarnational one. God came to us in the form of a man, Jesus Christ, and redeems us body and soul. The way we treat our bodies (and indeed all of Creation) says something about the way we regard the One Who gave it to us and Whose presence fills all things. That's the Gospel.

As the Benedictines teach, one of our tasks in life is to be a means by which God orders Creation, bringing it into harmony with His purposes. Sexuality is an inextricable part of that work.

Wendell Berry has written, "Sexual love is the heart of community life. Sexual love is the force that in our bodily life connects us most intimately to the Creation, to the fertility of the world, to farming and the care of animals. It brings us into the dance that holds the community together and joins it to its place."[2]

This is more important to the survival of Christianity than most of us understand. When people decide that historically normative Christianity is wrong about sex, they typically don't find a church that endorses their liberal views. They quit going to church altogether.

This raises critical questions: Is sex the linchpin of Christian cultural order? Is it really the case that to cast off Christian teaching on sex and sexuality is to remove the factor that gives—or gave—Christianity its power as a social force?

Though he might not have put it quite that way, Philip Rieff would probably have said yes. In *The Triumph of the Therapeutic*, he analyzes what he calls the "deconversion" of the West from Christianity. Nearly everyone recognizes that this process has been under way since the Enlightenment, but Rieff showed that it had reached a more advanced stage than most people—least of all Christians—recognized.

Rieff, writing in the 1960s, identified the Sexual Revolution—though he did not use that term—as a leading indicator of Christianity's demise. In classical Christian culture, he wrote, "the rejection of sexual individualism" was "very near the center of the symbolic that has not held." He meant that renouncing the sexual autonomy and sensuality of pagan culture and redirecting the erotic instinct was intrinsic to Christian culture. Without Christianity, the West was reverting to its former state.[3]

It is nearly impossible for contemporary Americans to comprehend why sex was a central concern of early Christianity. Sarah Ruden, the Yale-trained classics translator, explains the culture into which Christianity appeared in her 2010 book *Paul Among the People*. Ruden contends that it's profoundly ignorant to think of the Apostle Paul as a dour proto-Puritan descending upon happy-go-lucky pagan hippies, ordering them to stop having fun.

In fact, Paul's teachings on sexual purity and marriage were adopted as liberating in the pornographic, sexually exploitive Greco-

Roman culture of the time—exploitive especially of slaves and women, whose value to pagan males lay chiefly in their ability to produce children and provide sexual pleasure. Christianity, as articulated by Paul, worked a cultural revolution, restraining and channeling male eros, elevating the status of both women and of the human body, and infusing marriage—and marital sexuality—with love.

Christian marriage, Ruden writes, was "as different from anything before or since as the command to turn the other cheek." Chastity—the rightly ordered use of the gift of sexuality—was the greatest distinction setting Christians of the early church apart from the pagan world.[4]

The point is not that Christianity was only, or primarily, about redefining and revaluing sexuality, but that within a Christian anthropology sex takes on a new and different meaning, one that mandated a radical change of behavior and cultural norms. In Christianity, what a person does with their sexuality cannot be separated from what a person is. In a sense, moderns believe the same thing, but from a perspective entirely different from the early church's.

In speaking of how men and women of the early Christian era saw their bodies, historian Peter Brown says the body

> was embedded in a cosmic matrix in ways that made its perception of itself profoundly unlike our own. Ultimately, sex was not the expression of inner needs, lodged in the isolated body. Instead, it was seen as the pulsing, through the body, of the same energies as kept the stars alive. Whether this pulse of energy came from benevolent gods or from malevolent demons (as many radical Christians believed) sex could never be seen as a thing for the isolated human body alone.[5]

Early Christianity's sexual teaching does not only come from the words of Christ and the Apostle Paul; more broadly, it emerges from the Bible's anthropology. The human being bears the image of God, however tarnished by sin, and is the pinnacle of an order created and imbued with meaning by God.

In that order, man has a purpose. He is meant for something, to achieve certain ends. When Paul warned the Christians of Corinth that having sex with a prostitute meant that they were joining Jesus Christ to that prostitute, he was not speaking metaphorically. Because we belong to Christ as a unity of body, mind, and soul, how we use the body and the mind sexually is a very big deal.

Anything we do that falls short of perfect harmony with the will of God is sin. Sin is not merely rule breaking but failing to live in accord with the structure of reality itself.

The Christian who lives in reality will not join his body to another's outside the order God gives us. That means no sex outside the covenant through which a man and a woman seal their love exclusively through Christ. In orthodox Christian teaching, the two really do become "one flesh" in a way that transcends the symbolic.

If sex is made holy through the marriage covenant, then sex within marriage is an icon of Christ's relationship with His people, the church. It reveals the miraculous, life-giving power of spiritual communion, which occurs when a man and a woman—and only a man and a woman—give themselves to each other. That marriage could be unsexed is a total novelty in the Christian theological tradition.

"The significance of sexual difference has never before been contingent upon a creature's preferences, or upon whether or not God gave it episodically to a particular creature to have certain preferences," writes Catholic theologian Christopher Roberts. He goes on to say that for Christians, the meaning of sexuality has always depended on its relationship to the created order and to eschatology— the ultimate end of man. "As was particularly clear, perhaps for the first time in Luther, the fact of a sexually differentiated creation is reckoned to human beings as a piece of information from God about *who* and *what* it meant to be human," writes Roberts.[6]

Contrary to modern gender theory, the question is not *Are we men or women?* but *How are we to be male and female together?* The legitimacy of our sexual desire is limited by the givenness of nature. The facts of our biology are not incidental to our personhood. Marriage has to be sexually complementary because only the male-female pair mirrors the generativity of the divine order. "Male and female he made them," says Genesis, revealing that complementarity is written into the nature of reality.

Easy divorce stretches the sacred bond of matrimony to the breaking point, but it does not deny complementarity. Gay marriage does. Similarly, transgenderism doesn't merely bend but breaks the biological and metaphysical reality of male and female. Everything in this debate (and many others between traditional Christianity and modernity) turns on how we answer the question: Is the natural world and its limits a given, or are we free to do with it whatever we desire?

To be sure, there never was a golden age in which Christians all lived up to their sexual ideals. The church has been dealing with sexual immorality in its own ranks since the beginning—and let's be honest, some of the measures it has taken to combat it have been cruel and unjust.

The point, however, is that to the premodern Christian imagination, sex was filled with cosmic meaning in a way it no longer is. Paul admonished the Corinthians to "flee sexual immorality" because the body was a "temple of the Holy Spirit" and warned them that "you are not your own." He was telling them that their bodies are sacred vessels that belonged to God, who, in Christ, "all things hold together." Sexual autonomy, seemingly the most prized possession of the modern person, is not only morally wrong but a metaphysical falsehood.

History's Most Revolutionary Revolution

But our perception of that truth diminished long ago. Now we are on the far side of a Sexual Revolution that has been nothing short of catastrophic for Christianity. It struck near the core of biblical teaching on sex and the human person and has demolished the fundamental Christian conception of society, of families, and of the nature of human beings. There can be no peace between Christianity and the Sexual Revolution, because they are radically opposed. As the Sexual Revolution advances, Christianity must retreat—and it has, faster than most people would have thought possible.

In 1996, the Gallup polling organization conducted its first survey asking Americans what they thought of same-sex marriage. A whopping 68 percent opposed it. In 2015, just before the U.S. Supreme Court's *Obergefell* decision proclaiming a constitutional right to gay marriage, Gallup's poll revealed that 60 percent of Americans now support same-sex marriage.[7] This number will rise steadily as older generations die and make way for younger generations, who overwhelmingly favor LGBT rights.

Research shows that Millennials, both secular and religious, favor gay rights by enormous majorities. Those who have disaffiliated from Christianity say that the faith's negative attitudes toward homosexuality were a major factor. Strong majorities of Millennials who identify as Christian believe the church must change its views.

That being the case, you would think that churches that have liberalized their teachings on homosexuality, like Mainline Protestant denominations, or downplayed those teachings, like progressive Catholic parishes, would be booming. They're not. If anything, they are cratering faster than the more orthodox.

Future historians will wonder how the sexual desires of only three to four percent of the population became the fulcrum on which an entire worldview was dislodged and overturned. A partial answer is that the media are to blame. Back in 1993, a cover story in the *Nation* identified the gay rights cause as the summit and keystone of the culture war:

> All the crosscurrents of present-day liberation struggles are subsumed in the gay struggle. The gay moment is in some ways similar to the moment that other communities have ex-

perienced in the nation's past, but it is also something more, because sexual identity is in crisis throughout the population, and gay people—at once the most conspicuous subjects and objects of the crisis—have been forced to invent a complete cosmology to grasp it. No one says the changes will come easily. But it's just possible that a small and despised sexual minority will change America forever.[8]

They were right. Tying the gay rights cause to the civil rights movement was a strategic masterstroke. Though homosexuality and race are two very different phenomena, the media took the equivalence for granted and rarely if ever gave opposing voices a chance to be heard.

Though the unrelenting media campaign on behalf of same-sex marriage was critically important to its success, it wasn't the most important thing. Americans accepted gay marriage so quickly because it resonated with what they had already come to believe about the meaning of heterosexual sex and marriage.

We have gay marriage because the straight majority came to see sexuality as something primarily for personal pleasure and self-expression and only secondarily for procreation. We have gay marriage because the straight majority, in turn, came to see marriage in the same way—and two generations of Americans have grown up with these nominalist values on sex and marriage as normative.

To be modern, as we have seen, is to believe in one's individual desires as the locus of authority and self-definition. As philosopher Charles Taylor writes, "The entire ethical stance of moderns supposes and follows on from the death of God (and of course, of the meaningful cosmos)."[9]

Gay marriage and gender ideology signify the final triumph of the Sexual Revolution and the dethroning of Christianity because they deny Christian anthropology at its core and shatter the authority of the Bible. Rightly ordered sexuality is not at the core of Christianity, but as Rieff saw, it's so near to the center that to lose the Bible's clear teaching on this matter is to risk losing the fundamental integrity of the faith. This is why Christians who begin by rejecting sexual orthodoxy end either by rejecting Christianity themselves or by laying the groundwork for their children to do so.

"The death of a culture begins when its normative institutions fail to communicate ideals in ways that remain inwardly compelling," Rieff writes. By that standard, Christianity in America is in mortal danger.

If a remnant wants to survive, it must resist the Sexual Revolution. But how?

Don't Compromise to Keep the Young

Watering down or burying biblical truth on sexuality for the sake of keeping Millennials won't work. Mainline Protestant churches have tried this strategy, and they remain in demographic collapse. True, orthodox Christian churches are also struggling, but throwing biblical teaching overboard in an attempt to keep the boat afloat on rough seas is not the answer.

Even making the traditional teaching on sexual integrity an optional matter—either explicitly or implicitly, by not talking about it, or by turning a blind eye—is a mistake. It is impossible to bracket out Christianity's clear instruction on how to live a life of sexual integrity and separating it from the rest of the Christian life. It's hypocritical.

"Indifference toward sexual issues is going to mean the end of Christian orthodoxy," says an Evangelical friend, commenting on the attitude many Christians, even conservative ones, have.

True, a person can be completely chaste and still go to hell if his heart is cold. But that is not an argument for defying the Bible's clear teaching. Whether we like it or not, sex is at the center of contemporary culture, and it is tearing the church apart. You cannot avoid the fight, either in your own church or in your own family. To avoid taking sides is to take a side—and not that of the Bible.

Besides, watering down the truth for the sake of preserving or expanding the congregation is to make an idol of community.

Affirm the Goodness of Sexuality

Andrew T. Walker, a Southern Baptist lay leader of the Millennial generation, says he grew up in a good church but never heard a single sermon about Christian anthropology (i.e., what is man?) or biblical sexuality beyond conservative platitudes.

"I don't ever recall having a lesson about why my body is a good thing. No one ever explained to me why complementarity is important," Walker tells me. "We've been so driven by a culture of entertainment, but if you told most congregations that for the next few weeks, we're going to have a sermon series about biblical anthropology, the congregation wouldn't greet the idea enthusiastically," he continues. "This is wrong. That has to change if we're going to survive and pass down the faith.

"Tragically, I fear that the average Christian in America is no different than the average American—we just want to be told what to do and how to feel. This doesn't mean our churches need to be boring, but we'll need to find creative ways to go deep on important issues."

Walker is not alone in his experience. I have been attending church regularly for over twenty years, in both Catholic and Orthodox parishes around the country. I have yet to hear a sermon explaining in any depth what Christianity teaches about the human person and about the rightly ordered use of sex. For that matter, I recall only one sermon in all those years in which a priest endorsed the orthodox Christian view of sex.

Far too many pastors are scared to talk about sex. They need to get over it. It is hard to live chastely in this eroticized culture; pastors shouldn't make it harder by denying their people the teaching and support they need to be faithful. Silence from the pulpit, and from the church's ministers and teachers, conveys the message that sex and sexuality aren't important and that the church has nothing to offer on the matter.

This is ludicrous, even cruel. The church's teaching on the meaning of sex was liberating to me when I began to practice the faith as an adult. I had lived by the world's standards and had made a mess of my life and hurt others. Finally, backed into the corner by my own disordered desires, I surrendered to Christ.

To a twenty-five-year-old American man living in a big city, in a secular, hedonistic milieu, choosing chastity out of fidelity to Jesus is taking on a heavy cross. I hated it, but I wanted Christ more than I wanted to follow my own will. It was five years before I would marry at the end of an ascetic trek across a dry desert—a journey that I did not know would end one day in marriage.

Now, though, it is clear to me that sexual renunciation in obedience to biblical standards was precisely what I needed to purify my own heart and to prepare myself for marriage. As hard as it was to practice chastity, it was harder than it had to be because I never had the backing of the parish churches of which I was a part.

What would have helped? For one, the church needed to raise its own flag every now and then. That is, it would have been a source of strength to me in my struggle to be obedient had the pastor signaled to the congregation that sexual discipline is an important part of the Christian life.

For another, parish churches could have hosted classes for adult singles to explore in depth Christian teaching about sex and strategies for living out its teaching. It might also have turned into a small community of believers who could rely on each other for mutual support.

But I was not without fault myself. There is no rule that says a layperson cannot start such a group himself within the parish. I waited on somebody else to do it. My own passivity as a twentysomething Christian was a fault I now regret.

That's not the only way my passivity served me poorly. I did not try very hard to cultivate friendships with other orthodox Christians committed to walking the walk. In those days, I didn't fully appreciate how difficult it is to stay on the path of fidelity to Christian sexual morality when you are navigating it alone. I should have taken better care of myself.

For all those faults, I walked the line because I knew from experience that I did not want to go back to that particular Egypt. And as an adult convert, I had educated myself about what Christ expects from His followers regarding sexual behavior and how sex is woven into the whole tapestry of Christian teaching.

Being self-taught on Catholic sexual ethics made me unusual among most of the Catholics of my generation whom I knew. They had never had the fullness of the church's teaching on love and sexuality presented to them, if any sexual teaching was presented to them at all. It seemed to me that they had been formed—or rather, malformed—by priests and other adult Catholics who were ashamed of the church's teaching on sexuality and who downplayed it, perhaps to avoid confronting the young with truths they would find difficult. Over the years, I've come to see that a feel-good, self-centered approach to catechesis serves less as a gateway to mature Christianity than as a vaccination against it.

"When the culture places more emphasis on the needs of the self and less on social rules, more relaxed attitudes toward sexuality are the almost inevitable result," researcher Jean Twenge told the *Los Angeles Times*.[10]

There is an enormous disparity between Evangelical youth and Catholic youth on sexual matters. Surveys find that while Millennials as a group are much more liberal about sexual matters, Evangelicals are much more likely than Catholics to profess traditional Christian teachings. Indeed, Catholics are doing such a poor job forming their youth that Catholic Millennials are more likely to be sexual liberals than average Americans are.

Yet there is a growing movement within many churches to downplay or dismiss entirely the Bible's teachings on sexuality and instead emphasize fighting poverty, racism, and other forms of social injustice. This is a false choice. Social justice activism is laudable, but it does not earn you indulgences for sexual sin. Youth pastors especially need to make this clear.

Moralism Is Not Enough

As we have seen, many Americans believe that being a Christian is chiefly about treating God as a cosmic therapist and being happy with oneself and nice to others. That's a pseudo-Christianity. That said, a Christianity that reduces life in Christ to a moral and ethical code may be in one respect better than nothing—but it is not the Christian faith.

If the real challenge of the Sexual Revolution is cosmological, then a church that tries to meet it with middle-class moralism is bringing knives to a gunfight. The dry, brittle commands of moralism turn to ash in the face of the erotic drama revealed in the Bible.

Genesis tells us that from the very beginning, masculinity, femininity, and sex are created by God and bound to Creation. Man and woman become "one flesh," though remaining fully themselves, because this is how God regards the nature of the bond between Himself and each person.

This was something radically new in the world. As Pope Benedict XVI has written, "God's way of loving becomes the measure of human love. This close connection between eros and marriage in the Bible has practically no equivalent in extra-biblical literature."[11]

Throughout the Old Testament, its authors describe God's covenantal relationship with Israel in terms of marriage and infidelity. God loves Israel personally and through their covenant will bring forth the birth of the Messiah, who will redeem fallen Creation. Only in fidelity to the Lord, receiving His love and returning it to Him, can Israel know herself.

Jesus, born of a Virgin, fulfilled the law in His life, then emptied Himself out on the Cross in an act of perfect love for the salvation of all. Though the New Testament contains plenty of strong admonitions against sexual immorality, chastity for its own sake is never a goal. Rather, as we have seen, it is the means through which man's erotic instinct is channeled and redirected in continuing relationship with God.

Unbridled erotic passion creates chaos and disintegration. Eros that submits to Christ bears fruit in the gift of children, stable families, and communities. The contemporary Orthodox theologian Olivier Clément says that the spiritual secret of Christianity is that the love of God comes through the human body and flows throughout the universe to which it is joined. In Christianity, the individual's desire (eros) is purified and transformed into agape—unconditional, selfless love.

Dante's *Divine Comedy*, the greatest literary creation of the Middle Ages, is a staggeringly powerful portrait of the manifold dimensions of love: the pilgrim Dante's passion for Beatrice, and the glory transfiguring Creation when a man allows his desire for God to condition all his other loves. This is love as a glorious cosmic drama, transcending time and space, in which each individual joins with the eternal dance, sharing in "the love that moves the Sun and all the other stars."

To reduce Christian teaching about sex and sexuality to bare, boring, thou-shalt-not moralism is a travesty and a failure of imagination. While one may credit the courage of certain conservative pastors who don't shirk their duty to tell the truth about sex, those who jackhammer away at sexual immorality as if it were the only serious sin, or were somehow disconnected from a host of other sins of passion, distort the Gospel and undermine its credibility. This lamentable reductionism constitutes a failure to draw on the inexhaustible well of resources within the Christian theological and artistic tradition. In the end, it comes down to a matter of Christians having lost our own grand story about eros, cosmos, and theosis, the Greek word for "union with God," the ultimate end of the Christian pilgrimage.

"All of life is now being ordered by narratives and images that don't reflect the old boundaries," says sociologist Christian Smith. "Churches have something to say about this. They should go back again and again to the drinking well of the Gospel and offer a true alternative transcendent story. If they can't do that, if they remain saddled with moralism, then they better hang it up now."

If Christianity is a true story, then the story the world tells about sexual freedom is a grand deception. It's fake. As novelist Walker Percy advised, we have to attack the fake in the name of the real. Christians are going to have to become better tellers of our own story. Young people are not going to be argued into Christian chastity or brow-beaten by moralistic maxims. Beauty and goodness, embodied in great art and fiction, and in the lives of ordinary Christians, married and single, is the only thing that stands a chance.

Parents Must Be Primary Sex Educators

If we don't do it, the culture will do it for us. The pornification of the public square continues apace. To paraphrase the late, great media scholar Neil Postman, when children can access computers or smart-phones and watch hardcore pornography, childhood is over.

Mothers and fathers have to be far more aggressive in governing their kids' access to media and technology. But there is no way to keep them in a permanent bubble. When public schools in places like Wash-ington state are teaching gender ideology in kindergarten, parents cannot take anything for granted. We have to start talking about sex and sexuality with our children, early and often.

Kids today grow up in a culture that seeks to obliterate the natural family: one man and one woman, bound exclusively to each other, and the children they have together. It is now considered bigoted to say that the natural family is superior to any other arrangement. In schools today, and certainly in popular culture, kids are even told that gender is not a fixed category connected to biological sex. Besides, the culture of hooking up, and of divorce and unwed childbearing, is so normative today that you can't blame young people for their confusion. The new normal is that there is no normal.

"I worry all the time about my students, whether or not they will ever be able to sustain a family," a professor at a conservative Evangelical college told me. "Most of them have never seen what a traditional family looks like."

Along these lines, it's imperative that we raise our kids to know that children are a blessing without qualification and that fertility is not a disease.

It's hard to know how to start those conversations and where to take them. A terrific resource for families is *The Humanum Series*, six short movies, all available for free on YouTube, presenting the traditional Christian vision of sex, gender, marriage, and family.

Produced by the Vatican and featuring the participation of Christians and others from around the world, the *Humanum* videos explore the cosmic dimension of God's plan for the family, in profound but easy-to-understand words and images. They explore the meaning of marriage and sexuality, the role of the family, masculinity and femininity, how marriage helps people endure hardship, marriage and society, and more. None of the six *Humanum* videos lasts more than twenty minutes. They are not the least bit preachy and in fact are surprising in their sophistication and how they convey the joy of the traditional vision of sex, marriage, and family.

In my family, we watched them with our three children, ages sixteen, twelve, and nine. All the clips were appropriate for family viewing and served as a launch pad for discussions of their themes. There are few things more difficult for Christian parents than forming their children's moral imaginations about sex, not least because it is difficult to know how to articulate biblical truth in a winsome and appealing way. The *Humanum* films are a true gift to families—and to churches.

The Humanum Series reinforces with admirable skill the natural family ecology. Kids today grow up in a culture that seeks to obliterate the natural family: one man and one woman, bound exclusively to each other, and the children they have together. Christian parents must never assume that their children understand that the natural family is God's plan for humanity. We have to make this explicit in our teaching. We have to make it implicit too by modeling mutual respect, sacrifice, affection, and all the good things that come from a spiritually fruitful marriage.

Love and Support Unmarried People in the Community

Young Americans are waiting longer to marry, making it more likely that your church community has single Christians in it. As I said earlier, church can be a lonely place for singles. I didn't marry until I was nearly thirty and felt invisible in the parishes I attended as a single man.

It is understandable that churches hold marriage and family up as ideal forms of the Christian life, but doing so often devalues the lives and witness of those who do not receive the call to marriage. Married Christians tend to pity the unmarried among them, if they think of them at all. And it's all too easy for Christian singles, discouraged by the difficulty of their challenges, to slip into self-pity and bitterness.

A monastic life well lived exemplifies the spiritual fruits that can come from the unmarried state ordered to Christ.

"Everyone is searching for love. It's the most basic human desire. Whether one seeks that love in carnal pleasures, in material possessions, or God, everyone is seeking," says Brother Evagrius of Norcia. "The monastic life, in a nutshell, is giving up every other pleasure for the love of God. Everything in the monastic life is built around helping you to achieve that."

A congregation cannot be a monastery, but there is no reason why it should not reach out to hold its single members closer, as members of the church family. As Brother Augustine told me, there are days when he feels exhausted by the rigors of the monastic life—and on those days, he relies on the charity of his brother monks to carry him. Why can't we serve our unmarried community members in a similar way?

Moreover, if a parish community has the resources, it should consider establishing single-sex group houses for its unmarried members to live in prayerful fellowship as what you might call lay monastics. It is hard to live chastely in a culture as eroticized as ours, especially when there is so little respect for chastity. One expects this from the world, but the church must be different.

All unmarried Christians are called to live celibately, but at least heterosexuals have the possibility of marriage. Gay Christians do not, which makes their struggle even more intense.

Worse, too many gay Christians face rejection from the very people they should be able to count on: the church. The angry vehemence with which many gay activists condemn Christianity is rooted in large part in the cultural memory of rejection and hatred by the church. Christians need to own up to our past in this regard and to repent of it.

But that does not mean—and it cannot mean—that we should abandon clear, binding biblical teaching on homosexuality. Gay Christians, like all unmarried Christians, are called to a life of chastity. This is a heavy cross to bear, but one that cannot in obedience be refused.

Our gay brothers and sisters in Christ should not have to carry it alone. In recent years, several same-sex-attracted Christians living in fidelity to orthodox teaching have found their voice in the Spiritual Friendship movement. It is based on the writings of Saint Aelred of Rievaulx, a twelfth-century abbot.

"Aelred helped me to see that obedience to Christ offered more to me than just the denial of sex and romance," writes Ron Belgau, one of the movement's founders. "Christ-centered chaste friendships offered a positive and fulfilling—albeit at times challenging—path to holiness."[12]

That's an important point, for gay and single Christians alike. Too often chastity is presented only as saying no to sex. Though we can't deny the real and painful sacrifice the Christian ethic requires of unmarried believers, we should not neglect to teach and explore the good that may come from surrendering one's sexuality. Though monasticism had not yet developed when the New Testament was written, Jesus said that some are called by God to be chaste singles ("eunuchs for the kingdom of heaven"). This is a steep path to holiness, an especially treacherous one in our thoroughly eroticized culture, but a path to holiness it is for some. We have that on Christ's authority.

It is hard for single Christians to stay on that path, but again at least straight Christians have the prospect of marriage to comfort them. If we expect gay Christians to embrace celibacy, then in our churches, families, and individual lives we must give them love, respect, and friendship.

Moreover, gay Christians who reject traditional teaching must still be treated with love, because they too are image-bearers of Christ. Love wins, though not in the way the LGBT movement says. But it still wins. Christians don't dare forget it.

Fight Pornography with Everything You've Got

I once asked a Catholic priest friend to tell me the most common problem he deals with in the confessional. "Pornography," he said. "Nothing else is even close."

I've heard the same thing for years from other priests and pastors. The problem is overwhelming—and the church is no refuge. In 2014, the Barna Group published research showing that Christians are by and large no different from the rest of the population when it comes to using porn.[13]

Though porn use is up across demographic groups—in part because the Internet makes it far more accessible—researchers see a tectonic shift when it comes to young adults. Among adults aged eighteen to twenty-four, 96 percent of those surveyed by Barna do not think porn is negative. Nine out of ten teenagers agree. And though porn use is overwhelmingly a male problem, nearly one in five young adult women admit to watching it.

The moral and spiritual damage from porn use should be obvious. Porn dehumanizes, and it destroys the image of God in the faces of its performers. In turn, it trains its users to see others as depersonalized objects for sexual pleasure. It destroys the connection between sex and love. This is not news.

Recently, though, neuroscientists have discovered that pornography use has potentially devastating effects on the brain. Watching porn floods the brain's pleasure centers with dopamine. The more one uses porn, the more one has to use it, and more extreme versions of it, to get the same dopamine hit. Pornography literally rewires the brain, making it very difficult for longtime users to be aroused by actual human beings.

In 2015, a *Time* magazine cover story on the ubiquity of porn highlighted the experiences of young adult men who came of age after the smartphone was introduced in 2007 and who therefore had around-the-clock portable access to hardcore video porn. Said writer Belinda Luscombe:

> Their generation has consumed explicit content in quantities and varieties never before possible, on devices designed to deliver content swiftly and privately, all at an age when their brains were more plastic—more prone to permanent change—than in later life. These young men feel like unwitting guinea pigs in a largely unmonitored decade-long experiment in sexual conditioning.[14]

Men in the prime of their youth, who ought to have been virile, now report impotence and an inability to form normal relationships with women. Thus does the possibility for bringing children into the world, and creating families, die.

Christians, especially Christian parents, don't dare take this lightly. In addition to having the porn talk with their children early, parents should firmly resolve not to give kids smartphones with access to the Internet—or unmonitored Internet access, period. Parents have to watch the peer groups of their children closely and take strong, decisive action if porn enters the picture. If you discover that porn is part of your son's social life, you can't say, "Everybody does it." You must act decisively.

Cutting off potential access to pornography is not a foolproof solution, though. We have to raise our children to understand the connection between sex and love in the whole economy of Creation. This is not the kind of thing you can do with one or two sit-down sessions with your kids. It requires years of patient work, and it needs the active support of the church.

A cosmological response to the Sexual Revolution requires that we educate ourselves (and our children) in sexuality's social dimension. Not only is sex connected to the divine order, but it also binds individuals, families, and the community to each other.

"Sex, like any other necessary, precious, and volatile power that is commonly held, is everybody's business," says Wendell Berry.[15]

As with so many other things in contemporary society, we modern Americans see sex as wholly a private matter, one of individual rights. But this is false. The rules, rituals, and traditions of a community pertaining to sexuality, says Berry, intend "to preserve its energy, its beauty, and its pleasure; to preserve and clarify its power to join not just husband and wife to one another but parents to children, families to the community, the community to nature; to ensure, so far as possible, that the inheritors of sexuality, as they come of age, will be worthy of it."

Berry goes on to say that "if the community cannot protect this giving, it can protect nothing—and our time is proving it so."

Indeed. Our job as Benedict Option Christians is to form communities of healthy chastity and fidelity that can protect the gift and pass it on to the next generations. To do so, we have to master one of the most culturally transformative technologies in human history: the Internet.

CHAPTER 10

Man and the Machine

One warm spring weekend in 2016, I went to a Benedict Option conference at Clear Creek Abbey, a Benedictine monastery in deep rural Oklahoma. Once I arrived, I was unsettled to learn that we were so far from civilization, as it were, that cell phone reception was impossible. Wi-Fi was possible only if you went into a building on the conference site and stood in a certain place, or placed yourself in a single corner of the abbey's guest quarters, and hoped for the best. For that weekend, I was largely cut off from the outside world.

I was startled by how anxious this made me. Twenty years earlier I wouldn't have noticed. Not many Americans would have. In 2013, for the first time ever, over 90 percent of us had mobile phones, and by 2015, a stunning 64 percent of those were smartphones.[1] The Pew Research Center has called the cell phone "the most quickly adopted consumer technology in the history of the world."[2] Having a mobile connection has become so normal that we don't even notice it . . . until we don't have one.

Over the course of the weekend, every time there was the slightest lull in conversation, my hand reached into my pocket reflexively to pull out my iPhone and check e-mail, Twitter, Facebook, and the news. But it was not there. I was unplugged and disconnected, having had a digital fast inadvertently imposed on me by this monastic-themed conference. This unplanned exercise in asceticism was revealing—and I did not like what I saw.

As I sat listening to speeches, the moment my attention flagged even in the slightest, I went for my iPhone. The speakers were quite good, but I still found it difficult to give them my full attention. Am I always like this? Yes, alas, that's me. It had become so second nature that my addiction was invisible to me, in part because nearly everybody else I know does the same thing.

This is an enormous problem for all of us today but especially for Christians. That unanticipated technological weekend forced me to think hard about how the smartphone and the computer dominate my life—and what a massive challenge technology is to authentic Christian living in the twenty-first century.

There's the simple matter of individuals not being able to manage their smartphone use, using online access to watch pornography, or flopping onto a basement couch and playing video games all day instead of getting on with the business of life. But it's deeper than that. Online technology, in its various forms, is a phenomenon that by its very nature fragments and scatters our attention like nothing else, radically compromising our ability to make sense of the world, physiologically rewiring our brains and rendering us increasingly helpless against our impulses.

We think our many technologies give us more control over our destinies. In fact, they have come to control us. And this opens the door to the more fundamental point about technology: it is an ideology that conditions how we humans understand reality.

To use technology is to participate in a cultural liturgy that, if we aren't mindful, trains us to accept the core truth claim of modernity: that the only meaning there is in the world is what we choose to assign it in our endless quest to master nature. As we saw in an earlier chapter, the early modern period birthed the idea that science should be used to conquer nature "for the relief of man's estate," in Francis Bacon's words. And it was René Descartes who said that we could become "masters and possessors of nature" and whose philosophy taught Western man to think of nature (including the human body) as a kind of machine.

If we can use technology any way we like as long as the outcome results in our own happiness, then all reality is "virtual reality," open to construal in any way we like. There are no natural limits, only those that we do not yet have the technological capability to overcome. This point of view is ubiquitous in modernity but profoundly antithetical to orthodox Christianity.

Benedict Option families and communities who remain apathetic toward technology inadvertently undermine nearly everything they are trying to achieve. Technology itself is a kind of liturgy that teaches us to frame our experiences in the world in certain ways and that, if we aren't careful, profoundly distorts our relationship to God, to other people, and to the material world—and even our self-understanding.

Technology Is Not Morally Neutral

Most people assume that technology is nothing more than applied science, the moral meaning of which depends on what its user does with it. This is naïve. In a powerful address to a 2015 Catholic gathering in Philadelphia, philosopher of science Michael Hanby explained that "before technology becomes an instrument, it is fundamentally a way of regarding the world that contains within itself an understanding of being, nature, and truth."[3]

What is Hanby getting at? For thousands of years humans have used tools to affect their environment. What gave birth to technology as a comprehensive worldview was the sense, beginning with nominalism and emerging in the early modern era, that nature had no intrinsic meaning. It's just stuff. To Technological Man, "truth" is what works to extend his dominion over nature and make that stuff into things he finds useful or pleasurable, thereby fulfilling his sense of what it means to exist. To regard the world technologically, then, is to see it as material over which to extend one's dominion, limited only by one's imagination.

In the classical Christian understanding, true freedom for humankind, according to its nature, is to be found in loving submission to God. Anything that is not of God is slavery. In his 1993 book *Technopoly*, Neil Postman explained that premodern cultures allowed their metaphysical and theological convictions to direct how they used their tools. It is only in modern times, with the rise of technology, that our tools have turned the tables on us and gained the power to direct our metaphysical and theological convictions.

That's because Technological Man understands freedom as liberation from anything that is not freely chosen by the autonomous individual. This likely explains why Americans are so naïvely optimistic about technology. As philosopher Matthew Crawford has observed, the seeds of the technological worldview are embedded in the Enlightenment ideas upon which America was founded.

In one sense, technology truly is neutral. After all, the same bulldozer used to build a hospital can be used to build a concentration camp. More deeply, though, technology as a worldview trains us to privilege what is new and innovative over what is old and familiar and to valorize the future uncritically. It destroys tradition because it refuses any limits on its creativity. Technological Man says, "If we can do it, we must be free to do it." To the technological mind, questions of why we should, or should not, accept particular technological developments are hard to comprehend.

In a provocative but insightful formulation, Hanby says that the Sexual Revolution is what happens when we apply the ideology of technology to the human body. We have made biology subject to human will. Contraceptive technology sets women (and their male sexual partners) free to enjoy sex without fear of pregnancy. Reproductive technology extends the mastery of procreation by liberating conception from the body entirely.

Consider in vitro fertilization (IVF), a breakthrough technique allowing infertile couples to conceive. The 1978 birth of Louise Brown, the first "test tube baby," caused great controversy at the time, especially among religious leaders, many of whom denounced it as unnatural and warned that it would lead to the commodification of childbearing by separating conception from sexual union. But most Americans did not agree. A Gallup poll at the time found that 60 percent of the public approved of IVF.[4]

By 2010, when Robert G. Edwards, the British scientist who helped pave the way for IVF, won the Nobel Prize in medicine for his efforts, IVF was widely accepted. A 2013 Pew survey found that only 12 percent of Americans see IVF as morally wrong. The numbers are roughly the same with American Christians.[5]

As to the commodification of childbearing, consider the childless Tennessee couple who had donor eggs fertilized with the husband's sperm, creating ten embryos. Four babies later the couple decided they didn't want the remaining embryos and took to Facebook to offer them to a good home.

"We have six good-quality frozen six-day-old embryos to donate to an amazing family who wants a large family," the wife posted, according to the *New York Times*. "We prefer someone who has been married several years in a steady loving relationship and strong Christian background, and who does not already have kids, but wants a boat load."[6]

According to orthodox Christian teaching, these are six human persons. The embryo donation community has developed a cute euphemism for these unborn children: "frozen snowflakes."

Meanwhile British government statistics made public in 2012 revealed that 3.5 million embryos were created in UK laboratories since 1991, when record-keeping began.[7] Ninety-three percent never resulted in a pregnancy, and about half were thrown away without even trying. The United States has no reliable records for the sake of comparison, but with a population five times larger than Britain's, a parallel number would mean 17.5 million unborn human beings were brought into existence in a laboratory, with 16.2 million dying, and 8.8 million thrown into the trash can without an attempt at implantation.

Imagine every man, woman, and child in New York City, or the population of Houston times four, and you will understand the immensity of the death inside fertility clinics. That is, if you believe that life begins at conception, as 52 percent of Americans in a 2015 YouGov poll affirm.[8]

Clearly there are millions of Christians not putting two and two together. Many conservative Christians strongly oppose abortion and back laws restricting it. There is no movement to ban or restrict IVF, even though from the life-begins-at-conception point of view, it exterminates millions of unborn lives. What enables this hypocrisy? The technocratic mentality.

The argument goes like this: babies are good things, so anything technology does to help people have babies is therefore good. Love, as they say, wins. The technocrat decides what he or she wants and, once it is available via technology, rationalizes accepting it. Concealing what technology takes away from us is a feature of the technocratic worldview. We come to think of technological advances as inevitable because they are irresistible. Just as "truth" for the technocrat is what is useful and effective, what is "good" for him is what is possible and desirable.

Technological Man regards as progress anything that expands his choices and gives him more power over nature. Americans admire the "self-made man" because he has liberated himself from dependence on others by his own efforts and is his own creation. For Technological Man, choice matters more than what is chosen. He is not much concerned with what he should desire; rather, he is preoccupied with how he can acquire or accomplish what he desires. The seed that was planted in the fourteenth century with the triumph of nominalism reaches its full ripeness in Technological Man.

The Internet as the Floodgate of Liquid Modernity

The most radical, disruptive, and transformative technology ever created is the Internet. It is the ultimate facilitator of liquid modernity because it conditions the way we experience life ("as a swiftly moving stream of particles," says writer Nicholas Carr) and frames all our experiences. The Internet rapidly accelerates the political, social, and cultural fragmentation process that has been under way since the mid-twentieth century and profoundly compromises our ability to pay attention.

This is a bigger deal than it sounds like. As we learned in Chapter 5, media theorist Marshall McLuhan famously said, "The medium is the message," a cryptic statement that has confounded many. What he meant is that the changes a new medium cause in a culture are often more important than any information carried through that medium. Why? Because the medium alters the way we experience the world and interpret it.

To go through the screen of your computer or smartphone is to enter a world where you don't often have to deal with anything not chosen. You can be invisible on the Internet or create your own identity. There is no linear logic at work on the Internet: you can skitter from site to site, dipping in and out of social media, as you desire. I work as an online journalist and spend most weekdays doing exactly that.

And guess what? It's wonderful. It has made my life better in more ways than I can count, including making it possible for me to live where I want to live because I can work from home. The Internet has given me a great deal and does every day.

But the Internet, like all new technologies, also takes away. What it takes from us is our sense of agency. Matthew Crawford identifies a paradox intrinsic to the Internet as technology: it tells us that it is giving us more freedom and more choice, but in fact it is seducing us into passive captivity. The experience of inner compulsion I had at the abbey repeats itself in some small way every day.

There's a scientific explanation for that. At the neurological level, the Internet's constant distractions alter the physiological structure of our brain. The brain refashions itself to conform to the nonstop randomness of the Internet experience, which conditions us to crave the repetitive jolts that come with novelty. Writes Nicholas Carr:

> One thing is very clear: if, knowing what we know today about the brain's plasticity, you were to set out to invent a medium that would rewire our mental circuits as quickly and thoroughly as possible, you would probably end up designing something that looks and works a lot like the Internet.[9]

The result of this is a gradual inability to pay attention, to focus, and to think deeply. Study after study has confirmed the common experience many have reported in the Internet age: that using the Web makes it infinitely easier to find information but much harder to devote the kind of sustained focus it takes to know things.

Compounding the problem, the technological mentality denies that there is anything important to be known, aside from how to make things that help us realize our desires: in ancient Greek, *techne*, or "craftsmanship," versus *episteme*, or "knowledge gained through contemplation." *Techne* refers to knowledge that helps you do things, while *episteme* refers to knowledge of how things are, so that you will know what to do.

Both contemplation and action are necessary to human flourishing. The Middle Ages prized contemplation, which is why medieval societies, including products of their technological knowledge, were ordered to God. The icon, thought to be a symbolic window into divine reality, is an apt symbol of that age. Contemplation is alien to the modern mode of life. The iPhone, a luminous portal promising to show us the world, but really a mirror of the world inside our heads, is the icon of our own age.

Under the rule of technology, conditions that make authentic

Christian life possible disappear. And most of us have no idea what's happening.

Take on Digital Fasting as an Ascetic Practice

In the traditional Christian view, Truth, Goodness, and Beauty are objective realities, qualities of God and therefore intrinsic to Creation itself. To be free is to be able to see and participate in these supreme goods, thus realizing our true natures. As Christians, we behave virtuously not merely because God commands it but because acquiring virtue helps us to see Christ more clearly and in seeing Him, to reveal Him in turn to others. The early church sought nothing more than to see the face of God. Everything else followed.

If seeing the face of God, and becoming Christ-like in the process, is our greatest desire, then we must stay focused on that ultimate goal. In Dante's *Divine Comedy*, the pilgrim protagonist (also named Dante) learns that sin is disordered love. The source of all disorder is loving finite things more than the infinite God. Even loving good things, like family and country, can be a source of damnation if one loves them more than one loves God and seeks fulfillment in those things rather than in the Creator of those things.

It is very hard to stay focused on contemplating God. The pilgrim Dante discovers that he lost his way in life because he loved a woman, Beatrice, who was good, true, and beautiful, thinking that she was these things in herself. In the afterlife, Beatrice, who died young, chastises Dante, telling him that any good thing in her pointed to the Source of all goodness. His inability to see that led to his near-destruction.

William James, the founder of psychiatry, wrote, "My experience is what I agree to attend to. Only those items which I notice shape my mind." Our thoughts really do determine our lives. Tech writer Tim Wu, reflecting on James's insight, observes that religion has always understood that directing human attention toward what is holy is supremely important. This is why medieval Christendom was filled with prayers, rituals, fasts, and feasts: to keep life, both public and private, ordered around things divine.[10]

That was then. We are not going to return to a broad Christian culture as thick as that in the foreseeable future. But that doesn't let us Christians off the hook; it simply means that as individuals and communities, we are going to have to do a lot more work to keep our eyes focused on God.

Developing the cognitive control that leads to a more contemplative Christian life is the key to living as free men and women in post-Christian America.

The man whose desires are under the control of his reason is free. The man who does whatever occurs to him is a slave. Untold billions of dollars have been spent by advertisers over the past century to convince people that we can know our true identities only through fulfilling our desires. Say the advertisers, buy this object or experience, and you will know yourself—the self you want to be, not the self you are.

It doesn't work. Everything returns to the mean of everydayness. So we try something new, thinking this, finally, will be what makes us happy. On and on we go, flitting and darting our way through life, running from God and ourselves, terrified of quiet, of stillness, of our own thoughts. We are like the wandering monks Saint Benedict condemned in his Rule as the worst sort of monastic, led only by their own restless wills. "Of the miserable conduct of all such, it is better to be silent than to speak," wrote the saint.

Monks find true liberty by submitting to a rule of life, which is to say by ordering themselves to God in a structured way. And not only monks: almost anyone who lives by his own choice in a sustained, disciplined way will find true freedom. The woodworker who has given himself over to learning the traditions of his craft has far more liberty to exercise his creativity within the craft than the foolish amateur who thinks he can make it up as he goes along.

If you don't control your own attention, there are plenty of people eager to do it for you. The first step in regaining cognitive control is creating a space of silence in which you can think. During a deep spiritual crisis in my own life, the toxic tide of chronic anxiety did not began to recede from my mind until my priest ordered me to take up a daily rule of contemplative prayer. Stilling my mind for an hour of prayer was incredibly difficult, but it eventually opened up a beachhead in which the Holy Spirit could work to calm the stormy waters within.

A Jewish organization called Reboot promotes a nonsectarian concept they call "digital Sabbath." It's a day of rest in which people disconnect from technology—particularly computers, iPads, and smartphones—so that they can reconnect with the real world. The digital Sabbath is not a punishment but rather a means through which one can lay aside the world's cares (at least the ones communicated to us via digital technology).

This is akin to the ancient Christian habit of ritual fasting, which is still observed with relative strictness by many Eastern Orthodox Christians. Faithful Orthodox Christians observe Great Lent—the forty-day period before Holy Week—by abstaining from meat, fish, dairy, and other foods, according to their strength. They must also increase their prayer, repentance, and worship. As with Jewish observance of the Sabbath, none of this is meant to be punitive but is rather for the good of humankind.

"When a man leaves on a journey, he must know where he is going," writes the Orthodox priest Alexander Schmemann in his study of Lent.[11] This is why all serious believers must engage in periods of asceticism. They teach us to rid ourselves of accumulated distractions that keep our eyes from seeing our goal. Neil Postman, though a secular man, praises religious ascetics, saying that they "destroy" information that diverts their gaze from their ultimate end. To paraphrase the title of Postman's most famous book, the practices of religious ascetics prevent them from amusing themselves to spiritual death.

When we abstain from practices that disorder our loves, and in that time of fasting redouble our contemplation of God and the good things of Creation, we recenter our minds on the inner stability we need to create a coherent, meaningful self. The Internet is a scattering phenomenon, one that encourages surrender to passionate impulses. If we fail to push back against the Internet as hard as it pushes against us, we cannot help but lose our footing. And if we lose our footing, we ultimately lose the straight path through life. Christians have known this from generation to generation since the early church.

But with us, this wisdom has been forgotten. Laments Nicholas Carr, "We are welcoming the frenziedness into our souls."

Take Smartphones Away from Kids

My wife once asked a new Christian friend why she homeschools her children, given that they live in a good public school district. Said the friend, "The day my fifth-grade son came home from school and said his friends were watching hardcore porn on their smartphones was the day my husband and I made the call." It wasn't the school's fault. Smartphones were forbidden there. The boys were accessing pornography on their free time—and there wasn't a thing school authorities could do about it.

When parents hand their children small portable computers with virtually unlimited access to the Internet, they should not be surprised when their kids—especially their sons—dive into pornography. Unfortunately, with boys at least, it's in the nature of the hormone-jacked beast. Moms and dads who would never leave their kids unattended in a room full of pornographic DVDs think nothing of handing them smartphones. This is morally insane.

No adolescent or young teenager should be expected to have the self-control on his own to say no. Earlier in this book, we discussed the catastrophic impacts pornography can have on the brains of addicts. According to the University of New Hampshire's Crimes Against

Children Research Center, 93 percent of boys and 62 percent of girls have seen online pornography in adolescence.[12] It may be impossible to guard their eyes constantly, but it is irresponsible of parents not to try. Plus, parents in peer groups should work together to enforce a smartphone ban among their kids.

Moreover, teenagers are far too immature to understand the serious legal trouble they can get into with sexting. In many jurisdictions, sending sexually explicit images of minors counts as transmitting child pornography. Is it fair to put an impulsive tenth grader in the same category as a pervert? No, but that's a call for the district attorney and the judge. Even if your child avoids conviction, to be dragged through the legal process with the prospect of sex offender status hanging over his head, potentially for the rest of his life, can be financially and emotionally devastating to a family.

Finally, though most teens who sext will never find themselves in legal jeopardy, the moral dimension can be ruinous. The habit trains kids to objectify the opposite sex, treating them as commodities, and to regard their own sexuality as something to be marketed for status. A single illicit image that hits social media can destroy a teen's reputation and set them up for bullying and abuse.

Aside from the risk of pornographic content, there is the critical problem of what too much online exposure does to a young person's brain. If we don't treat our homes and schools as monasteries, strictly limiting both the information that comes to our kids (for the sake of their own inner formation), as well as their access to brain-altering technologies, we are forfeiting our responsibilities as stewards of their souls—and our own.

Did you know that Apple Computer founder Steve Jobs did not let his children use iPads and strictly limited their access to technology? Jobs was not the only one.

Chris Anderson, a former top tech journalist and now a Silicon Valley CEO, told the *New York Times* in 2014 that his home is like a tech monastery for his five children. "My kids accuse me and my wife of being fascists and overly concerned about tech, and they say that none of their friends have the same rules," Anderson said. "That's because we have seen the dangers of technology firsthand. I've seen it in myself, I don't want to see that happen to my kids."[13]

If that's how Silicon Valley tech geniuses parent, how do we justify being more liberal? Yes, you will be thought of as a weirdo and a control freak. So what? *These are your children.*

"The fact that we put these devices in our children's hands at a very young age with little guidance, and they experience life in terms of likes and dislikes, the fact that they basically have technology now as a prosthetic attachment—all of that seems to me to be incredibly short-sighted and dangerous," says philosopher Michael Hanby.

"It's affecting their ability to think and to have basic human relationships," he said. "This is a vast social experiment without precedent. We have handed our kids over to this without knowing what we are doing."

Keep Social Media Out of Worship

Some churches encourage Tweeting and texting during worship services. The idea is that this is simply another way to share the Gospel. They may be right as a general matter, but it's a huge mistake to invite this technology into worship.

For one thing, there is zero chance that people Tweeting and texting during church will restrict themselves to commentary on the sermon or Scripture readings. More importantly, the last place anyone needs to have his attention divided is during Sunday worship. Social media divides our attention with the razor's-edge efficiency of a sushi chef. Many people, especially the young, live all week immersed in the fragmented headspace that is today's norm. Bringing social media into Sunday worship exacerbates the problem, in part by denying that it is a problem in the first place.

Neuroscience has demonstrated that remembering a thing depends on sustaining attention to it. Engaging in social media during worship all but guarantees that anything the pastor says will be ephemeral. Plus, encouraging social media use during worship works against the contemplative state of mind one needs to bring into church.

More deeply, pastors and worship leaders who justify incorporating social media into worship should ask themselves: *How does this serve the Gospel?* If "sharing the Gospel" means simply disseminating information about Jesus, then that makes sense. But we see that becoming a disciple of Christ is about submitting to formation, not absorbing information. In that sense, social media acts like a gale-force wind that prevents the seed of the Gospel from taking root in the soil of one's soul.

Do Things with Your Hands

For over a decade, my friend Andrew Sullivan was one of the most prolific and influential bloggers on the Internet. Then one day in 2015, at the height of his fame and success, he suddenly dropped out and fell below the radar.

A few months later, when we both happened to be in Boston, Andrew and I met for coffee. I could hardly believe how good he looked. He was fit and glowing and had a startling sense of serenity about him. Andrew told me this was the fruit of getting off the Internet.

A year later, in a *New York Magazine* essay, Andrew explained his dramatic epiphany:

> Every minute I was engrossed in a virtual interaction I was not involved in a human encounter. Every second absorbed in some trivia was a second less for any form of reflection, or calm, or spirituality. "Multitasking" was a mirage. This was a zero-sum question. I either lived as a voice online or I lived as

a human being in the world that humans had lived in since the beginning of time.

And so I decided, after 15 years, to live in reality.[14]

It is not feasible for most of us to abandon the Internet entirely. But at the very least we can impose on ourselves a discipline similar to the Benedictine monks, who, observing the Rule, strictly limit themselves to particular tasks during certain hours.

We can also do more things with our hands. Put that way, it sounds almost childish, but there's a serious point here. Technology enables us to treat interaction with the material world—people, places, things—as an abstraction. Getting our hands dirty, so to speak, with gardening, cooking, sewing, exercise, and the like, is a crucial way of restoring our sense of connection with the real world. So is doing things face to face with other people.

We have to work hard to fight back against the technology that makes our everyday lives so easy, so that we can be human beings who live in reality. Brother Francis of Norcia says heaving big sacks of grain in his monastery work has been great for him "because it helps me remember that the human person is body and spirit, not just a spirit."

Question Progress

On the other side of that equation, the body is not simply wetware, a biological form of the computer. The habit of thinking mechanistically about the body causes us to let down our moral and ethical guard. Technological progress is not the same thing as moral progress—and in fact, can be its opposite.

In a tense conversation about bioethics, a prominent Christian medical researcher said to me, "The things we are going to be facing in the next decade or so shock the conscience.

"My colleagues can't see it," he continued, referring to scientists he works with. "Most of them aren't Christians, but even the Christians, when I try to engage them on the topic, I get nothing but blank stares."

These are scientists whose minds have been captured and disarmed by technology, which trains us to think of ourselves in instrumental terms. In the early twentieth century, the most progressive minds in the American establishment embraced eugenics—the pseudoscience of improving the race through controlled breeding. Leading church-men endorsed the idea, saying it would improve society through ap-plied science. It fell to Catholics and Protestant fundamentalists to object to eugenics on grounds of human dignity.

Eugenics fell into disgrace after the world saw what the Nazis did with these racial theories. Now, in the twenty-first century, eugenics is making a comeback, thanks to rapidly advancing biotechnology that promises to give parents the ability to make designer babies. Will con-temporary Christians find their prophetic voice? Not if they have or-dered their minds according to the technological imperative.

The connection between a future technologically driven dystopia and the suburban shopping mall is closer than you think. As we saw in Chapter 1, sociologist Christian Smith found that only 9 percent of Millennials surveyed thought consumerism was a serious moral issue. For most Americans, desire is self-justifying. For consumers, if you can afford it, why not buy it? For citizens of a technocracy, if the technol-ogy exists to give you what you want, no one has a right to object.

The mind of Technological Man cannot resist his heart's desires, because he has been trained by his culture not to question them. Tech-nological Man comes to believe that the limits on what he can do to nature lie primarily in his capacity to subdue it to his will. The Chris-tian must rebel against this. The only impregnable fortress is meta-physical, the conviction that meaning transcends ourselves and is grounded in God. There are boundaries beyond which we cannot go if we want to live.

Thinking that the world mediated by technology is the real world is a fatal error. We don't see reality then; we only see ourselves. If we do not understand this, if we don't believe that all things exist independently of our desires, that there is a world beyond our heads, then there is no reason to pay attention, because there is nothing to contemplate. If feeling defines reality, then contemplation is useless, and so is resistance. If we live as if boredom were the root of all evil, we will not be able to fight back, and if we do not fight back, we will find that our machines have mastered us. Perhaps they already have.

In Chapter 1, we saw that authentic Christianity has been taken over by a parasitical form of spirituality called Moralistic Therapeutic Deism, one effect of which is to culture Christians to believe that God blesses whatever makes them happy. In this way, technology becomes a kind of theology. It is a protean theology, because the god to whom it bears witness is the ever-changing Self that is seeking liberation from all limits and unchosen obligations.

Every time the church embraces a new fad, especially trends that turn worship into electronic spectacle, it yields more of its soul to this false theology. Before long—and we may be at this point already in some places—the church becomes fully possessed by the spirit of this world. Authentic orthodox Christianity can in no way be reconciled with the Zeitgeist. To the extent the church invites the technological mindset to take up residence within it, the conditions for Christianity will cease to exist.

The core reason is that immersion in technology causes us to lose our collective memory. Without memory, we don't know who we are, and if we don't know who we are, we become whatever our momentary passions wish us to be.

No regime is trying to steal our cultural memory and Christian identity from us. We are giving it away ourselves. Neil Postman counseled a strategy of resistance, saying that "a resistance fighter understands that technology must never be accepted as part of the natural order of things." Otherwise the war is over.

If Christians today do not stand firm on the rock of sacred order as revealed in our holy tradition—ways of thinking, speaking and acting that incarnate the Christian in culture and pass it on from generation to generation—we will have nothing to stand on at all. If we don't take on everyday practices that keep that sacred order present to ourselves, our families, and our communities, we are going to lose it. And if we lose it, we are at great risk of losing sight of the One to whom everything in that sacred order, like a divine treasure map, points.

That has been the main argument of this book. In these pages, I have attempted to sound the alarm for conservative Christians in the West, warning them that the greatest danger we face today does not come from aggressive left-wing politics or radical Islam, as many seem to think. Those are dangers that our Christian brothers and sisters in China, Nigeria, and the Middle East face. For us, the greatest danger comes from the liberal secular order itself. And our failure to understand this reinforces our cultural captivity and the seemingly unstoppable assimilation of the next generations.

The Benedict Option is not a technique for reversing the losses, political and otherwise, that Christians have suffered. It is not a strategy for turning back the clock to an imagined golden age. Still less is it a plan for constructing communities of the pure, cut off from the real world.

To the contrary, the Benedict Option is a call to undertaking the long and patient work of reclaiming the real world from the artifice, alienation, and atomization of modern life. It is a way of seeing the world and of living in the world that undermines modernity's big lie: that humans are nothing more than ghosts in a machine, and we are free to adjust its settings in any way we like.

"It is easy for me to imagine that the next great division of the world will be between people who wish to live as creatures and people who wish to live as machines," writes Wendell Berry. Let's take our stand on the side of creatures, and the Creator.

Conclusion: The Benedict Decision

*Instead of a fortified castle built in the middle of
the land, we must think of an army of stars thrown
into the sky.*

—Jacques Maritain, on the church in modernity

O n a cold January night, I sat with Pastor Greg Thompson in a
cozy Virginia pub, sipping from a steaming cup of hot toddy,
talking with him about the Benedict Option. Thompson, at the time
the senior pastor of a Charlottesville Presbyterian congregation, is
cautious about the movement, out of concern that American Christians will be drawn to it out of fear. Though fear in the face of these
turbulent times is understandable, Thompson said, the Benedict Option ultimately has to be a matter of love. "The moment the Benedict
Option becomes about anything other than communion with Christ
and dwelling with our neighbors in love, it ceases to be Benedictine,"
he said. "It can't be a strategy for self-improvement or for saving the
church or the world."

Thompson's remarks highlight a key challenge for Benedict Option
Christians going forward: How do we live in joy and confidence even
though the world seems to be collapsing around us? How do we navi-

gate the arks we build safely between the twin illusions of false optimism and exaggerated fear?

The image of the church as an Ark floating atop tempestuous waters of destruction is one of great antiquity in the history of the Christian faith. This iconic concept of the church's self-understanding must be recovered with vigor.

But there's another biblically sound way to think about the waters that flood the earth, one that is just as important to the Benedict Option project as the Noah's Ark story.

During the Babylonian captivity of the Hebrews, God granted the Prophet Ezekiel a vision of the restored Holy City of Jerusalem. In the vision, a mysterious man leads the prophet into a rebuilt Temple. Ezekiel sees a stream of water issuing forth from the altar, flowing out of its openings and into the world outside. It deepens and widens the farther it spreads from the Temple, until it has become a river that no one can cross. Everywhere this water flows, abundant life follows.

The traditional Christian interpretation of Ezekiel's vision holds that it was fulfilled on Pentecost, when God poured out the Holy Spirit on the gathered disciples, inaugurating a new era with the birth of the church. Through the church—the restored Temple—would flow the living waters of salvific grace.

The church, then, is both Ark and Wellspring—and Christians must live in both realities. God gave us the Ark of the church to keep us from drowning in the raging flood. But He also gave us the church as a place to drown our old selves symbolically in the water of baptism, and to grow in new life, nourished by the never-ending torrent of His grace. You cannot live the Benedict Option without seeing both visions simultaneously.

Love is the only way we will make it through what is to come. Love is not romantic ecstasy. It has to be a kind of love that has been honed and intensified through regular prayer, fasting, and repentance and, for many Christians, through receiving the holy sacraments. And it must be a love that has been refined through suffering. There is no other way.

In my travels in search of the Benedict Option, I found no more complete embodiment of it than the Tipi Loschi, the vigorously orthodox, joyfully countercultural Catholic community in Italy recommended to me by Father Cassian of Norcia. Motoring with Tipi Loschi leader Marco Sermarini through the hills above his city, I asked him how the rest of us could have what his community has discovered.

Start by getting serious about living as Christians, he said. Accept that there can be no middle ground. The Tipi Loschi began as a group of young Catholic men who wanted more out of their faith life than Moralistic Therapeutic Deism.

"That used to be my life," said Marco. "I didn't know the teaching of Jesus Christ was for *all* my life, not just the 'religious' part of it. If you recognize that He is the Lord of all, you will order your life in a radically different way."

What Marco and his friends found, to their great surprise, was that everything they needed to live faithfully together had been right in front of them all along. "We invented nothing," he said. "We discovered nothing. We are only rediscovering a tradition that was locked away inside an old box. We had forgotten."

Driving through the achingly beautiful towns and fields overlooking the Adriatic, Marco pulled his SUV over on the side of a narrow country road and led me to a steeply plunging hillside. It was covered with olive trees. This was the Sermarini family olive grove. As a boy, Marco's ninety-one-year-old grandfather helped his own father harvest olives from these trees. Marco was raised doing the same, and now he and his own children collect olives yearly and press their oil for the family's use.

This, I said to Marco, is stability.

He shrugged, then looked out pensively over his trees.

"I don't know what's going to happen next in life, but in the meantime, we have to fight for the good," he told me. "The possibility of saving the good things in the world is only that: a possibility. We have to take the chances we have to set a rock in the earth and to keep this rock steady."

We walked back to the SUV, climbed in, and drove on. My friend continued to wax philosophical about stability in a world of change.

"Nothing we make in this life will be eternal, but we have to build them as if they will be eternal," Marco continued. "That's what God wants. If you promise yourself to a woman for a lifetime, that is a way of making the eternal present here in time."

We have to go forward in confidence that the little things we do might, in time, grow into mighty works, he explained. It's all up to God. All we can do is our very best to serve him.

Sometimes Marco lies in bed at night, worrying that his efforts, and the efforts of his little Christian community, won't amount to much in the face of so much opposition. He is anxious that the current will be too strong to resist and will tear them apart.

"I know from the olive trees that some years we will have a big harvest, and other years we will take few," he said. "The monks, when they brought agriculture to this place a thousand years ago, they taught our ancestors that there are times when we have to save seed. That's why I think we have to walk on this road of Saint Benedict, in this Benedict Option. This is a season for saving the seed. If we don't save the seed now, we won't have a harvest in the years to come."

It was getting late in the afternoon. I was afraid I would miss my bus to the Rome airport. Shouldn't we be going? I asked.

"*Grande* Rod, don't worry, my friend!" he said. "You worry too much. You will make it!" And off we sped, down the winding road toward the sea.

As the sun went down in the western sky, we spoke once more about the challenge facing orthodox Christians in the West and how daunting it seems. Marco left me with these unforgettable lines.

"In Italy, we have a saying: 'When there is no horse, a donkey can do good work.' I consider myself a little donkey," he said. "There are so many purebred horses that run nowhere, but this old donkey is getting the job done. You and me, let's go on doing this job like little donkeys. Don't forget, it was a donkey that brought Jesus Christ into Jerusalem."

Grande! So we little donkeys go on, walking the pilgrim path in the way of Benedict, out of the ruined imperial city, to a place of peace where we can be still and learn to hear the voice of our Master. We find others like us and build communities, schools for the service of the Lord. We do this not to save the world but for no other reason than we love Him and know that we need a community and an ordered way of life to serve Him fully.

We live liturgically, telling our sacred Story in worship and song. We fast and we feast. We marry and give our children in marriage, and though in exile, we work for the peace of the city. We welcome our newborns and bury our dead. We read the Bible, and we tell our children about the saints. And we also tell them in the orchard and by the fireside about Odysseus, Achilles, and Aeneas, of Dante and Don Quixote, and Frodo and Gandalf, and all the tales that bear what it means to be men and women of the West.

We work, we pray, we confess our sins, we show mercy, we welcome the stranger, and we keep the commandments. When we suffer, especially for Christ's sake, we give thanks, because that is what Christians do. Who knows what God, in turn, will do with our faithfulness? It is not for us to say. Our command is, in the words of the Christian poet W. H. Auden, to "stagger onward rejoicing."

The Benedictine monks of Norcia have become a sign to the world in ways I did not anticipate when I began writing this book. In August 2016, a devastating earthquake shook their region. When the quake hit in the middle of the night, the monks were awake to pray matins, and they fled the monastery for the safety of the open-air piazza.

Father Cassian later reflected that the earthquake symbolized the crumbling of the West's Christian culture, but that there was a second, hopeful symbol that night. "The second symbol is the gathering of the people around the statue of Saint Benedict in the piazza in order to pray," he wrote to supporters. "That is the only way to rebuild."

The tremors left the basilica church too structurally unstable for worship, and most of the monastery uninhabitable. The brothers evacuated the town and moved to their land up the mountainside, just outside the Norcia walls. They pitched tents in the ruins of an older monastery and continued their prayer life, interrupted only by visits to the town to minister to its people.

The monks received distinguished visitors in their exile, including Italy's then-prime minister Matteo Renzi and Cardinal Robert Sarah, who heads the Vatican's liturgical office. Cardinal Sarah blessed the monks' temporary quarters, celebrated mass with them, then told them that their tent monastery "reminds me of Bethlehem, where it all began."

"I am certain that the future of the Church is in the monasteries," said the cardinal, "because where prayer is, there is the future."

Five days later, more earthquakes shook Norcia. The cross atop the basilica's facade toppled to the ground. And then, early in the morning of Sunday, October 30, the strongest earthquake to hit Italy in thirty years struck, its epicenter just north of the town. The fourteenth-century Basilica of St. Benedict, the patron saint of Europe, fell violently to the ground. Only its facade remained. Not a single church in Norcia remained standing.

With dust still rising from the rubble, Father Basil knelt on the stones of the piazza, facing the ruined basilica, and accompanied by nuns and a few elderly Norcini, including one in a wheelchair, he prayed. Later amateur video posted to YouTube showed Father Basil, Father Benedict, and Father Martin running through the streets of the rubble-strewn town, looking for the dying who needed last rites. By the grace of God, there were none.

Back in America, Father Richard Cipolla, a Catholic priest in Connecticut and an old friend of Father Benedict's, e-mailed the sub-prior when he heard the news of the latest quake. "Is there damage? What is going on?" Father Cipolla wrote.

"Yes, damage much worse," Father Benedict replied. "But we are okay. Much to tell you, but just pray. I am well, and God continues to purify us and bring very good things."

The next morning, as the sun rose over Norcia, Father Benedict, who would soon take over as prior from the retiring Father Cassian, sent a message to the monastery's friends all over the world. He said that no Norcini had lost their lives in the quake because they had heeded the warnings from the earlier tremors and left town. "[God] spent two months preparing us for the complete destruction of our patron's church so that when it finally happened we would watch it, in horror but in safety, from atop the town," the priest-monk wrote.

Father Benedict added, "These are mysteries which will take years—not days or months—to understand."

Surely that is true. Indeed, when I left Norcia earlier that year, I envied the monks the security of their mountain fastness. But I was wrong. There is no place on this Earth entirely safe from catastrophe. When the earth moved, the Basilica of St. Benedict, which had stood firm for many centuries, tumbled to the ground. Only the facade, the mere semblance of a church, remains. But notice this: because the monks headed for the hills after the August earthquake, they survived. God preserved them in the holy poverty of their canvas-covered Bethlehem, where they continued to live the Rule in the ancient way, including chanting the Old Mass. Now they can begin rebuilding amid the ruins, their resilient Benedictine faith teaching them to receive this catastrophe as a call to deeper holiness and sacrifice. God willing, new life will one day spring forth from the rubble.

Because they lived the Benedict Option in the good times, they built within themselves the stability and resilience to endure the worst time—and to begin again, in God's time.

"We pray and watch from the mountainside, thinking of the long three years Saint Benedict spent in the cave before God decided to call him out to become a light to the world," wrote Father Benedict. *"Fiat. Fiat."*

Let it be. Let it be.

He who has ears to hear, let him hear what the Spirit is saying to the churches.

Acknowledgments

This book has been a long time in coming and is the fruit of over a decade of conversation among friends all over the country. I wish to thank them all, in particular Patrick Deneen, Caleb Stegall, Jake Meador, Frederica Mathewes-Green, Michael Hanby, Ryan Booth, Philip Bess, Leroy Huizenga, Kale Zelden, Ross Douthat, Michael Brendan Dougherty, Denny Burk, Andrew T. Walker, Andy Crouch, Chris Roberts, Marco Sermarini, Russell Arben Fox, Becky Elder, James Card, Ralph C. Wood, Lance Kinzer, Conor Dugan, Jeff Polet, Mark T. Mitchell, Robert Duncan, Caleb Bernacchio, Matthew Lee Anderson, Alan Jacobs, Gabe Lyons, Jason McCrory, Joe Hartman, Mark Meador, Matt Bonzo, James Matthew Wilson, Christopher Roberts, and the late Roger Pfau.

Special thanks go to Ken Myers, the happy genius behind the *Mars Hill Audio Journal*, which has been the most formative influence on my thinking as a Christian trying to make sense of our post-Christian culture. This book is nothing but a series of footnotes on the work Ken has done over the years. If the only thing it achieves is introducing more thoughtful Christians to the riches of the *Journal*, then I will be satisfied.

Acknowledgments

Thanks to Clint Barron, Ryan T. Anderson, and others who read early versions of this manuscript, and thanks to the communities around Wichita's Eighth Day Books and the Clear Creek Abbey in rural Oklahoma for their warm hospitality and witness. At the risk of sounding grandiose, I also want to express my gratitude for the life and work of Joseph Ratzinger, Pope Benedict XVI, who I consider the second Benedict of the Benedict Option.

My literary agent, Gary Morris, is all that a writer could hope for, and the work he has done to make this and every other book I've written come into being is something I cannot ever repay. Bria Sandford, this book's editor, has been a delight to work with and was especially helpful in teaching me how to explain all this monkish stuff to Evangelicals like her. Many of the ideas in this book have been honed in conversation with readers of my blog at the website of *The American Conservative*. I thank my readers there for their encouragement and constructive criticism. I also thank my bosses at *TAC*, especially Jeremy Beer and Daniel McCarthy, for their unfailing support, and with the profoundest gratitude, I thank Howard and Roberta Ahmanson for their continued generosity. I thank my wife Julie and kids Matthew, Lucas, and Nora, for their infinite patience. It is not easy to have a writer in the family, but I hope my children understand one day that this book is for the sake of their future.

Finally, I lack the words to express my gratitude to the monks of Norcia for opening their hearts and their monastery to me. None of us could have reckoned that by the time this book was finished, their basilica and monastery would be in ruins. These men of God are living the way of the Cross now, but I am confident that God will use them in a special way to bear His light unto the world. Amid all the world's sorrow, confusion, and pain, the Norcia monks and their jolly hobbitlike friends, the Tipi Loschi, remind me of the command of the elder in Revelation 5: "Do not weep, for the Lion of the Tribe of Judah, the Root of David has triumphed." Because they believe it, and because they live it, so can I live it and believe it. So can we all.

Notes

Chapter 1: The Great Flood

1. Ephraim Radner, "No Safe Place Except Hope: The Anthropocene Epoch," *Living Church*, July 28, 2016, http://living church.org/covenant/2016/07/28/no-safe-place-except-hope-th e-anthropocene-epoch/.
2. Michael Lipka, "Millennials Increasingly Are Driving the Growth of 'Nones,'" Pew Research Center, May 12, 2015, http://www.pewresearch.org/fact-tank/2015/05/12/millennial s-increasingly-are-driving-growth-of-nones/.
3. Christian Smith and Melinda Lundquist Denton, *Soul Searching: The Religious and Spiritual Lives of American Teenagers* (New York: Oxford University Press, 2005).
4. Christian Smith and Patricia Snell, *Lost in Transition: The Dark Side of Emerging Adulthood* (New York: Oxford University Press, 2011), 86.
5. Alasdair MacIntyre, *After Virtue,* 3rd ed. (Notre Dame, IN: University of Notre Dame Press, 2007), 263.

Chapter 2: The Roots of the Crisis

1. Robert Rector, "Marriage: America's Greatest Weapon Against Child Poverty," Heritage Foundation Special Report #117, September 5, 2012. Using U.S. government statistics, the report also says that marriage drops the probability of child poverty by 82 percent, http://www.heritage.org/research/reports/2012/09/mar riage-americas-greatest-weapon-against-child-poverty).

2. Charles Taylor, *A Secular Age* (Cambridge, MA: Belknap Press of Harvard University Press, 2007), 12.

3. C. S. Lewis, *The Discarded Image: An Introduction to Medieval and Renaissance Literature* (New York: Cambridge University Press, 2012), 203.

4. David Bentley Hart, *The Experience Of God: Being, Consciousness, Bliss* (New Haven, CT: Yale University Press, 2013), Kindle ed., 62.

5. Lewis, *Discarded Image*, 222.

6. Brad S. Gregory, *The Unintended Reformation: How a Religious Revolution Secularized Society* (Cambridge, MA: Belknap Press of Harvard University Press, 2012), 99.

7. John Adams, *Letter to the Massachusetts Militia, 11 October 1798*, U.S. National Archives, http://founders.archives.gov/docu ments/Adams/99-02-02-3102.

8. Zygmunt Bauman, *Liquid Modernity* (Malden, MA: Blackwell, 2000).

9. Philip Rieff, *The Triumph of the Therapeutic: Uses of Faith After Freud*, 40th anniversary ed. (Wilmington, DE: ISI Books, 2006), 19.

10. Stephen L. Gardner, "The Eros and Ambitions of Psychological Man," ibid., 244.

11. Charles Taylor, *The Ethics of Authenticity* (Cambridge, MA: Harvard University Press, 1992), 14.

12. Ursula K. Le Guin, *A Wizard of Earthsea* (New York: Houghton Mifflin, 2012), 51.

Chapter 3: A Rule for Living

1. Esther de Waal, *Seeking God: The Way of St. Benedict* (Collegeville, MN: Liturgical Press, 2001), 15.
2. This book uses the Leonard Doyle translation that the Order of St. Benedict uses on its Web site (http://www.osb.org/rb /text/toc.html). The Benedictines adapted it by making every other chapter in the Rule use female pronouns, but this has been changed to the original male pronouns to avoid confusion.
3. Romano Guardini, *The End of the Modern World* (Wilmington, DE: ISI Books, 1998), 210.
4. Ibid., 202.
5. Zygmunt Bauman, "From Pilgrim to Tourist, or, A Short History of Identity," in *Questions of Cultural Identity*, ed. Stuart Hall and Paul du Gay (Thousand Oaks, CA: SAGE Publications, 1996), 24.
6. Dietrich Bonhoeffer, *Life Together: The Classic Exploration of Christian in Community* (New York: Harper One, 2009), 8.
7. Léon Bloy, quoted in Peter Kreeft, *Prayer for Beginners* (San Francisco: Ignatius Press, 2000), 39.

Chapter 4: A New Kind of Christian Politics

1. Yuval Levin, *The Fractured Republic: Renewing America's Social Contract in the Age of Individualism* (New York: Basic Books, 2016), 178.
2. Patrick J. Deneen, *Conserving America?: Essays on Present Discontents* (South Bend, IN: St. Augustine's Press, 2016), 3.
3. Scott H. Moore, *The Limits of Liberal Democracy: Politics and Religion at the End of Modernity* (Downers Grove, IL: IVP Academic, 2009), 15.
4. Václav Havel, "The Power of the Powerless," trans. Paul Wilson, in *The Power of the Powerless: Citizens Against the State in Central-Eastern Europe*, ed. John Keane (Armonk, NY: M. E. Sharpe, 1985).
5. Benda's concept has an interesting predecessor in the early church. Historian Peter Brown says that the letters of Saint Cy-

prian, Bishop of Carthage (martyred in 258), "show how the Church had begun to function as a fiercely independent body— a veritable 'city within the city.'" See Peter Brown, *The Rise of Western Christendom: Triumph and Diversity, A.D. 200-1000* (Malden, MA: Wiley-Blackwell, 2013), 62.

6. Václav Benda, "The Meaning, Context and Legacy of the Parallel Polis," trans. Paul Wilson, in *The Long Night of the Watchman: Essays by Václav Benda, 1978–1989*, ed. F. Flagg Taylor IV (South Bend, IN: St. Augustine's Press, 2017).

Chapter 5: A Church for All Seasons

1. Robert Louis Wilken, "The Church as Culture," *First Things*, April 2004, https://www.firstthings.com/article/2004/04/the-church-as-culture.

2. Russell Moore, *Onward: Engaging the Culture Without Losing the Gospel* (Nashville, TN: B&H Books, 2015), 27.

3. Ralph C. Wood, *Contending for the Faith: The Church's Engagement with Culture* (Waco, TX: Baylor University Press, 2003), 2.

4. James K. A. Smith, *Desiring the Kingdom: Worship, Worldview, and Cultural Formation* (Grand Rapids, MI: Baker Academic, 2009).

5. Robert Inchausti, *Subversive Orthodoxy: Outlaws, Revolutionaries, and Other Christians in Disguise* (Grand Rapids, MI: Brazos Press, 2005), 143.

6. Paul Connerton, *How Societies Remember* (New York: Cambridge University Press, 1989), 72.

7. Simon Chan, *Liturgical Theology: The Church as Worshiping Community* (Downers Grove, IL: InterVarsity Press, 2006), 159.

8. Ibid., 149.

9. Stanley Hauerwas and William H. Willimon, *Resident Aliens* (Nashville, TN: Abingdon Press, 2014), 78.

10. Wendell Berry, *Sex, Economy, Freedom, and Community: Eight Essays* (New York: Pantheon, 1994), 108.

11. Matthew Crawford, *The World Beyond Your Head: On Becoming an*

Individual in an Age of Distraction (New York: Farrar, Straus, and Giroux, 2015), 257.

12. Robert Louis Wilken, "Evangelism in the Early Church: Christian History Interview—Roman Redux," in *Christian History* 57 (1998), http://www.christianitytoday.com/history/issues/issue-57/evangelism-in-early-church-christian-history-interview.html.

13. Richard Wurmbrand, *In God's Underground* (Bartlesville, OK: Living Sacrifice Book Company, 2004), Kindle ed., loc. 661.

Chapter 6: The Idea of a Christian Village

1. Sociologist Robert Nisbet observed in the work of the Jewish philosopher Martin Buber, the Catholic philosopher Jacques Maritain, the Protestant theologians Emil Brunner and Reinhold Niebuhr, and the Anglican theologian and priest Vigo Auguste Demant: "'When the relations between man and God is subjective, interior (as in Luther) or in timeless acts and logic (as in Calvin) man's utter dependence upon God is not mediated through the concrete facts of historical life,' writes Canon Demant. And when it is not so mediated, the relation with God becomes tenuous, amorphous, and unsupportable." Nisbet, *The Quest for Community* (Wilmington, DE: ISI Books, 2010), 11.

2. Ibid., 223.

3. Judith Rich Harris, *The Nurture Assumption: Why Children Turn Out the Way They Do* (New York: Free Press, 2009), 165.

4. Ibid., 179–85.

5. Ibid., 189.

Chapter 7: Education as Christian Formation

1. Charles J. Chaput, "Yeshiva Lessons," *First Things*, August 2012, https://www.firstthings.com/article/2012/08/yeshiva-lessons.

2. Patrick Deneen, "How a Generation Lost Its Common Culture," *Minding the Campus*, February 2, 2016, http://www

.mindingthecampus.org/2016/02/how-a-generation-lost-its-co
mmon-culture/.

3. Philip Rieff, *Fellow Teachers* (New York: Harper & Row, 1973),
    quoted in Jeremy Beer, "Pieties of Silence," *American Conservative*,
    October 23, 2006, http://www.theamericanconservative.com/
    articles/pieties-of-silence/.

4. National Center for Health Statistics, *Health, United States, 2015:
    With Special Feature on Racial and Ethnic Health Disparities* (Wash-
    ington: U.S. Government Printing Office, 2016), table 51, 194–
    96; Centers for Disease Control and Prevention, *MMWR
    Surveillance Summaries.* 65, no. 6 (June 10, 2016), table 69, 119.

5. Judith Rich Harris, *The Nurture Assumption: Why Children Turn Out
    the Way They Do* (New York: Free Press, 2009), 194.

6. Terence P. Jeffrey, "1,773,000: Homeschooled Children Up
    61.8% in 10 Years," CNSNews.com, May 19, 2015, http://www
    .cnsnews.com/news/article/terence-p-jeffrey/1773000-homesc
    hooled-children-618-10-years.

7. Peter Jesserer Smith, "Keeping the Faith on College Campuses,"
    National Catholic Register, April 15, 2013, http://www.ncregister
    .com/daily-news/keeping-the-faith-on-college-campuses#ixzz
    2QjYllhb9.

Chapter 8: Preparing for Hard Labor

1. William Perkins, "A Treatise on the Vocations," cited in Patrick
    J. Deneen, *Conserving America? Essays on Present Discontents* (South
    Bend, IN: St. Augustine's Press, 2016), 33.

2. Ibid., 34.

3. David Gushee, "On LGBT Equality, Middle Ground Is Disap-
    pearing," Religion News Service, August 22, 2016, http://reli
    gionnews.com/2016/08/22/on-lgbt-equality-middle-ground-is-
    disappearing/.

Chapter 9: Eros and the New Christian Counterculture

1. Wendell Berry, "What Is Sex For?: Interview with Wendell Berry," *Modern Reformation*, November–December 2001, 38–41, http://allsaintsaustin.typepad.com/files/what-is-sex-for-1.pdf.

2. Wendell Berry, *Sex, Economy, Freedom, and Community: Eight Essays* (New York: Pantheon, 1994), 133.

3. Philip Rieff, *The Triumph of the Therapeutic: Uses of Faith After Freud*, 40th anniversary ed. (Wilmington, DE.: ISI Books, 2006), 12.

4. Sarah Ruden, *Paul Among the People: The Apostle Reinterpreted and Reimagined in His Own Time* (New York: Pantheon, 2010).

5. Peter Brown, *The Body and Society: Men, Women, and Sexual Renunciation in Early Christianity* (New York: Columbia University Press, 2008), xlv–xlvi.

6. Christopher C. Roberts, *Creation and Covenant: The Significance of Sexual Difference in the Moral Theology of Marriage* (New York: T&T Clark International, 2007), 213.

7. Heather Mason Keifer, "Gallup Brain: The Birth of In Vitro Fertilization," Gallup.com, August 5, 2003, http://www.gallup.com/poll/8983/gallup-brain-birth-vitro-fertilization.aspx.

8. Andrew Kopkind, "The Gay Moment," *Nation*, May 3, 1993.

9. Charles Taylor, *A Secular Age* (Cambridge, MA: Belknap Press of Harvard University Press, 2007), 588.

10. Jean Twenge, "The Paradox of Millennial Sex: More Casual Hookups, Fewer Partners," *Los Angeles Times*, May 9, 2015, http://www.latimes.com/science/sciencenow/la-sci-sn-millennials-sex-attitudes-20150508-story.html.

11. Benedict XVI, *Deus caritas est*, encyclical letter, December 25, 2005, http://w2.vatican.va/content/benedict-xvi/en/encyclicals/documents/hf_ben-xvi_enc_20051225_deus-caritas-est.html.

12. Ron Belgau, "Spiritual Friendship in 300 Words," Spiritualfriendship.org, August 29, 2012, https://spiritualfriendship.org/2012/08/29/spiritual-friendship-in-300-words/.

13. "Pornography Use Among Self-Identified Christians Largely

Mirrors National Average, Survey Finds," CNSNews.com, August 27, 2015, http://www.cnsnews.com/news/article/penny-starr/pornography-use-among-self-identified-christians-largely-mirrors-national.

14. Belinda Luscombe, "Porn and the Threat to Virility," *Time*, April 11, 2016, quoted in Conor Friedersdorf, "Is Porn Culture to Be Feared?," *Atlantic*, April 7, 2016, http://www.theatlantic.com/politics/archive/2016/04/porn-culture/477099/.

15. Wendell Berry, *Life Is a Miracle: An Essay Against Modern Superstition* (Washington, DC: Counterpoint, 2001), 55.

Chapter 10: Man and the Machine

1. "Cell Phone Ownership Hits 91 Percent Adults," Pew Research Center, June 6, 2013, http://www.pewresearch.org/fact-tank/2013/06/06/cell-phone-ownership-hits-91-of-adults/.

2. "U.S. Smartphone Use in 2015," Pew Research Center, April 1, 2015, http://www.pewinternet.org/2015/04/01/us-smartphone-use-in-2015/.

3. Michael Hanby, "The Truth Shall Set You Free: Liberal Order and the Future of Christian Freedom," address delivered at St. Charles Borromeo Seminary, Philadelphia, December 7, 2015, text shared with author by Hanby.

4. Neil Postman, *Technopoly: The Surrender of Culture to Technology* (New York: Vintage, 1993), 184.

5. "Abortion Viewed in Moral Terms: Fewer See Stem Cell Research and IVF as Moral Issues," Pew Research Center, August 15, 2013, http://www.pewforum.org/2013/08/15/abortion-viewed-in-moral-terms/.

6. "Industry's Growth Leads to Leftover Embryos, and Painful Choices," *New York Times*, June 17, 2015, http://www.nytimes.com/2015/06/18/us/embryos-egg-donors-difficult-issues.html.

7. Andrew Hough, "1.7 Million Human Embryos Created for IVF Thrown Away," *Daily Telegraph*, December 31, 2013, http://

www.telegraph.co.uk/news/health/news/9772233/1.7-million
-human-embryos-created-for-IVF-thrown-away.html.

8. "Three-quarters Say Longmont Attack Is Murder," YouGov
   .com, April 7, 2015, https://today.yougov.com/news/2015
   /04/07/three-quarters-say-longmont-attack-murder/.

9. Nicholas Carr, *The Shallows: What the Internet Is Doing to Our Brains*
   (New York: W. W. Norton, 2011), 116.

10. Tim Wu, *The Attention Merchants: The Epic Scramble to Get Inside Our
    Heads* (New York: Knopf, 2016), 344. Wu's mention of how the
    monastic life focuses one's attention, in contrast to the scattering
    forces of life in modernity, is worth a book on its own.

11. Alexander Schmemann, *Great Lent: Journey to Pascha* (Crestwood,
    NY: St. Vladimir's Seminary Press, 1974), 11.

12. Nick Bilton, "Parenting in the Age of Online Pornography," *New
    York Times,* January 7, 2015, http://www.nytimes.com/2015/01/08
    /style/parenting-in-the-age-of-online-porn.html?_r=0.

13. Nick Bilton, "Steve Jobs Was a Low-Tech Parent," *New York
    Times*, September 10, 2014, http://www.nytimes.com/2014
    /09/11/fashion/steve-jobs-apple-was-a-low-tech-parent.html.

14. Andrew Sullivan, "I Used to Be a Human Being," *New York*,
    September 18, 2016, http://nymag.com/selectall/2016/09/an
    drew-sullivan-technology-almost-killed-me.html.

Index

Index

Index

Index

Index

Index